Simply The

PC Edition

GH00738919

by
John Daw

Simply The Book

PC Edition

ISBN 07457 0302 X

Published by:

Kuma Books Ltd
12 Horseshoe Park
Pangbourne
Berks
RG8 7JW

Tel 0734 844335
Fax 0734 844339

Dedication

I would like to thank my wife Gillian and our daughters
Sophie-Dawn, Kiri-Marie and Jessica for their whole
hearted support of this project. A special thanks to Adam
Fullalove for his dedicated hard work and loyalty.
And I dedicate this book to all those who have searched
for a chance to understand computers.

John Daw

WELCOME

Welcome to Simply The Book, a system that has been devised for people that are scared of computers, many of whom feel that they are not adequate enough to grasp this futuristic item.

The book has proven particularly useful to the novice, who knows just enough to create phenomenal mistakes which can lead to both capital outlay and a severe lack of performance. It is our belief that most computers which have been purchased are not running at anywhere near their optimum speed, primarily because the vendors of these machines simply do not understand how to impart the basic knowledge required by the buyer in any would-be start up purchase.

We have also found that many of the functions explained in this publication are used frequently by those that are more enlightened to computing.

With the computer illiterate person in mind, the book has been carefully constructed to ensure that every function required to do any particular task is clearly and precisely written in commonly used day to day language. I.e. DOS becomes translated as the commander of all operations considered or undertaken by the computer. We have also attempted wherever possible to colour code and clearly define the individual keys and functions that need to be undertaken throughout the publication. i.e. STEP(1), STEP(2), STEP(3), STEP(4) etc.

WHAT DO YOU GAIN BY OWNING "THE BOOK"!

Firstly of course you will be able to solve problems that are otherwise not understandable in any conventional manual supplied with the purchase of a personal computer or software package. You will also have a built-in system that allows you to make a telephone call for technical support should the need arise. These numbers can be found throughout the publication strategically placed to coincide with the relevant problems. You quote the page number from "THE BOOK" and the problem, and we feed back the answer. This service is absolutely free as it comes included with the purchase and personal registration of "THE BOOK".

In the first place "THE BOOK" sets out to give clear understandable training in the Disc Operating Systems of DOS and Windows. These two systems are at present the main governing bodies in today's Personal Computer environment. We would envisage that your requirement to understand individual programs will come later in your itinerary, therefore over the next 18 months once you have purchased and registered your copy of "THE BOOK" you will receive updates to this already substantial amount of information together with the complete sections required in understanding the following programs. These are:- Wordperfect 5.2 for Windows, Microsoft Word for Windows, Wordstar for Windows, Lotus 123 for Windows, Quatro Pro for Windows, and a special graphics section covering most of the major packages available on the market today. These sections will also carry updates from time to time together with built-in phone assistance, and it's all absolutely free.

CONGRATULATIONS on owning "Simply THE BOOK".
Your initial reference number is ....

CONTENTS

SECTION	PAGE

WHAT IS A COMPUTER ?

Please Note:- This section is for the complete novice, information further on will clearly be important to those more enlightened.

An interesting question isn't it? The word computer conjures up numerous different thoughts in countless different people. This is primarily because there are two major groups of people in Europe today, those that have been taught from an early age about computers as part of their school curriculum and the older generation who simply haven't. This is leaving a tremendous void that will obviously diminish as the next generation takes over. There are however those who have made it their business to understand the workings of a computer; although they were not born in the computing era, they did see it to be the future, and grasped the opportunity to learn.

A computer essentially is a form of abacus or adding machine, the difference is that the abacus relied upon the human brain to move the beads, whereas the computer has the capacity to think and move them for itself, provided it is given the information and know-how to do so. Not only can the computer think or move the beads for itself it can also do it at far greater speed than conventional methods; in short the computer is a sophisticated calculator that deals only in numbers and nothing else in it's primary state.

So how can this be?. If the computer deals with numbers then where do the pictures on the screen come from?

The machine has the capacity to convert the shapes and pictures we recognise into it's own numeric picture. It can then convert it's own numeric information into something that we can understand using the various components that make up a personal computer.

Although interesting we feel it is unnecessary to explain precisely how these functions take place inside the computer. It is rather more the purpose of the book to explain how to make the the computer perform instructions and work for you!

THE COMPONENTS OF A PERSONAL COMPUTER (P.C.)

Basically the personal computer (P.C.) is split into three parts, a communication device that allows you to talk to the computer called the "Keyboard", the brain called the "Computer" and the T.V.like screen called the "Monitor" or "Video Display Unit". See Figure (1) Below.

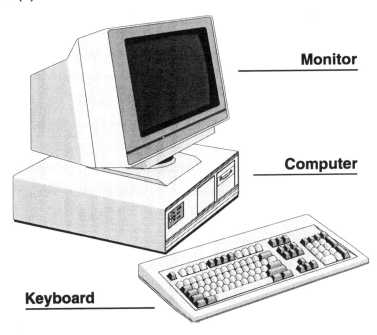

Monitor

Computer

Keyboard

Figure (1)

THE KEYBOARD

Because the keyboard is basically constructed the same way as a conventional typewriter with added keys, its primary function is to "type" messages to the computer. Some of these messages have already been pre-arranged by the inventors of your computers commanding system (DOS). These commands are shown overleaf in Figure(2) which acts as a guide helping you to understand where the keys appear on the keyboard and more importantly their purpose.

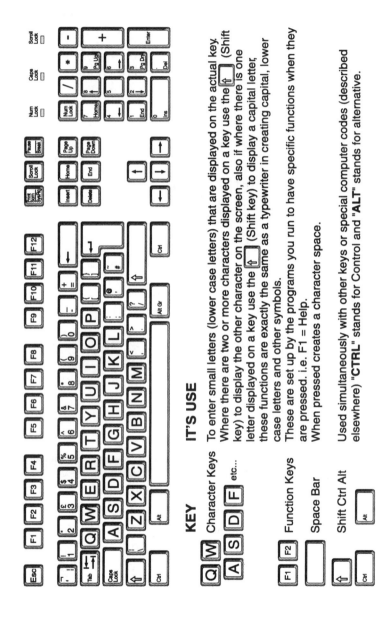

KEY

Character Keys

Q W

A S D F etc...

Function Keys

F1 F2

Space Bar

Shift Ctrl Alt

IT'S USE

To enter small letters (lower case letters) that are displayed on the actual key. Where there are two or more characters displayed on a key use the ⬆ (Shift key) to display the other character on the screen, also if where there is one letter displayed on a key use the ⬆ (Shift key) to display a capital letter, these functions are exactly the same as a typewriter in creating capital, lower case letters and other symbols.

These are set up by the programs you run to have specific functions when they are pressed. i.e. F1 = Help.

When pressed creates a character space.

Used simultaneously with other keys or special computer codes (described elsewhere) **"CTRL"** stands for Control and **"ALT"** stands for alternative.

14

Cursor Keys		Use the arrows displayed on the keys to move the cursor (flashing line) in the direction shown on top of the cursor keys. This isn't available when the numeric keypad is being used. (See Numlock).
Home End PageUp PageDown		These keys are used to view your work i.e. to move the cursor to the beginning or the end of a document using PageUp or PageDown or to move the cursor to the beginning or end of the line using Home or End.
Carriage Return		Creates another line or paragraph when you are typing or editing text, but this key is also used to send commands to your P.C. I.e When you are formatting a disk the computer will ask you a question similar to this: **"Format (Y/N)"** you reply **"Y"** then Carriage Return, also if you wish to view a directory you would type **"Dir"** then Carriage Return.
Tab Key		Moves the cursor to the next Tab Stop inserting spaces which have been predetermined.
Backspace Key		Deletes the character to the left of the cursor. (Remember the cursor is the flashing line)
Delete Key		Deletes the character to the right of the cursor. (Remember the cursor is the flashing line)
Escape Key		Used by most programs to indicate when you wish to stop using them. Esc stands for Escape.

KEY | IT'S USE

Insert Key — Used to switch between inserting or overwriting characters that are already on the screen.

Numlock Key — Used to swap between using the main keyboard numbers and the numeric keypad numbers on the right hand side of your keyboard. See Figure(1)

CapsLock Key — When Capslock is depressed i.e. turned on, a light is displayed on the top right hand side of your keyboard. Now all the lower case characters become capital letters when pressed without using the shift key until the Capslock is turned off i.e. pressed again.

Scroll Lock Key — Used by some programs to make the cursor keys move the text on the screen behind the cursor (i.e to the left, also note the light displayed on the top right hand side of the keyboard) this rather than the cursor moving over the text, press again to return to normal cursor movement (light is turned off).

Break Key — Can be used with the "**CTRL**" Key on some programs to exit.

Print Screen Key — Tells your computer's printer to print the current page displayed on the screen.

Note:- Not all programs will use the keys in exactly the same way. For more information please phone **(0860) 325144**

16

Using the keyboard is simply a matter of pressing keys either on their own or in conjunction with two or more others at the same time. When you use them on their own you get lowercase letters (little letters) of the alphabet or the lower portion of the two characters written on the keys; When you press "**Shift**" ⬆ at the same time you get uppercase letters (Capital Letters) or the upper portion written on the key. i.e. if you press "**8**" 8 on it's own you get the letter "**8**" if you press "**Shift**" and "**8**" ⬆ 8 simultaneously you will get "***".

The "**CapsLock key**" [Caps Lock] works like the shift lock key on a typewriter, but it only affects the letters (A-Z). Your P.C. keyboard also has a number of additional keys, there are twelve "**F**" keys known as "**Function Keys**" these are seen at the top of your keyboard marked F1 [F1] through to F12 [F12], many programs used on your machine will utilise these keys as quick reference i.e. F1 is nearly always used for help.

You also have two erase keys which are "**Backspace**" [←] and "**Delete**" [Delete], a "**Carriage return**" [↵] key which either makes a new paragraph or new line whilst editing a document. It can also send your reply back to one of the computer's questions or allows you to Enter (Send) a command into the computer; there is also an "**Escape key**" [Esc] which normally allows you to stop what you are doing when you want to.

Most of the time you will use the keys in the central section of your keyboard, most of these keys are the same as a typewriter and can be used on their own or in conjunction with the "**Shift**" ⬆ or "**CTRL**" [Ctrl] keys.

If you have any problems with using your keyboard please telephone (0860) 325144.

It is a good idea to spend some time getting used to where all of the keys are, for instance:- note where 1,2,3,4,5,6,7,8,9,0 are, along your keyboard. Should you wish to become more proficient in the use of your keyboard, we thoroughly recommend several inexpensive teaching programs. Future updates to this book will coincide with these programs.

For more information dial (0860) 325144.

THE COMPUTER

The main body of the computer consists of a case containing surprisingly few major components see Figure(3). There is a power supply and a motherboard with several micro-chips soldered onto its circuit board which act as the brains of the computer; There is also a storage area, used to hold and keep information permanently called the hard disk. Hard disks vary in size and have different capacities of storing information. There are also several boards plugged into the motherboard which act as sockets when you connect your various pieces of external equipment to the computer into i.e.the monitor, mouse and printer.

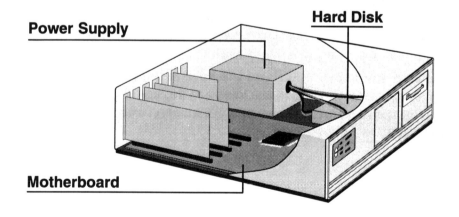

Figure (3)

Imagine holding your hand up with your fingers spread in a parallel position in between which are four magnetic spinning disks. If your finger tips were magnets capable of understanding what these disks were saying then you would effectively be holding a hard disk and your brain (the motherboard) would process any information read from it and in turn write back to the hard disk (your hand) any new or updated information that it needs to permanently store; the information stored on your hard disk (hand) can be called upon at any time in the future with absolutely no loss of information. In short it's like having a form of photographic memory.

We have all seen floppy disks, the names of which seem surprisingly common to everyone see Figure(4), below:-

5¼" Floppy Disk

3½" Floppy Disk

Figure (4)

A floppy disk to most people means computers. There are two types of commonly used floppy disks, the 5 1/4"and 3 1/2"; in your computer you will have one or two types of floppy disk drives which are the reading devices for floppy disks. You will learn that your computer identifies with these drives through your commanding operating system (DOS) and gives them different names. Normally there are two drives in a computer, the Hard Disk Drive commonly referred to as Drive C: and the floppy disk drive commonly referred to as Drive A:, if there are two floppy disk drives in your machine then normally the physically larger size drive is referred to as Drive B: the computer will recognise the drives as follows:-

1.44mb 3½" Floppy Disk Drive   **= Drive A:**
1.2mb 5¼" Floppy Disk Drive   **= Drive B:**
Hard Disk   **= Drive C:**

If you require the use of any of these drives, simply type "**A:**" then press the return key or "**B:**" then press the return key or "**C:**" then press the return key.

THE I.O. CARD

In order for your Floppy or Hard Disk Drives to communicate with the Motherboard (Brain) they must first connect and pass through an I.O. Card (In-Out Card) if you can imagine a postman delivering letters to houses in a street, he needs to know all the names and numbers of the houses so he can deliver his letters and in turn who has sent the letter so that he can pass back any reply of information to the sender. However if someone unscrewed all the numbers in the street he would find it impossible to deliver the letters (messages), in fact the postman would simply stand there totally confused.

In short the I.O.card is the postman in the computer and recognises where to send or receive information after being given the sender's and receiver's address. I.O. stands for in-out i.e. information given to and sent from the computer.

As well as being responsible for passing information to and fro between the Floppy Disk Drive, Hard Disk Drive and the Computer, the I.O.Card gives other devices direct access to the computer such as a mouse, joystick or printer. These devices can be connected to the respective ports supplied on the I.O.Card at the rear of the computer. i.e **COM1** (Communication port1),**COM2** (Communication Port2) and **LPT1** (Parallel Printer Port). See Figure(5)

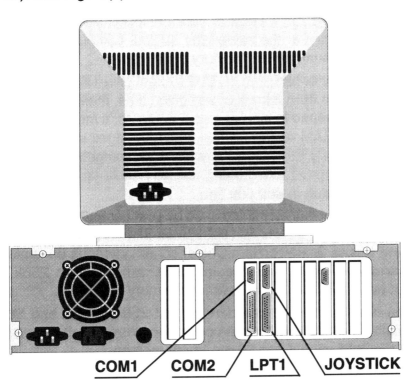

Figure (5)

MEMORY

A standard P.C. comes supplied with 1024k of memory which is split up into 640k of conventional memory (working memory for DOS) which your basic command system (DOS) relies upon to function, and 384k of extended memory which can be accessed by a specialist memory interpreter (Memory Manager), in short an assistant to the computer's commander (DOS).

There are slots in the motherboard designed to take extra memory, and this is called **RAM** which stands for Random Access Memory, this means that any amount of information you require can be accessed instantly by the use of this memory provided there are enough RAM chips inserted to cope with it all; If you insert more RAM in your computer you can access more information at the same time as your computer is able to hold bigger chunks in it's memory, for instance:-

If your computer had 1mb of RAM it might give it the capacity to read one page from a book at any given time, therefore it would surely make sense to increase your computer's memory capacity to 4mb of RAM so that it could read four pages at a time. This would obviously drastically increase your computer's processing/handling speed with it being able to handle up to four times more information at any one time.

The groups of memory chips used by your computer are known as **SIMMS** and the slots that hold these SIMMS (RamChips) are called Buses. SIMMS (Ram Chips) come in various denominations according to your requirements, ranging from 256k of memory per SIMM to 8000k (8mb) memory per SIMM.

You may by now be wondering what 256k, 8000k and 8mb means. To explain we have prepared the following table explaining the units used when talking about memory.

TYPE	DEFINITION
1bit=	1 byte of information. This effectively is the smallest denominator of memory and can be explained in terms of a light bulb being on or off (1 or 0).
1Kb=	1,000 bytes of information, 1Kb stands for One KiloByte.
1Mb=	1,000 kilobytes of information (1,000Kb), 1Mb stands for One MegaByte.
1Gb=	1,000 Megabytes of information (1,000Mb), 1Gb stands for One GigaByte.

To explain briefly how memory and extended memory works, you need to imagine a filing cabinet full of files. Firstly if you were to open the top drawer of a filing cabinet see Figure(6) and look through the contents of its files it would take you approximately 1 hour. If you wanted to read through all three drawers of the filing cabinet it would take you three times as long, however the computer is capable of using RAM to access all three drawers at the same time which could in this case speed the process up by 300%.

  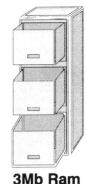

1Mb Ram   **2Mb Ram**   **3Mb Ram**

Figure (6)

THE VIDEO/GRAPHICS CARD and MONITOR (VDU)

Another important part of your computer is the **Video Card**, which effectively translates the computer's information into something you can see on the monitor (pixels). Your computer's monitor is connected to the computer via a port situated at the back of your computer on the graphics card; the monitor works exactly like a Television Screen in that the glass part (The Tube) has had all the air sucked out of it to create a vacuum. There is a mesh situated just behind the front of the screen inside the vacuum, and at the rear of the vacuum are three coloured guns (unless your monitor is Black & White). These guns are controlled by the computer to fire at the mesh and so light the screen up in controlled areas. We feel that it is not important to understand the exact method, however most of the images you see on the screen are directed to your **Monitor** (VDU) in this way. Please see Figure (7).There are various types of graphics card with the capacity to display varying amounts of colour and information.

R G B Coloured Guns

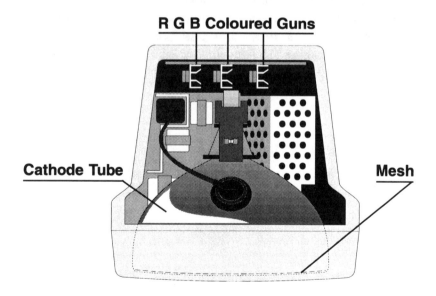

Cathode Tube

Mesh

Figure (7)

CONCLUSION

By now you will have realised that your computer is not as sophisticated as you first imagined. We have described methods of talking to and controlling your computer (Keyboard, Mouse and Joystick) and methods of receiving information (Monitor and Printer) all of which are controlled by a central brain (The Motherboard), which can read or write information to it's own storage cabinets (Hard Disks and Floppy Disk Drives) by using memory (SIMMS).

If you require any more information on this section please telephone (0860) 325144.

You will be delighted to know that after this section we will give you practical step by step guides in pursuing and solving tasks on your personal computer; but before this is started it is important to understand what MS-DOS actually is.

MS-DOS stands for Microsoft's Disk Operating System and as the name implies the system simply commands and operates a disk in conjunction with your computer's brain; for instance if you were introduced to a new job, quite often you would need to know certain words and terms that you had never heard before, but if you were to take the time to analyse these new instructions they could be described in a language you were both familiar with and fully understand.

In short, technical people use technical language more often than not to justify their expertise. It is our intention to make MS-DOS as user-friendly as possible by simplifying the terms utilised by the program writers themselves.

MS-DOS the program, often called the application program or software is a series of instructions pre-written to work with your computer in a language that it can understand, in order that it may perform tasks. For example the program might tell your computer to sort through a list of names, putting them into alphabetical order; or it might tell your computer to add up a sequence of numbers on an accounting sheet. There are many other examples of commands that in the first part you tell MS-DOS which in turn tells your computer to carry out the command.(MS-DOS commands everything that happens within the computer and responds to pre-written programs designed to run with it.)

You will note that when purchasing certain programs they are termed as DOS programs which means they will only run providing a version of MS-DOS is present on the computer; this surely means that if you understand how MS-DOS performs its command procedures, you will eventually use your application programs more effectively.

Programs are usually called applications or software. They are a series of instructions written in computing language (language that a computer can understand). These instructions are stored in files that tell your computer what to do; A file held in a directory on your hard disk is a collection of information exactly like a letter found in a folder inside your filing cabinet. The folder (directory) for instance might contain an office memo or sales figures that can be examined at will by a master controller, namely you; MS-DOS performs exactly the same task required in sorting out one letter (file) from a folder (directory) but much more quickly. It is therefore logical that each file should be given a name before it can be found, for instance:- just as each letter and folder in your filing cabinet has a name or label, so must each file and directory on a disk have a name or label.

A standard MS-DOS filename has two parts, a filename and an extension. A filename can be from 1-8 characters in length typed in small or capital letters (MS-DOS automatically converts filenames to capital letters) after which comes an extension (max.3 characters) these two parts form the necessary filename needed for MS-DOS to recognise the file;

For instance a valid filename would be **LETTER.TXT** (The Name of the file is **LETTER** and the Extension is **.TXT**).

It is always important to remember that MS-DOS provides a kind of yellow pages to browse through, in order that you may identify the location of a specific file or program; These yellow pages are called directories. When you look in a directory on your MS-DOS master disk you will see lots of files with extension names primarily .exe or .com. These extension names mean

.exe=executable and .com=command thus anywhere you see .exe or .com extensions the computer understands that these files are programs that can be run as programs through MS-DOS. There are many other types of files which have other extension names which are covered later on in this book.

MS-DOS allows you to run different types of applications, ranging from spreadsheets to word processing and graphics packages; it has standard commands that can be easily understood both by yourself and the computer. For instance "**dir**" means view the current directory, "**dir/w**" means view the directory across the screen in columns, "**dir/p**" means view the directory piece by piece (one screen at a time). Simple isn't it?

In order for you to understand these terms Section 3 of this book will bring you an easy but comprehensive basic knowledge of communicating with MS-DOS.

By this time you should understand what MS-DOS actually is and it is time to get started in a step by step guide of communicating with your computer commander MS-DOS.

Installing/understanding your command system (MS-DOS)

Most computers when purchased come with MS-DOS but if you wish to update your system or do not have MS-DOS installed on your computer then you should read and follow the instructions below.

When you buy MS-DOS you will receive a manual and some floppy disks, the manual will clearly state which version of MS-DOS you have purchased. Because there have been several upgrades since MS-DOS was first written it is highly unlikely that you will need to know about any MS-DOS package lower than version 5.

We recommend that if you are currently running a version lower than DOS 5 you purchase an update. If you telephone our hot-line number **(0860) 325144** you will receive special discounts due to your purchase of this book.

We have therefore designed your start up procedures as if you were installing the latest versions of DOS 5, 6 and 6.2.

Before you can use an MS-DOS operating system you must first check that your machine is capable of running it, i.e. your machine must be an I.B.M. or Compatible personal computer (P.C.). We also recommend that you use a 386 style computer or above to obtain the optimum benefits from your computer.

Lets get on!

In order to setup your computer with MS-DOS, first of all remove the floppy disks from the polythene packaging and note that if you are using the smaller size disks (3.5") there are three disks, if you are using the larger size disks (5 1/4") there will be five disks. For this purpose we will assume you are using the smaller size disks as these are now far more popular and are virtually standard.

"**Disk1**" is marked "**Setup Disk**", and this is the first disk that you should insert in your floppy disk drive. On the label you will see that it states the series and the storage capacity of the disk, together with the version. The second disk is marked "**Disk2**" and the third disk is marked "**Disk3**", and this is the order you should use them in.

INSTALLATION PROCEDURE FOR MS-DOS.

STEP(1)

Ensure that your computer is turned off, and if you are updating to a newer version of DOS, i.e. DOS 6 from 5 make sure you have two spare blank floppy disks. These disks must be the same type (format) as your MS-DOS installation disks.

STEP(2)

Put **Disk 1** (Setup Disk) into your floppy drive A:

Turn your computer on and it will automatically run the MS-DOS setup program (If you have a problem with running the setup disk telephone **(0860) 325144** as there could be a problem with your hardware setup)

STEP(3)

Provided the disk has successfully started your machine just simply read and follow the instructions given.

First of all you will see a message on the screen stating that MS-DOS is in Setup mode. The Setup mode will give you three main options marked with three small square white dots on a blue background. At the bottom of the screen is a white band with the following written across it:-

"**ENTER-Continue**" "**F1=Help**" "**F3=Exit**" "**F5=Remove Colour**" "**F7=Install to a Floppy Disk**"

You will not need use F5 or F7 unless you have a monochrome screen or do not have a hard disk. The three main options will read as follows:-

To Set up MS-DOS Now, press the enter/return key.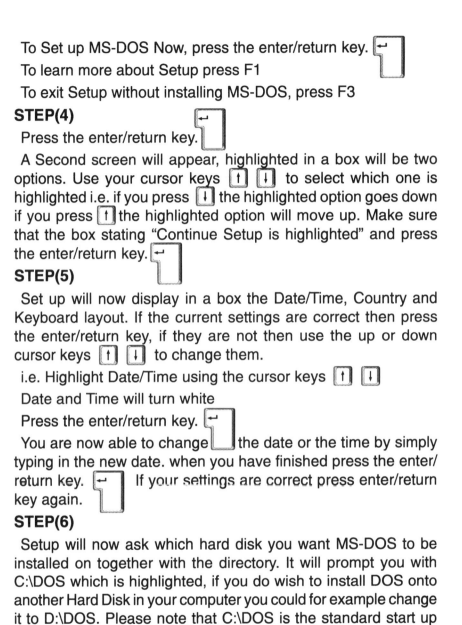

To learn more about Setup press F1

To exit Setup without installing MS-DOS, press F3

STEP(4)

Press the enter/return key.

A Second screen will appear, highlighted in a box will be two options. Use your cursor keys to select which one is highlighted i.e. if you press the highlighted option goes down if you press the highlighted option will move up. Make sure that the box stating "Continue Setup is highlighted" and press the enter/return key.

STEP(5)

Set up will now display in a box the Date/Time, Country and Keyboard layout. If the current settings are correct then press the enter/return key, if they are not then use the up or down cursor keys to change them.

i.e. Highlight Date/Time using the cursor keys

Date and Time will turn white

Press the enter/return key.

You are now able to change the date or the time by simply typing in the new date. when you have finished press the enter/return key. If your settings are correct press enter/return key again.

STEP(6)

Setup will now ask which hard disk you want MS-DOS to be installed on together with the directory. It will prompt you with C:\DOS which is highlighted, if you do wish to install DOS onto another Hard Disk in your computer you could for example change it to D:\DOS. Please note that C:\DOS is the standard start up (Boot-up) drive in nearly all of today's computers.

Press the enter/return key.

Setup will now start to install in this case DOS-6, a yellow bar will gradually grow across the screen above which is a message showing the current percentage of the installation carried out.

After a few minutes MS-DOS will ask you to insert Disk2, so remove Disk1 from the floppy drive and insert Disk2 into the drive.

Press the enter/return key.

After a few more minutes the MS-DOS installation program will ask you to insert Disk3, remove Disk2 from the floppy drive and insert Disk3 into the drive.

Press the enter/return key.

STEP(7)

When MS-DOS has finished installing itself the Yellow bar will be fully extended across the screen.

Press the enter/return key.

MS-DOS will now ask you to restart your computer. To do so press the enter/return key, your computer will now restart with MS-DOS installed onto your hard disk. **Easy wasn't it?**

SPECIAL NOTES ON UPDATING FROM DOS-6 to 6.2

We strongly recommend that you upgrade from DOS-6 to DOS-6.2 as there are several problems with MS-DOS 6 that could cause problems especially if you intend to or are using Double-space. (Double-space is Microsoft's own program that doubles the storage capacity of your hard disk, i.e. you can make an 80mb Hard Disk store nearly as much information as a standard 160mb Hard Disk)

To install the DOS-6.2 upgrade please follow the following steps

STEP(1)

Make sure you have a blank disk labelled **"Uninstall1"**, if your floppy drive's capacity is anything below 1.44mb make sure you have two disks handy.

Type at the C:\ Prompt **"md makesys"** return

Type **"cd makesys"** return

STEP(2)

Insert your DOS 6.2 upgrade disk into floppy drive A:

Type **"copy A:*.*"** return

STEP(3)

Type **"Makesys"** return

STEP(4)

Type **"Y"** return

STEP(5)

Type **"Y"** return but **"N"** if DOS is installed on a different drive.

STEP(6)

Type **"Setup"** return

Press return

(Make sure you have your blank disks ready)

Press return

Press return

Type **"Y"**

STEP(7)

Insert your blank disk marked uninstall1

Press return

Press return to restart the machine using DOS 6.2.

STEP(8)

Type **"cd makesys"**

Type **"del."** return

Type **"Y"** return

Type **"cd .."** return

Type **"rd makesys"** return

STEP(9)

Type "**cd old_dos.1**" return

Type "**del.**" return

Type "**Y**"

Type "**cd ..**"

Type "**rd old_dos.1**"

You have now successfully installed DOS-6.2. Fun wasn't it. You should now feel confident knowing that you have upgraded to the latest version of DOS. By the way, always make a backup of your master Program/Install Disks.

MAKING A COPY OF A DISK OR SET OF DISKS.

We strongly recommend at this stage that you make a complete copy of all your original program/installation disks. Make sure that after you have made copies (backups) of all your disks that you label them correctly and store the originals in a safe separate place away from your other disks.

IF YOU ARE USING DOS-5

STEP(1)

Ensure you have enough disks to copy all of your original disks.

Type "**DISKCOPY A: A:**" return

STEP(2)

Insert your original disk into Drive A:, this is the source disk

Press return

STEP(3)

When asked, remove your original disk from drive A: and insert your blank disk (target disk) labelling it to match your original disk.

Press return

STEP(4)

Repeat Steps(2)and(3) until the following message appears

"Copy another diskette (Y/N)"

STEP(5)

If you wish to copy another disk type **"Y"** remove disk and repeat Steps(1) to (5) if you do not wish to copy another disk type **"N"** and proceed to Step(6)

STEP(6)

Your disk/s will now have been successfully copied onto the blank disks you have supplied.

Always keep your original disks in a safe separate place.

Use your copies rather than the originals.

IF YOU ARE USING DOS-6+

STEP(1)

Ensure you have enough disks to copy all of your original disks.

Type **"DISKCOPY A: A:"** return

STEP(2)

Insert your original disk into Drive A:, this is the source disk

Press return

STEP(3)

When asked to remove your original disk from drive A: and insert your blank disk (target disk) labelling it to match the original disk.

Press return

STEP(4)

You will now be prompted with a message

"Do you want to make another duplicate of this disk"

Type **"N"**

STEP(5)

Now you will be asked **"Copy another diskette (Y/N)"**

If you wish to copy another disk type "**Y**" remove the disk and repeat steps(1) to (5) if you do not wish to copy another disk type "**N**" and proceed to Step(6)

STEP(6)

Your disk/s will now have been successfully copied onto the blank disks you have supplied.

Always keep your original disks in a safe separate place.

Use your copies rather than the originals.

If you have had any difficulties following this section and need additional help please telephone (0860) 325144

MAKING AN EMERGENCY BOOT-UP DISK

Before carrying out any major alterations or tweaks to your computer it is always a good idea to make an EMERGENCY BOOT-UP DISK which will successfully start your computer from Drive A:. If you accidentally delete the root directory of Drive C: and totally wipe out the all important files, **"command.com"**, **"config.sys"** and **"autoexec.bat"** files which are essential if your computer is to start correctly.

A Boot-up disk can be left in your computer when you first turn it on, re-boot it or press the reset button. It will start the computer with the same configuration as your standard hard drive boot-up sequence, it can do this because the computer's main start-up files are all duplicated onto it; the only differences you will find when booting up from your Boot-up disk are as follows:

a) A Boot-up disk is much slower at booting up (starting) your computer than your hard drive due to its slower disk access and transfer times.

b) After booting your computer from a floppy boot-up disk it is impossible for you to format any floppy disk inserted into the same floppy drive, for instance: if you were to boot-up from a floppy boot-disk in drive A: you would not be able to format any floppy disk in drive A:, unless you successfully managed to re-start the computer from another drive i.e. your hard drive C..

MAKING YOUR OWN EMERGENCY BOOT-UP DISK
IN DOS

Insert a blank or spare 1.44mb disk into your floppy diskette drive marked A:, make sure that if you have any important files on the floppy disk you have carefully copied them somewhere safe, as when you make a Boot-up disk all information on the disk is completely erased.

STEP(1)

At the DOS prompt type the following:-

"**Format A:\ /s**" the /s command informs the computer to copy the necessary hidden boot-up files to the floppy disk after formatting it, these are needed in order for the computer to start properly from the floppy Boot-up disk.

The following message will now appear.

"Insert new diskette for drive A:"

"and press ENTER when ready..."

Again if you are sure that the disk you have inserted in drive A: has no important files on it or is perferably empty, press enter. However if you are at all not sure then press the "**CTRL**" and "**C**" keys simultaneously and repeat STEP(1) after you have safely copied all of your important files either on to another disk or have found a clean or empty disk.

If you pressed enter at the prompted question the computer will start clicking away as it slowly formats your disk. You can now use your disk.

Note:-If you are using DOS 5.0 or above you can speed the process up by typing:

("**Format A:\ /q/s**" instead of "**Format A: /s**", the extra parameter tells DOS 5.0 or higher to quick format the disk if the disk has previously been formatted, this improves formatting times on average by about 300% or more.)

When the computer has finished formatting the floppy disk it will display a message like this:-

"Format Complete"

"System transferred"

The system files are the computer's own "Hidden" boot-up files and they are vital as if you do not inform the computer to copy them it will not boot from your floppy drive A; in this case your Boot-up disk.

After the system files have been copied the computer will display a message similar to this:-

Volume label (11 characters, ENTER for none)?

Either type in a name for your disk then press enter or simply press enter to leave your disk's name blank. At this point, the computer will ask if you want to **"Format another ? (Y/N)"**. If you want to make another Boot-up disk take out the current disk in drive A:\ and put in another blank or empty disk then type **"Y"** if you do not need another Boot-up disk type **"N"**.

STEP(2)

Now you can test to see whether your computer can load from your newly created Boot-up disk, to do this leave the disk in drive A: and reset the computer by either pressing the **"RESET"** button normally situated on the front panel of your computer or by preferably pressing the **"CTRL"** **"ALT"** and **"DEL"** keys simultaneously. You computer will now restart, and after a short while you will be left with a prompt from the computer similar to this:-

Enter new date (mm-dd-yy):

Press enter twice and you will now be left at the DOS prompt.

STEP(3)

The next step is to copy onto your Boot-up disk all of the neccesary configuration files and drivers needed to Boot-up your computer correctly. Simply type the following:-

"Copy C:*.sys A:\\" return

"Copy C:*.bat A:\\" return

"Copy C:\dos*.sys A:\\" return

"Copy C:\dos\emm386.exe A:\\" return

"Copy C:\dos\smartdrv.exe *.* A:\\" return

"Copy C:\dos\setver.exe A:\\" return

"Copy C:\dos\msav.exe A:\\" return

"Copy C:*.* A:\\" return

Please note that if you are prompted by the computer at any time to overwrite a file you should type "**N**". If you cannot fit all of your Root directory of your Drive C:\ onto your Boot-up disk you should now have sufficient files to be able to Boot-up safely.

STEP(4)

Now type "**Edit A:\config.sys**" return

A screen will now appear looking something like this:-

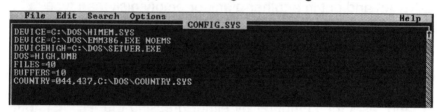

DEVICE=C:\DOS\HIMEM.SYS

DEVICE=C:\DOS\EMM386.EXE NOEMS

DEVICEHIGH=C:\DOS\SETVER.EXE

DOS=HIGH,UMB

FILES=40

BUFFERS=10

COUNTRY=044,437,C:\DOS\COUNTRY.SYS

DEVICEHIGH=C:\DOS\DISPLAY.SYS

Using your arrow keys and the delete key try changing your config.sys file so that it looks like the example shown below:-

DEVICE=**A**:\HIMEM.SYS

DEVICE=**A**:\EMM386.EXE NOEMS

DEVICEHIGH=**A**:\SETVER.EXE

DOS=HIGH,UMB

FILES=40

BUFFERS=10

COUNTRY=044,437,**A**:\COUNTRY.SYS

DEVICEHIGH=**A**:\DISPLAY.SYS

STEP(5a)

To test whether your computer's new Boot-up disk works properly after changing the "**A:\config.sys**" file you must first save and exit the file editor and then leave the Boot-up disk in drive A:\ whilst you "**RESET**" the machine or press "**CTRL**" "**ALT**" and "**DELETE**" keys simultaneously, **DO NOT REBOOT** your machine until you have completed STEP(5b).

STEP(5b)

To save your changed "**A:\config.sys**" file and exit the editor program simply press the "**ALT**" and "**F**" keys simultaneously. This will bring up the File drop down menu, now press "**X**". The computer will prompt you with the message "**Save file on exit?**" "**<YES> <NO>**" type "**Y**" and the computer will exit the editor program after saving your "**A:\config.sys**" file leaving you at the Dos prompt. Now you can safely reboot your machine as explained earlier in STEP(2).

STEP(6)

Now that you have successfully re-configured your CONFIG.SYS file, you must now edit and re-configure your AUTOEXEC.BAT file. Type the following "**edit A:\autoexec.bat**"

LOADHIGH C:\DOS\SMARTDRV.EXE

@ECHO OFF

Prompt pg

PATH=C:\DOS;C:\;C:\WINDOWS;C:\TEMP;C:\MOUSE;

SET TEMP=C:\TEMP

LOADHIGH C:\DOS\SHARE.EXE

LOADHIGH MOUSE

Using your arrow keys and the delete key try changing your config.sys file so that it looks like the example shown below:-

LOADHIGH **A:**\SMARTDRV.EXE

@ECHO OFF

Prompt pg

PATH=**A:**\;C:\DOS;C:\;C:\WINDOWS;C:\TEMP;C:\MOUSE;

SET TEMP=C:\TEMP

LOADHIGH **A:**\SHARE.EXE

LOADHIGH MOUSE

STEP(7)

Now save and exit the editor program by again pressing the "**ALT**" and "**F**" keys simultaneously then press "**X**". The computer will again prompt you with the following message "**Loaded File is not saved. Save it now?**" Type "**Y**" and the editor program will save your file and exit leaving you at the DOS prompt.

STEP(8)

RESET your Machine with your Boot-up disk in drive A.

You should now be able to run your computer normally from drive A:\, even if you have accidentally deleted the root directory of Drive C:\.

If you want to know more about using your Emergency Boot-up disk see the section marked "**WHAT TO DO IN CASE OF AN EMERGENCY**" later on in this book. (Please refer to the CONTENTS page or INDEX for the relevant page number).

If you have had any difficulties following this section and need additional help please telephone (0860) 325144

USING THE KEYBOARD WITH YOUR COMPUTER (BASIC MS-DOS COMMANDS)

The first things you will need to know are listed as follows:

A. **HOW TO VIEW THE CONTENTS OF A DIRECTORY (Browsing through the Yellow Pages)**

B. **HOW TO CHANGE BETWEEN DIRECTORIES**

C. **HOW TO CREATE OR DELETE DIRECTORIES**

D. **HOW TO CHANGE FROM ONE DRIVE TO ANOTHER**

E. **HOW TO COPY FILES**

F. **HOW TO COPY A GROUP OF FILES**

G. **HOW TO RENAME FILES**

H. **HOW TO DELETE FILES**

I. **HOW TO FORMAT A FLOPPY DISK**

A. HOW TO VIEW THE CONTENTS OF A DIRECTORY

This one is easy! Simply type "**dir**" then return. It's easy to remember as "**dir**" simply means directory in abbreviated form.

If you wish to see the directory displayed across the screen in rows type "**dir/w**" return, the "/w" command stands for across the width of the screen.

If you wish to see the directory in parts type "**dir/p**" return for the first part then press return to see the next part. Now keep on pressing return until you have viewed all of the directory. Please see Figures(1a) and (1b).

Please note that in Figures (1a) and (1b) the top of your directory reads "**Volume in Drive C is (name of drive)**" together with the volume serial number, below which a list of files in the directory can be seen.

Figure (1a) Using the "Dir/w" Command

```
Volume in drive C is SCANTECH
Volume Serial Number is 1B90-6E54
Directory of C:\

[ADDSTOR]        [DOS]           [TEMP]          [WINDOWS]       [BATS]
AUTOEXEC.BAT     COMMAND.COM     DEVSWAP.COM     EMM386.EXE      HIMEM.SYS
MOUSE.COM        MOUSE.SYS       SETVER.COM      SETVER.EXE      SSTORDRV.SYS
WINA20.386       CONFIG.SYS
        17 file(s)           342,083 bytes
                          14,983,168 bytes free

C:\>_
```

Figure (1b) Using the "Dir" Command

```
Volume in drive C is SCANTECH
Volume Serial Number is 1B90-6E54
Directory of C:\

ADDSTOR      <DIR>              07-28-92   11:11p
DOS          <DIR>              07-18-92    8:38a
TEMP         <DIR>              08-16-93   12:48p
WINDOWS      <DIR>              07-18-92    8:24a
BATS         <DIR>              01-21-94    1:20p
AUTOEXEC BAT              203   01-25-94   12:20p
COMMAND  COM           54,619   09-30-93    6:20a
DEVSWAP  COM            1,720   08-16-92    1:00a
EMM386   EXE          115,294   03-10-93    6:00a
HIMEM    SYS           14,208   03-10-93    6:00a
MOUSE    COM           28,886   11-13-91    4:04p
MOUSE    SYS           29,762   11-08-91   10:59a
SETVER   COM            6,901   04-09-91    5:00a
SETVER   EXE           15,804   04-09-91    5:00a
SSTORDRV SYS           65,010   08-16-92    1:00a
WINA20   386            9,349   03-10-93    6:00a
CONFIG   SYS              327   02-02-94    1:08p
        17 file(s)          342,083 bytes
                         14,983,168 bytes free

C:\>
```

The list comprises of files which have a title (of no more than eight letters), and an extension (of no more than three letters), after which there is a column showing the size of the file in bytes, and a column showing the date when the file was created or changed last. You will note that in one column "**<DIR>**" appears, this line refers to a seperate sub-directory of the directory currently shown; for instance if you had a folder with lots of letters in it, which also contained another folder with some more letters in it, the second folder would be called a sub-folder, and so a directory inside another directory is called a sub-directory. Please refer back to Figures (1a) and (1b).

You will note that throughout using your computer you will start at a command prompt, in this case "**C:\>**", typing a command always proceeds after this prompt. You must press the **enter/ return** key after every command you type, if the command is wrong the message "**Bad Command or Filename**" will appear, this will continue to happen until you enter a correct command.

Type "**ver**" (version), then press the return key at the prompt sign, MS-DOS will now display the version of DOS installed in your computer. (It's a good idea to know the version of your basic disk operating system as DOS version numbers will be commonly referred to in this publication.)

B. HOW TO CHANGE BETWEEN DIRECTORIES

O.K., lets start from the "**C:**" prompt. Type "**Dir**" return, this will show you the root directory found on your hard drive. If you were to then type "cd " (Change Directory) and then the name of a valid directory directly afterwards you would change to that directory. Let's try it:.

At the "**C:**" prompt type "**Dir**" return, a screen similar to the one shown in Figure(1b) will appear, now type "**cd dos**" return. The computer will now display the "**C:\DOS**" prompt, meaning that you are now in the directory of DOS, if you now type "**dir**" return you will note that the files shown have changed (just like turning the page of a book) See Figure(2), If you type "**cd ..**" return you will be taken back to the root directory "**C:**" again.

Figure (2)

49

So lets quickly try it again:-

Type "**cd dos**" return

Now type "**cd ..**" return, to bring you back again.

This rule applies to any directories whilst running in a standard DOS mode; therefore if you were to view the Root Directory from the "**C:**" prompt using the "**dir**" command, and saw that there was a sub-directory listed called for instance "**THE-BOOK**", you could change into that directory and view it's contents by simply typing "**cd THE-BOOK**" return then "**dir**" return, to get out of the directory all you would have to do is to type "**cd ..**" return.

C. HOW TO CREATE OR DELETE DIRECTORIES

Right, now let's try to create a directory. From the "**C:**" prompt you need to type "**md** " (Make Directory) and then the name you wish the directory to be called i.e."**test**" then press return.

Type "**md test**" return.

You will have now created a new directory called "**TEST**", to prove this type "**dir**" return, you will now see the "**TEST**" direc-tory listed as a Sub-directory of your Root directory. Please see Figure(3) for an example.

```
Volume Serial Number is 1B90-6E54
Directory of C:\

ADDSTOR      <DIR>           07-20-92   11:11p
DOS          <DIR>           07-18-92    8:38a
TEMP         <DIR>           08-16-93   12:48p
WINDOWS      <DIR>           07-18-92    8:24a
BATS         <DIR>           01-21-94    1:20p
TEST         <DIR>           02-10-94    8:26p
AUTOEXEC BAT              203 01-25-94   12:20p
COMMAND  COM           54,619 09-30-93    6:20a
DEUSWAP  COM            1,720 08-16-92    1:00a
EMM386   EXE          115,294 03-10-93    6:00a
HIMEM    SYS           14,208 03-10-93    6:00a
MOUSE    COM           28,886 11-13-91    4:04p
MOUSE    SYS           29,762 11-08-91   10:59a
SETUER   COM            6,901 04-09-91    5:00a
SETUER   EXE           15,804 04-09-91    5:00a
SSTORDRV SYS           65,010 08-16-92    1:00a
WINA20   386            9,349 03-10-93    6:00a
CONFIG   SYS              327 02-02-94    1:08p
        18 file(s)          342,083 bytes
                         14,981,120 bytes free

C:\>
```

Figure (3)

To view your "**TEST**" directory type "**cd test**" return, you are now inside the newly created "**TEST**" directory.

Type "**dir**" return to view it.

Well done, easy isn't it!

Now let's put something into your newly created directory.

Type "**copy C:*.***" Return (copy literally stands for Copy)

This command will copy all of the files from your root directory into the directory you are currently in. (In this case C:\TEST).

Now let's try deleting your newly created directory (C:\TEST).

Please note you cannot delete a directory which still has files inside it, if you do try the following message will appear:-

"**Invalid path, not directory,**"

"**or directory not empty.**"

To try this out type "**cd ..**" Return

Then type "**rd test**" Return (rd stands for Remove Directory)

The message shown above will now appear, in order to remove the directory we must first go back into the "**TEST**" directory, delete all the files in it, then change back into the root directory and then use the "**rd test**" command to finally delete the "**TEST**" directory, lets try it:

Type "**cd test**" Return

Now type "**del.**" Return, the following message will now appear

"**All files in directory will be deleted!**"

"**Are you sure (Y/N/)?**"

Make sure that you are in the "**C:\TEST**" directory by checking that you are at the "**C:\TEST**" prompt and then type "**Y**" Return to delete all of the files.

Now type "**cd ..**" Return to go back into the root directory

Finally type "**rd test**" Return

These steps will have removed both the files in the "**TEST**" directory and the directory itself from your root directory.

We have now learned how to create and change directories, we have also learned how to look at them. All these basic commands with many others may be found in the section marked **"MS-DOS COMMANDS QUICK REFERENCE GUIDE"** later on in this book, now lets go on to changing drives.

D. HOW TO CHANGE FROM ONE DRIVE TO ANOTHER

We learned earlier that there are normally only two drives in a standard computer a 3½" Floppy drive and a Hard Disk probably in the region of 40mb+ (however it is possible to increase your hard disk size to well in excess of over 2Gb per drive). The two drives are normally labelled **Drive A:** being the small floppy disk and **Drive C:** being the hard disk that stores the main bulk of your computer's information, there could well be a second floppy disk drive such as a 5¼" disk drive. These are not commonly used as they have now all but been replaced by the smaller 3½" Floppy Drives, but if you do have one on your computer it will be labelled as **Drive B:**. Also If you have an extra hard disk it will be labelled as **Drive D:** and so on.

Changing drives is very useful, for instance: if you wanted to work with files spread across different disk drives, such as moving information from your main **Drive C:** (Hard Disk) to **Drive A:** (Floppy Disk) initially you would need to use the following commands to change drives. In this case make sure your machine shows the "**C:**" prompt before starting:

Insert a floppy disk which has some files on it into Drive A:

Type "**A:**" return

You are now in the root directory of drive A:

Now type "**dir**" return and the screen will display the files on the floppy disk in Drive A:.

To return to your main hard disk Drive C: you should now type "**C:**" return, this will now leave you at the "**C:**" prompt.

If you try to change onto floppy drive A: without inserting a floppy disk the following message will appear:

"Not Reading Drive A"

"Abort, Retry, Fail?"

If you wish to carry on simply insert a floppy disk and type "**r**" for retry, or if you wish to cease the operation type "**f**" you would now be left with the prompt "**Current drive no longer valid>**" to return to Drive C: (Hard Disk) you would now type "**C:**" return.

To change on to another drive i.e. Drive B: you would insert in this case a large 5¼" floppy disk into Drive B: and then type "**B:**" return, please note that because Drive C: is always present in your machine you do not have to insert any floppy disks or otherwise to return to Drive C:, all you have to do is type "**C:**" return.

E. HOW TO COPY FILES BETWEEN DRIVES.

Being able to copy files from one drive to another is extremely useful, for instance if you wanted to transfer a letter to a friend's personal computer you could copy from your Hard Disk onto a Floppy Disk, and then your friend could then copy it from the Floppy Disk onto his or her Hard Disk or simply view the file from the floppy disk.

You can also use floppy disks to store all of your hard disk's information in case anything disastrous happens to your hard disk. These disks would be in the form of a numbered set of disks and would be called a back-up.

Right, let's copy a file. First of all if you want to copy information from drive C: to drive A: you must follow these instructions: In this case we are going to copy the "**autoexec.bat**" file from your root directory to a floppy disk in Drive A:.

STEP(1)

Insert a floppy disk into drive A: and make sure you are in the root directory of drive C: by typing "**cd C:**" return.

STEP(2)

View the contents of the directory by typing "**dir**" return and select which file you wish to copy onto drive A:, in this case we will use the "**autoexec.bat**" file.

STEP(3)

Type "**copy autoexec.bat A:**" return, your file will have now been copied onto your floppy disk in drive A:

If the file you wanted to copy was in another directory such as "**C:\\Files**" you could select it for copying simply by first changing into that directory and then telling DOS to copy it to Drive A:, for instance. In this case we are going to first make a directory called "**Files**", copy some files into it pretending that these are your working files and then copy one of the files onto a floppy disk.

STEP(1)

Type "**md files**" return (Make a directory called "files")

STEP(2)

Now type "**cd files**" return (Change to the files directory)

STEP(3)

Type "**copy C:*.***" (Copy all of the root directory into the current directory in this case "C:\\Files")

STEP(4)

Type "**dir**" return or "**dir/w**" return or "**dir/p**" return to view all of your files.

STEP(5)

Now after selecting the file you want to copy in this case we will use the "**config.sys**" file you would type "**copy config.sys A:**" return

STEP(6)

Your file will have now been copied onto Drive A: to check this type "**dir A:**" return (Show the directory of drive A: and all its contents).

You should now see at least two files on your floppy disk, the **"autoexec.bat"** file we copied on to it earlier and the **"config.sys"** file that we have just copied.

Finally just to explain exactly where the directory of FILES is please see Figure(4) below.

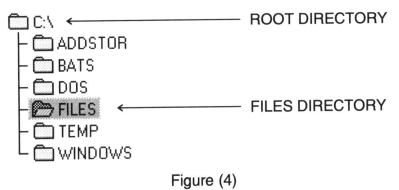

Figure (4)

F. HOW TO COPY A GROUP OF FILES

In this section you will use wild cards to copy groups of files from one directory to another (in this case the DOS to the files directory)

In a card game a wildcard matches any card in the deck, the same applies in MS-DOS by an asterisk "*" matching any character in that position and all other positions that follow it. If you play cards you will understand this but if you don't then imagine a universal bolt, that will screw onto any nut because it's thread adapts itself to the thread on the bolt, and this is effectively how a wild card works in DOS.

If you wanted to copy a group of files with a similar name, using wild cards would be easier and quicker than copying each file individually. To help you understand wildcards and their use in DOS we have compiled the following steps.

STEP(1)

To start with, make sure your command prompt looks like this "**C:\DOS**", you can do this by typing "**cd C:\dos**" return.

Now then, do you remember the various extensions that you normally find on files, ".com" ".txt" ".exe" and so on? Well let's try copying a group of files which all have the extension ".txt" from the "**DOS**" directory to the "**FILES**" directory.

STEP(2)

To view all the files in the DOS directory that end in the extension ".txt" you must type the following "**dir *.txt**" return, remember the "*" denotes a wildcard. (Please note there is a space before the "*" but not after it.) A list similar to the one seen in Figure(5) will appear because the command has simply told MS-DOS to list all the files in the "**DOS**" directory that end in the extension ".txt", the "*" will match any characters before the ".txt" option.

```
C:\>cd dos

C:\DOS>dir *.txt

 Volume in drive C is SCANTECH
 Volume Serial Number is 1B90-6E54
 Directory of C:\DOS

APPNOTES TXT         8,723 04-09-91    5:00a
NETWORKS TXT        20,463 03-10-93    6:00a
OS2      TXT         6,358 03-10-93    6:00a
README   TXT        76,705 09-30-93    6:20a
        4 file(s)         112,249 bytes
                       14,981,120 bytes free

C:\DOS>_
```

Figure (5)

STEP(3)

As you can see MS-DOS has listed all the files that end in ".txt" extensions, the wildcard has told MS-DOS to ignore all the different beginnings of the files and focus only on the extension ".txt". Now lets copy all the files with a ".txt" extension to the "**C:\Files**" directory.

Type "**copy *.txt C:\files**" return, this command now copies all the files in the current directory that have a "**.txt**" extension to the directory of "**C:\FILES**". To check that this has happened change to the FILES directory by typing "**cd C:\files**" return and then type "**dir**" return, a screen similar to the following screen will now appear. Please see Figure(6).

```
.              <DIR>           02-10-94   9:19p
..             <DIR>           02-10-94   9:19p
AUTOEXEC BAT         203 01-25-94  12:20p
COMMAND  COM      54,619 09-30-93   6:20a
DEVSWAP  COM       1,720 08-16-92   1:00a
EMM386   EXE     115,294 03-10-93   6:00a
HIMEM    SYS      14,208 03-10-93   6:00a
MOUSE    COM      28,886 11-13-91   4:04p
MOUSE    SYS      29,762 11-08-91  10:59a
SETVER   COM       6,901 04-09-91   5:00a
SETVER   EXE      15,804 04-09-91   5:00a
SSTORDRV SYS      65,010 08-16-92   1:00a
WINA20   386       9,349 03-10-93   6:00a
CONFIG   SYS         327 02-11-94  11:29a
APPNOTES TXT       8,723 04-09-91   5:00a
NETWORKS TXT      20,463 03-10-93   6:00a
OS2      TXT       6,358 03-10-93   6:00a
README   TXT      76,705 09-30-93   6:20a
       18 file(s)      454,332 bytes
                    14,510,080 bytes free

C:\FILES>
```

Figure (6)

As you can see the files with a "**.txt**" extension that you listed earlier have now all been successfully copied to the files directory. Now in the future when someone mentions about wildcards you will understand exactly what they are and what they can do.

G. HOW TO RENAME FILES

You may want to rename a file if the information in it changes or you simply prefer another name. To rename a file you would type "**rename (the name of the original file and its extension) (the new name of the file and its extension)**" return, for instance if your filename was "**menu.txt**" and you wanted to change it to "**buffet.txt**" you would type the following:

"**Rename menu.txt buffet.txt**" return

This will rename your file, and you can also use a wildcard to rename groups of files in exactly the way you used it to copy groups of files, to do this you would simply type **"rename buffet.* starters.*"** return. This command specifies that all the files that begin with **"buffet"** should be renamed to **"starters"**, however they will still keep their extensions.

To rename all the files in a current directory whose names end in the extension **".txt"** to **".doc"** simply do the following:

STEP(1)

In this case we will name all of the **".txt"** files in the files directory to **".doc"** files. So first make sure that you are in the files directory by typing **"cd C:\files"** return

STEP(2)

Now type **"dir *.txt"** return, a list of files with the **".txt"** extension will appear on the screen.

STEP(3)

Type **"rename *.txt *.doc"** return, this will immediately rename all of the **".txt"** files to **".doc"** files, to confirm this type **"dir"** return and view the changes.

Now lets try another one, this time just renaming one file.

STEP(1)

Type **"rename autoexec.bat autoexec.tmp"** return

STEP(2)

Type **"dir"** return to view the directory and as you can see the **"autoexec.bat"** file has now been renamed to **"autoexec.tmp"**.

By now you may be wondering what to do with all of these files taking up your valuable disk space? Well it's simple. All you have to do is delete them! **"How do I delete them?"** I hear you ask. Just read the next section and all will be explained!.

H. HOW TO DELETE FILES

It is obviously important to explain how to remove a file that you no longer need or want on your Drive. To delete a file you must use the "**del**" command which stands for delete.

STEP(1)

Before you begin, make sure that you are on your hard drive and that the command prompt looks like this:- "**C:\FILES**". Again just to make sure type "**cd C:\files**" return.

STEP(2)

Type "**Dir**" return to view all of the files in your "**C:\FILES**" directory.

Now then what do we want to delete from it ? Let's assume you wanted to delete the newly named "**autoexec.tmp**" file that we made earlier.

STEP(3)

Again make sure that you are in your files directory and that you are at the "**C:\files**" prompt as deleting files can be a very risky business, especially if you are in the wrong directory. In fact the most common failures on the computer come from people being over-indulgent in their spring cleaning. For instance, deleting just about everything that doesn't seem to look very big or important, which is more often than not a vital part of a program or worse still your computer's operating system. Anyway let's get on.

Type "**del autoexec.tmp**" return, you have now instantly deleted that file, and it is very, very easy, so again be extremely careful when deleting files.

STEP(4)

To confirm that you have deleted the file type "**dir**" return.

If you wish to delete a group of files, in this case all the files you renamed earlier with the extension of "**.doc**" you would do the following:

STEP(1)

Type "**del *.doc**" return, that's it!

Also if you wanted to delete all the files in a directory you would type either "**del *.***" return, or "**del.**" return. Let's give it a go and delete all of your files in the "**C:\FILES**" directory.

STEP(2)

Type "**del *.***" return or "**del.**" return. Both of these commands, will give you the prompted message:

"All the files in your directory will be deleted!"

"Are you sure (Y/N)?"

You can either reply "**Y**" return for YES or "**N**" return for NO. Remember always use extreme caution when deleting anything from your hard disk.

Finally just to finish off and leave your disk tidy change back to the root directory and remove the files directory that we have been using.

O.K. just in case you haven't got the idea of it yet:

Type "**cd ..**" return, now type "**rd files**" return. Easy isn't it ?

I. HOW TO FORMAT A FLOPPY DISK

(IN DOS)

Insert a blank or unneeded 1.44mb disk into your floppy diskette drive marked A, make sure that if you have any important files on the floppy disk you have safely copied them to a safe place as when you format a disk all information on the disk is completely erased.

To format a floppy disk simply follow the following steps shown overleaf.

STEP(1)

At the DOS prompt type the following

"**Format A:**" return

The following message will now appear.

"**Insert new diskette for drive A:**"

"**and press ENTER when ready...**"

Again make sure that the disk you have inserted in drive A has no important files on it or is empty. If so, press enter. If you are not sure then press "**CTRL**" and "**C**" simultaneously and then change the floppy disk or copy the files on it to a safe place, then repeat STEP(1)

STEP(2)

If you have pressed enter at the prompted question the computer will start clicking away as it slowly formats your disk.

Note:-If you are using DOS 5.0 or above you can speed the process up by typing:

"**Format A:\\ /q**" return instead of "**Format A:**" return

The extra parameter tells DOS 5.0 or higher to quick format the disk if the disk has previously been formatted, this improves formatting times on average by about 300% or more.

STEP(3)

When the computer has finished formatting the floppy disk it will display a message like this:-

"**Format Complete**"

"**Volume label (11 characters, ENTER for none)?**"

Either type in a name or press enter at this point. The computer will now ask you if you want to "**Format another ? (Y/N)**", if you want to format another disk take out the current disk in drive A:\\ and put in another blank or empty disk then type "**Y**". If you do not need to format another disk type "**N**".

SO LETS SUMMARISE ON WHAT WE'VE DONE SO FAR:

(1) **"dir"** allows you to view a directory in any drive on any disk.

(2) **"cd"** allows you to change directories.

(3) **"md"** allows you to make a directory.

(4) **"rd"** allows you to remove a directory.

(5) **"copy"** allows you to copy a file or group of files

(6) **"rename"** allows you to rename files

(6) **"del"** allows you to delete files

(7) **"format"** allows you to format hard or floppy disks

If you have had any difficulties following this section and need additional help please telephone (0860) 325144

MANAGING YOUR COMPUTER'S FILING CABINETS
(File Management)

A file is a group of information held in the form of a file on your computer. It also enables MS-DOS to tell the difference between one collection of information and another. I.e. If you typed a letter in a word processing program you would save your letter in its own file, just as you would save a copy of a handwritten or typed letter in your filing cabinet. Every file has a name and extension which indicates what type of information it contains.

The files on your computer come from lots of different sources and some of them are not created by you because they come from MS-DOS and other programs. They contain codes and other information to enable your computer and its programs to run. For example each of the files used by MS-DOS contains information about the commands MS-DOS will understand, like the files you create MS-DOS has named them in order that it may understand the contents of each file. It is not therefore difficult to understand that in time there will be hundreds, thousands even tens of thousand of files on your computer which can make it difficult to locate one specific file, just as it would be difficult to find the correct nut in a box containing thousands of different sized nuts. By far the better thing to do would be to label or colour all the nuts of the same size so they can be found more easily and the different sizes can be recognised more quickly.

MS-DOS needs to identify thousands of files in pretty much the same way, for instance storing groups of files in different directories makes it easier to find files. All the main programs files that come in MS-DOS are stored in a separate directory called DOS, therefore if both you or the computer need to find a DOS related file you both know where to look. Like files, directories can be created by you or an application, giving you the chance to separate your information into different identifiable titles. Directories would be hard to find or recognise if you didn't know which one you were in "**Then how**" you ask "**can you be in a directory ?**".

Well think of your computer as a garage, and when your computer is turned off you are outside the garage, when your computer is turned on you are inside the garage. As long as you are in the garage you are in one of the areas able to assist you in fixing or working on your car, in the same sense as long as your computer is on you must be in a directory and can easily find the files you need to assist your task.

MS-DOS indicates which directory you are in by displaying it at the command prompt, for example if you were in the directory of DOS it would be shown at the prompt as "C:\DOS".

The directory you are in is called the current directory. Knowing which directory you are in obviously helps you to find specific files you need whilst working between directories. Sub-directories are directories inside of directories (Files inside Files), a directory with another with another directory in it is called a sub-directory. By creating sub-directories you can arrange your files more easily; for example if you had a directory containing a word processor you could make a sub-directory to hold your actual working files. This would ensure that you could easily find your own files as they would not get mixed up with the word processor's own program files.

You do not have to be in the directory that contains the files you want, but if you are the commands you need to type will be shorter, however we hope you will become more comfortable in typing longer commands as you work through the book.

Practically speaking all directories are actually sub-directories, that is a directory within a directory apart from one, this is called the root directory. We have learned that the root directory is simply the first shoot that connects a plant to the ground or the first directory that connects all programs to the computer, just to emphasize that for a moment, let's just take a quick look at what we have said.

If you imagine a full grown plant or tree, the root would be the only part connected to the ground and the stem or trunk would be in fact the pathway to send information to and from the root. In the same way the computer can be termed as the ground, and the trunk is the pathway needed to send information, that is why from time to time you will hear the word path mentioned in sending information to a particular directory or file. If you look further along a branch on a tree you will see there are smaller branches or twigs that grow from it and then even smaller twigs that grow from those, a sub-directory divides in the same way.

Please see Figure(1) below.

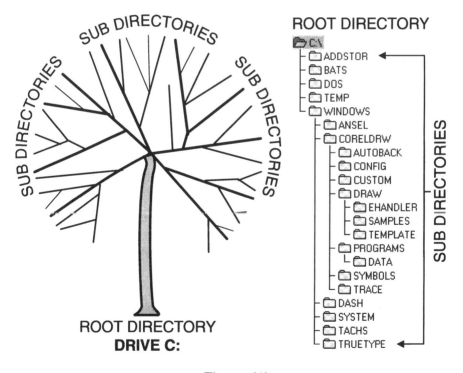

Figure (1)

DRIVES

Just as a directory holds a collection of files, a drive which is represented by a letter holds a group of directories. Drives are nearly always associated with a piece of computer hardware called a disc, and a disc in fact is a piece of flat metal or plastic on which information is stored, the most common types of discs are hard disks, which are situated inside your computer. We have already mentioned the difference between different drives but you should also understand that there are differences between discs also. The command prompt indicates the current drive being used, if you see "**C:**" then drive C is being used if you see "**A:**" then drive A is being used and so on. If the drive you are using is drive A and the directory you are in is "**BOOK**" then the command prompt would appear as follows "**A:\BOOK\>**". You have already learned how to change from drive to drive but let's refresh your memory:

If you want to used drive A at the "**C:**" prompt you type "**A:**" return and then "**dir**" return to view the directory of drive A: not forgetting to insert a floppy disc in drive A: before you type the command. Drive B: and drive C: can be accessed in exactly the same way by simply changing the letter i.e. from the "**A:**" prompt you would type "**C:**" return to get back on to C: drive and so on. If you have more than one hard disk, use a CD-ROM or have a network, additional drive letters will also be used, "**D: E: F:**" and so on. Please note that every drive no matter what type it is will always have a root directory and will be initially named by a letter of the alphabet.

PATHS

As previously explained a path is the course that leads from the root directory of a drive to another directory holding the file you want to use, please refer back to Figure (1).

Figure (2) clearly shows you the path in colour which DOS would take if you typed "**cd C:\windows\coreldrw\programs**" return

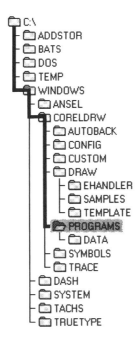

PATH=C:\WINDOWS\CORELDRW\PROGRAMS

Figure (2)

NAMING FILES AND DIRECTORIES

All files and directories except for the root directory on each drive must have a name, there are some simple rules laid out by DOS as to what form and size these names may take. The rules for naming files and directories are as follows.

(1) The name can be up to eight characters long and in addition to that you may include an extension of no more than three characters, however between the name and the extension you must insert a dot. i.e. "**letter.txt**"

(2) All names are not capital or lower case letter sensitive. In fact you can type them however you wish, as they will automatically be converted to uppercase anyway.

(3) You can only use the letters between A to Z and 0 to 9 plus the following special characters:

" _ " Underscore,   " ^ " Caret   "$" Dollar Sign
" ~ " Tilde   " # " Hash   "&" Ampersand
" - " Hyphen   "{ }" Braces   "@" At Sign
" ' " Apostrophe   "%" Percentage Sign
" ` " Single Quotation Mark   " ! " Exclamation Mark
"( )" Brackets   **No other special characters are acceptable to DOS.**

You cannot have spaces, commas, backslashes or periods (dots) except for the dot that separates the extension from the filename.

(4) You may not have two or more files in the same directory which have the same name, you may also not have two subdirectories with the same name in the same directory.

Right then, I think we have covered most points in getting to know your disk operating system or commander as we have called it. You will find that you will learn much more by actually using your system, and clearly it is inevitable that problems will occur. You might for instance wipeout DOS completely or be over indulgent in deleting files. Whatever happens, making mistakes bears one fine quality (you are learning by them) and if you become completely stuck you can dial (0860) 325144 quoting your personal reference number and the page number in the book which is relevant to your problem. However DOS has it's own help system that basically falls into two categories, it is a good idea to understand how this works; the **"MS-DOS HELP"** is a complete on-line reference for MS-DOS commands including notes and examples and **"COMMAND LINE HELP"** which displays the structure of a command without leaving the command prompt. Please read the next section **"USING MS-DOS HELP"** which explains how to use MS-DOS Help.

USING MS-DOS HELP

To start help at the **"C:\"** prompt type **"Help"** return and a con-tents table will appear. You will note (DOS-6) there are green luminous brackets highlighting the various topics of DOS that are covered, and that on the right hand side of the screen there is a sliding scale which has a black bar in the middle and arrows at the top and bottom.

If you press the down arrow you will note that the bar starts to move down the sliding scale whilst the screen does the same. A flashing cursor on the left hand side of the screen will also start to move down showing which help topic on the screen you can currently select. If you press the up arrow the cursor will start to move up again, you will note that every time the bar moves up or down the number in the bottom right corner of the screen changes, this denotes the line number, to move across the screen use the right direction arrow key, and you will be able to select any of the help topics available in MS-DOS help simply by pressing the return/enter key when your cursor is directly over the topic you wish to select. Please see Figure(1) below.

Figure (1)

At the top of your screen are the words **"File"**, **"Search"** and **"Help"**, if you press the **"ALT"** key the word File will turn black, if you then press your left or right arrows you will move the black marker between **"File"**, **"Search"** and **"Help"**; lets leave the black marker on **"Help"** and press the down arrow key, a drop-down menu will appear with two titles on it namely **"How to use MS-DOS Help"** and **"About..."**, if you press your left arrow you will select **"Search"** its drop-down menu will appear with two more titles reading **"Find..."** and **"Repeat Last Find"**, if you press your left arrow yet again you will select **"File"** and it's drop-down menu will appear reading **"Print..."** and **"Exit"** which of course when confirmed by pressing the enter/return key exits MS-DOS Help.

You can also use a mouse (if you have one installed) to highlight any area of the screen simply by moving the small white pointer that appears when a mouse is present to the area you want to select, then simply press the mouse button and the relevant help section will appear.

Please note that in order for a mouse to work with any DOS based program you must have connected the mouse to the computer and correctly installed the necessary software needed to run it. (Mouse driver must be installed and resident in memory) If you need help on installing a mouse please see the relevant section marked **"INSTALLING A MOUSE (MS-DOS)"**.

OK. Lets try selecting a help topic, in this case we will be selecting the **"<Expand>"** topic.

STEP(1)

Move your cursor or mouse so that it is directly over the **"<Expand>"** help topic, press return or click on the mouse.

(Please note, you can use the **"Tab"** key which automatically places the cursor over each of the help topics on the screen. To move the cursor forwards along the help topics press **"Tab"**, to move backwards through the topics keep the **"Shift"** key pressed and press the **"Tab"** key, until the cursor highlights your topic.)

STEP(2)

Another screen will appear (See Figure(2)) with the help file displayed, you can scroll through the documents pages of help text by either using the up and down arrow keys or by using the Page Up and Page Down keys.

Figure (2)

STEP(3)

Alternatively you can print the help file by selecting "**Print**" in the "**File**" drop down menu, simply press *Alt" and "**F**" simultaneously, (or click onto the "File" menu with your mouse) the "**File**" drop down menu will appear with "**Print...**" highlighted in black. Press return (or click) and a message will appear asking you where you want to print your current help topic, the default setting will be to your current printer, so press return (or click on O.K.). The help file will now be sent to your printer.

STEP(4)

To Exit the help topic simply press the "**Escape**" key or the "**Alt**" and "**C**" keys simultaneously. If you want to exit MS-DOS Help completely just press the "**Alt**" and "**F**" keys simultaneously then press "**x**" for exit.

It is interesting to note that MS-DOS version 6 and upwards includes several programs that can manage, protect and improve the performance of your computer. There is a back-up system that actually allows you to take files you no longer use and store them elsewhere just in case you need access to them at a later date. This can also safeguard all your computer's files by them being safely backed up onto floppy disks.

There is also an anti-virus system that helps take away the possibilities of losing data from destructive computer viruses, computer viruses can be transported from one computer to another via floppy disks or interconnecting systems (networks), just as colds are transferred from person to person. It is therefore important to use the anti-virus utility from time to time especially when receiving data produced on another computer; please note that magazine free disks are usually checked for all known viruses and are badged to say so, but if you are still wary then it is still a good idea to virus check them yourself before using them.

There is also a Microsoft defragmenter and Smartdrive program, and these minimise the time it takes for your computer to access the hard disk and transfer information, increasing the overall computing speed.

Finally Microsoft "**Undelete**" is capable of retrieving lost files that may have been mistakenly deleted; In order to keep your computer in top working order we advise you to use these programs regularly.

To help you understand which program you might need for a particular job we have produced the following table.

IF YOU WANT TO	DO THIS	MORE INFORMATION
a) Create more free space on your hard disk	a) Use a disk compression program or delete unwanted files.	a) "FREEING DISK SPACE" See Page(x)
b) Find lost bits of information that use up hard disk space.	b) Use the "Chkdsk" command or a defragmenting program.	b) "OPTIMISING YOUR HARD DISK" See Page(x)
c) Make your computer read information from your hard disk more quickly	c) Use Smartdrive or another disk caching device	c) "INCREASING DISK SPEED" See Page(x)
d) Free space and ensure that files are retrievable if your hard disk fails or you accidentally delete them.	d) Use a backup program	d) "BACKING UP YOUR HARD DISK" See Page(x)
e) Safeguard against viruses damaging your computer files or performance just as we use toothpaste against decay.	e) Use an anti-virus program	e) "ANTI-VIRUS PROGRAMS" See Page(x)
f) Access files more efficiently	f) Use MS-DOS(6) "Defrag" or a similar optimization program	f) "OPTIMISING YOUR HARD DISK" See Page(x)
g) Recover files that you have destroyed or deleted accidentally or not.	g) Setup or use the "undelete" command.	g) "RECOVERING DELETED FILES" See Page(x)

By now you will have realised that there are only two major components that your computer uses to store information, the floppy disk and the hard disk, and between them they provide both temporary and long term storage.

As you now know information on disks is stored magnetically, in the same way that sound is stored on a cassette tape. If you can imagine the available space on a hard disk being represented by a large magnet and the information you store on it as thousands of pins, when the pins completely cover the magnet they will eventually start to fall off, even though for a time they will stick to one another. When you store files on a hard disk they too use up some of the available magnetic space. This magnetic space is measured as a capability to store megabytes of information. If you have an eighty megabyte disk (80Mb) and store on it eighty megabytes worth of files any further information you wish to store will simply not be allowed on the disk.

It is therefore important that your hard disk always has some free or empty space, as you will need empty space to save documents and other data files. Also the program that you are using may wish to create temporary files and store them on your hard disk whilst it is running, and these programs need to create these temporary files in order to run correctly.

Please note: To keep track on how much disk space you have available you should use the "**chkdsk**" and "**dir**" commands. i.e.

At the "**C:**" prompt either type "**Chkdsk**" return or "**Dir**" return and the amount of disk space used/left will be shown.

There are only two ways to make more disk space available, you can either delete unwanted files by using the delete command, or you can compress the files that exist on your hard disk.

Please note: the delete command should be used with great care as it can prove quite destructive, sometimes causing a complete computer failure.

Let's for a moment consider disk compression. If you have ever witnessed dehydrated food that has simply had all the moisture sucked out of it, you will notice that it will shrink to sometimes less than three quarters of its size. With special care it is possible to shrink food without damaging its nutritional value, and by adding water at a later date it will literally explode into its original size and edibility. In the same way a disk compression program shrinks the size of the original information (file) by squashing it on the disk and when the DOS commander asks to read the file it automatically expands the information (file) back to it's original state.

DELETING UNWANTED FILES

First of all you must be absolutely sure that you don't want the files any more. You might want to delete the files because you no longer use the program or data files on it, or you might want to delete files that were left on your disk temporarily due to your program breaking down (crashing). You might want to delete files that were installed by MS-DOS that you don't need to use, and lastly there could be bits of information that have lost their identity and don't know where they belong which you want to remove. **Please Remember:** Always keep as much disk space free as possible.

These are the steps you should take to delete files:

At the "C:\" prompt type "**dir/p**" return and make a note of the files or programs you no longer want (please remember that when you delete a program there are sometimes other directories found inside the programs directory, these are called sub-directories and need to be deleted before you can completely delete the programs directory from the hard disk. Please see Figure(1).

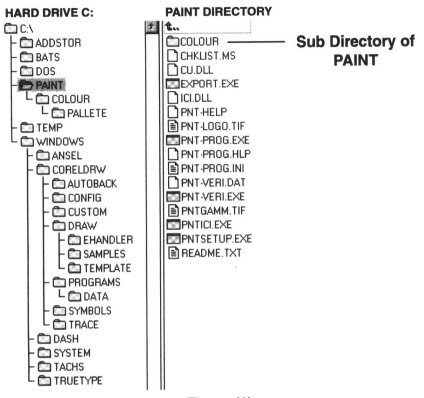

Figure (1)

Let us therefore try and delete the program shown in Figure(1) called "**PAINT**" which has a sub directory in it called "**COLOUR**" which itself has a sub directory called "**PALLET**". This is how you would proceed.

STEP(1)

At the "**C:**" prompt type "**cd paint**" return (The directory of the program that you want to delete)

STEP(2)

At the "**C:\paint**" prompt type "**cd colour**" return (Sub-Directory of the program)

STEP(3)

At the "**C:\paint\colour**" prompt type "**cd pallet**" return (Sub-Directory of Colour)

You can now start deleting the files in pallet.

STEP(4)

Type "**dir**" return and you will be shown the files in the current directory ("**C:\paint\colour\pallet**").

STEP(5)

Type "**del *.***" return, a message will appear reading:

"All files in the directory will be deleted"

"Are you sure (Y/N)?"

Type "**Y**" for yes or "**N**" for no, please remember that if you type "**Y**" that's it and all the files will be lost forever, and that it can be a real pain getting them back.

STEP(6)

Type "**cd ..**" return

We are now at the "**C:\paint\colour**" prompt and are about to delete the sub-directory inside "**COLOUR**" namely "**PALLET**".

Type "**rd pallet**" return ("rd" stands for remove directory)

STEP(7)

At the "**C:\paint\colour**" prompt type "**del *.***" return

Type "**Y**" return for yes

STEP(8)

Type "**cd ..**" return

You are now in the directory of "**C:\paint**".

At the "**C:\paint**" prompt type "**rd colour**" return

STEP(9)

Type "**del *.***" return

Type "**Y**" return for yes

STEP(10)

Type "**cd ..**" return

You can now completely delete the paint directory by typing "**rd paint**" return at the "**C:**" prompt. You will have now deleted all three directories, if you only had one directory to delete you would only follow Steps**(1)**,**(9)** and **(10)**.

Now let's suppose that instead of deleting the whole of the paint program you only wanted to delete a single file from the "**PAINT**" directory called "**readme.txt**". (See Figure(1)) To delete this file you would simply do the following.

Select the directory where the file exists, if the file existed in "**C:\PAINT**" you would type "**cd paint**" return.

At the "**C:\PAINT**" prompt type "**dir**" return and make sure that the file you wish to delete (in this case "**readme.txt**") exists in the directory. Please note that to delete this file you will have to use the name and the extension of the file, not just the name.

At the "**C:\PAINT**" prompt type "**del readme.txt**" return and the file will be deleted. Now type "**cd ..**" return to get back to the root directory and that's it.

Can we finally say that deleting files should only be considered when you have planned what you intend to do with your computer, and only when you are absolutely certain that (as in the above case) you do not require the program on your hard disk. However before you delete any programs from your hard disk it is always advisable to make a copy of them on to a floppy disk(s), just in case you want to use it again. Well, that just about concludes deleting.

For further information about deleting files and getting to grips with the various basic disk commands please see the section **"USING THE KEYBOARD WITH YOUR COMPUTER (BASIC MS-DOS COMMANDS)"**

TO DOUBLE YOUR HARD DISK'S STORAGE CAPACITY.

The program MS-DOS Double-space frees up space on your hard and floppy disks by squashing the data that is on them. Double-space is both easy to setup and use, but please remember that Double-space will only compress by 50%. In other words you can get twice as much information on the same disk or 100% extra space. (Other optimization programs such as Superstor-Pro and Staker-4 can compress by up to 400% and have proved to be reliable). However please understand nothing is ever perfect and if you use Double-space over a period of time your hard disk will slow down, affecting the computer's overall performance.

If you run Double-space for the first time, the Double-space setup program will automatically start. During the Double-space setup it is possible to select either "**Express setup**" or "**Custom setup**". This means that you can either accept the "Express setup" configuration that is standard and accepted by the program or use "Custom setup" to select specific programs that you wish to compress. When you choose the "Custom setup" the settings which you determine yourself can be changed should you wish to do so, however we strongly recommend that unless you have good reason for using the "Custom setup" you should choose "**Express setup**" option, especially if you are not totally conversant with the way your computer works. So let's install Double-space by using the "Express setup", using the following steps.

STEP(1)

Come out of all running programs including "**MS-DOS SHELL**" and "**WINDOWS**".

Please note that when using "**Microsoft Windows**" on a "**386**" or above computer you should make sure that a "**Permanent Swap File**" has been created on your hard disk before running the Double-space compressing program. If you do not understand about "Permanent Swap Files" please read the relevant

"**Permanent Swap File section**" shown later in the Windows section of this book.

STEP(2)

At the root directory "**C:**" prompt type "**Dblspace**" return

A welcome screen will appear.

STEP(3)

Press return and a Double-space screen will be displayed.

STEP(4)

Choose the "**Express setup**" option using your arrow keys and then press enter. Double-space will then display a screen confirming your choice that will also estimate the amount of time it will take to compress your hard disk. (Please note: if you have two hard drives you will have to determine which hard drive you want to compress i.e. Drive C: or D:)

STEP(5)

To compress drive C: highlight the "**C:**" option in black and press return (Please note: the colours displayed on your screen can at times vary from the ones stated in this book, especially if you select the customise colours option at the start of the program)

STEP(6)

Please be sure that if you run or intend to run "Microsoft Windows in 386 Enhanced mode" that it is already set up on your hard disk and that you have created a "**Permanent Swap File**" on your hard disk. Make sure that Double-space has both recognised and reserved some uncompressed space on your hard drive for it.

STEP(7)

You are now running Double-space, the program is now defragmenting and compressing your hard drive at virtually the same time. This process could take several minutes or several hours depending on the speed of your hard disk and processor and the amount of information already stored on your hard disk.

You will be delighted to know that Double-space checks and re-checks the quality of the data it compresses, and the process is therefore absolutely safe. For example: if you suffer a power cut whilst Double-space is compressing your hard disk, Double-space will recover itself when power is restored and complete the compression of your hard disk with no loss of information.

Please Note:

1.) During the compression process Double-space setup re-starts your computer twice (**Don't be alarmed**).

2.) When Double-space setup has finished, a screen is displayed showing how long compression took and how much space your newly compressed drive contains (Double-space has not finished until you see this screen).

STEP(7)

To come out of Double-space after it has compressed your hard drive simply press return. **Please note:** after you have used Double-space your computer's drives will be configured differently i.e.

1.) Drive C: will be compressed and will contain more free space than it did before, (but remember you cannot use double-space twice on the same drive)

2.) Your computer will have a new drive that is not compressed. This drive is used to store files that must not be compressed, for instance the "**Windows Permanent Swap File**" as it does not work properly if it is located on a compressed drive. If the "Windows Permanent Swap File" was previously located on drive C:, Double-space will have located a small part of your hard disk to create a separate drive and store the Permanent Swap File on it. This drive will probably be called "**Drive D:**" or "**Drive E:**" depending on whether you have one or two hard disks installed in your computer.

Don't be alarmed if you see an extra drive appear on your computer, you have not gained an extra hard disk!

Please also note: Now you have compressed your hard disk, you will have created a compressed volume file called a "**CVF**" it will appear in your root directory as "**dblspace.000**" or higher (dblspace.001). Do not tamper with a CVF, if you do you will almost certainly lose all the files on your compressed drive.

Please note we have written an in depth study about CVF's, if you wish to obtain a copy of these updates then please telephone **(0860) 325144.** As this is an uncommon request there will be an extra fee of £6.50.

Finally you can work with your compressed drive just as you would with an uncompressed drive, saving, copying, deleting etc., it all works in exactly the same way. However there are some thing's you can now do that you couldn't do with an uncompressed drive. For example you can now change the size of your compressed drive, you couldn't normally do this with an uncompressed drive, and you can compress floppy disks. Please see the next section.

USING DOUBLE-SPACE WITH FLOPPY DISKS

You can use Double-space to create more storage space on a floppy disk if you have Double-space installed on your hard disk.

Please note: In order to use a compressed floppy disk to transfer information from one computer to another, both computers **must** have the same version of Double-space installed.

Before you can use Double-space on a floppy disk you must make sure your floppy disk is formatted and has at least 650kb of free space on it, Double-space cannot compress a 360k disk, an unformatted disk or a disk that is full. To compress a floppy disk follow these steps.

STEP(1)

Insert a disk into a floppy disk drive either A: or B:

STEP(2)

At the "**C:**" prompt type "**Dblspace**" return

The Double-Space Main Menu will appear.

Choose the "**Existing Drive**" option then press return

Double-space will now scan your computer and then display a list of drives that can be compressed. If the list does not include the drive you have your disk in, then please make sure that the disk is formatted and possesses at least 650Kb of free disk space.

STEP(3)

Use the up and down arrow (cursor) keys to select the floppy disk drive you want to compress, then press return.

Double-space then displays a screen confirming that everything is OK and that the drive you wish to compress has been selected. To compress the floppy disk press "**C**" return, Double-space will now compress your floppy disk.

STEP(4)

You can now use your newly compressed floppy disk in exactly the same way as you would use a normal uncompressed disk. **Please note:** That your compressed floppy disk has already been recognised (mounted) by Double-space, if you wish to use your floppy disk after re-starting your computer you must first tell Double Space to mount the floppy disk before you can use it again.

Please remember that before your compressed floppy disk is mounted (recognised) the disk will look full. If you change to drive A:\ by typing "**A:**" return and type "**dir**" return you will note a file called "**readthis.txt**". This file briefly explains how to mount a floppy disk, and you can read this file by using the edit program included in DOS. i.e. Type "**edit A:\readthis.txt**" return and the file will appear on your screen. You can scroll through the file by either using the **Up** and **Down** arrow keys or the **Page Up** and **Page Down** keys; To exit the program press the "**ALT**" and "**F**" keys simultaneously followed by "**x**" to exit.

USING CHKDSK (DOS 3.3+) AND DEFRAGMENTER (6+)

When you have been using your computer for a period of time i.e. a few months, the information that programs read and write to and from your hard disk becomes broken or fragmented, that is to say they disconnect themselves from a whole body into fragments or pieces, like a jigsaw puzzle starting as a full picture and then thrown ad-lib around the floor. When a file is broken into fragments the pieces are stored in different locations on the disk, but this scattering of information does not affect how the computer reads it as your files will still be complete when they are re-opened. However it does take much longer to read the pieces as they are scattered around the hard disk, and therefore they need to be found, stuck together and then read.

The MS-DOS 6+ defragmenter simply allows your computer to work at its optimum speed by putting your files back into order leaving them as whole chunks of information on the hard disk, in other words it puts the puzzle back together.

To defragment the files on your computer's hard disk please follow the procedures below.

STEP(1)

At the "C:\" prompt type "**Chkdsk/f**" return

The computer will come up with a message showing a list of information about your hard disk. Please see Figure(1) overleaf.

If you are asked the following question

"**Convert lost chains to files?**"

Type "**Y**" for yes then return.

This will have converted any lost bits of information into deletable files, now get rid of them and free up some disk space.

Type "**cd C:**" return

Type "**Del *.chk**" return

```
C:\>chkdsk

Volume SCANTECH    created 02-10-1994 1:05p
Volume Serial Number is 1B90-6E54

 104,820,736 bytes total disk space
  16,173,056 bytes in 3 hidden files
      92,160 bytes in 25 directories
  75,460,608 bytes in 1,525 user files
  13,094,912 bytes available on disk

       2,048 bytes in each allocation unit
      51,182 total allocation units on disk
       6,394 available allocation units on disk

     655,360 total bytes memory
     623,504 bytes free

Instead of using CHKDSK, try using SCANDISK.  SCANDISK can reliably detect
and fix a much wider range of disk problems.  For more information,
type HELP SCANDISK from the command prompt.

C:\>
```

Figure (1)

STEP(2)

Now type "**defrag**" return. A screen will appear see Figure(2)

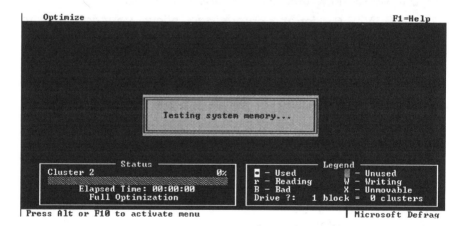

Figure (2)

Select the Drive you wish to defragment by pressing the up and down arrow (cursor) keys, highlighting each drive in black, when you have selected the drive for defragmentation either press return or use the right arrow (cursor) key to highlight the "OK" option in white, then press return.

The computer will tell you the amount of hard disk it wishes to defragment. Make sure that the "**defragment**" option is high-lighted and press return.

Your computer will now proceed to defragment the selected drive and will prompt you when it has finished.

To exit the program type "**Alt+x**" return.

ALTERNATIVE DEFRAGMENTATION PROGRAMS

There are various other defragmentation programs available in today's P.C. market place, such as "**OPTUNE**", "**PC TOOLS**" and "**NORTON UTILITIES**" etc. If you would like more informa-tion about other optimisation programs please telephone our hotline number to find out more.

If you require any more information on this section please telephone (0860) 325144.

USING SMARTDRIVE

Smartdrive is automatically installed on your computer when you are using DOS 5 or above. It is a memory resident program and is designed to shorten the time your computer takes to read the information from the hard disk. You can use smartdrive if your computer has a hard disk together with some free extended memory, you will not be able to use "**smartdrv.exe**" if it doesn't, that is unless you are using MS-DOS 6.2+ which can work on CD-ROM drives.

Smartdrive uses an area of your computer's extended memory to store information which it reads or writes to your hard disk. A program or application can access this information in the extended memory faster than it could from your hard disk. When certain resources in a system are needed smartdrive can temporarily store the information and then write it to your hard drive, this process is called "**disk caching**". You can normally see whether smartdrive is installed on your system by looking for smartdrive telling you that it is installed when your computer boots-up (starts). If a smartdrive message doesn't appear when your computer starts you can make another check to see whether it is installed by editing the autoexec.bat file and the command should be present in one of the lines. If you need help on doing this then please follow these steps.

STEP(1)

At the "**C:**" prompt type "**edit C:\autoexec.bat**" return then a screen similar to Figure(1) should appear.

```
 File   Edit   Search   Options                                    Help
                               AUTOEXEC.BAT
LOADHIGH C:\DOS\SMARTDRV.EXE
PROMPT $p$g
PATH C:\DOS;C:\;C:\WINDOWS;C:\TEMP;C:\MOUSE;
SET TEMP=C:\TEMP
LOADHIGH C:\DOS\SHARE.EXE
LOADHIGH MOUSE
```

Figure (1)

STEP(2)

Check to see whether smartdrive is present. It should look something like the first line in Figure(1).

If the line isn't there simply add it in by using the cursor keys to first move the cursor to the top of the screen, then press return and type in the first line shown in Figure(1).

STEP(3)

Now exit the MS-DOS EDITOR program by pressing the "**ALT**" and "**F**" keys simultaneously, now press "**x**" for exit, the computer will prompt you with the following message:

"**Loaded file is not saved. Save it now?**"

Type "**Y**" for "**<YES>**" and the file will be automatically saved.

STEP(4)

Now all you have to do is re-boot your computer, by either pressing the "**RESET**" button or by turning the computer off, waiting for a few seconds then turning it back on again.

A Smartdrive message should now appear when your system re-starts.

If you require any more information on this section please phone (0860) 325144.

Backing up really means to make a duplicate copy, and to be certain that the new copy is not accessed in every day use.

Why should we do this ? Well, if your Hard Disk fails (Crashes) all the information that was stored on it could be wiped into oblivion, and if you have not saved that information anywhere else it would be lost forever. A Hard Disk failure could make all information held on the Hard Disk inaccessible and it can take up to 2,000 hours of work to replace lost information on to a new or corrected hard disk.

Making copies or backups is simply an investment. It safeguards your time and effort, because within minutes you can restore the data you that have lost back to your hard disk from your backup disk. You will probably hear the terms grandfather and great grandfather disks. This simply means that if you take your data and pass it on to a first copy, that first copy becomes essentially the next generation passed down from the original (the grandfather). If you then take a copy of your copy it will have been passed down once again and this copy will be known as the Great Grandfather. **Please note:** We recommend that you constantly update your backup disks on at least a Monthly basis to help eliminate the risk of severe data loss.

MS-DOS Version 6 and upwards includes two Backup Programs: **"Backup for MS-DOS"** which you can run from the MS-DOS command prompt and **"Back Up for Windows"** which you can run from Microsoft Windows; The Help option in both programs includes a clear and defined outline for the command procedures and has dialogue boxes that appear throughout. **Please note:** Later on in this book we will be talking about making backups in the Windows environment, don't worry too much as the section is in our view particularly easy to understand.

Right then, what can you back up to?

Well you can back up to floppy disks as we have already mentioned, but the disks must be in a standard MS-DOS format, remembering that if they are not MS-DOS will automatically convert them. You can also format a disk in backup format, and this allows you to store more data faster, using less space. Secondly the MS-DOS device drivers allow you to copy files to a device (i.e Tape Streamers etc.), providing of course MS-DOS supports that particular backup device. For example **"Back Up"** supports Network Drives, Removable Drives and Tape Drives. It is widely felt that these devices will not be used by single users such as yourself and we have therefore not mentioned any of these devices within The Book.

TYPES OF BACKUP

There are three types of Backup or ways in which you can save your data.

1.) A Full Backup, which allows you to select your files before starting the back up sequence.

2.) An Incremental Backup, this allows you to back up only the files that have been changed or added since the last backup, this obviously saves you time as you only have to back up the files that have been changed.

3.) A Differential Backup, this backs up only the files that have changed since your last back up, and does not include any files that may have been added to your system in the meantime. Generally you will only require the use of a **Full Backup** every month ensuring that **all** your files are backed up. This means that you can easily restore any file from your backup disks, however there can be a substantial time disadvantage when backing up large amounts of data. If you have a fairly large and full hard disk we recommend you use the **Incremental** or **Differential** back up options, and can supply you with more information on these features for a small fee if you **Telephone (0860) 325144.**

When you run the MS-DOS backup program for the first time, your computer will give you a message telling you that it is about to run a compatibility test. This means that **Back Up** wants to test and adjust itself to your computer's hardware configuration (It is rare that any two computers are set up exactly the same). This makes absolutely sure that your backup will be reliable, as the DOS Commander in your computer will understand precisely how it should run your backup procedure.

O.K. lets start up backup for the first time.

STEP(1)

Make sure that you have two spare floppy disks ensuring that there is nothing on them of importance and that all floppy disks have been removed from your floppy disk drives.

At the "**C:**" Prompt type "**Msbackup**" Return

STEP(2)

A message will appear with a box headed "**Alert**" another message below will say:

"**Backup requires configuration for this computer**"

Underneath which will be an option to either:

"**Start Configuration**" or "**Quit**" out of the program.

You can select either option by using your left or right arrow keys, the option you have selected will be highlighted in white and the option you have not selected will remain grey.

Highlight the "**Start Configuration**" option and press return.

STEP(3)

A new screen will appear please see Figure(1)

Check to see that the options shown on the screen are correct, if you need to change any of these options, you can do so by using the arrow keys to move around the various option boxes using Return to change them.

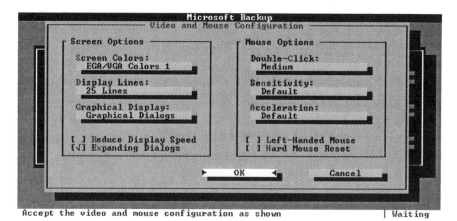

Figure (1)

Normally it is not necessary to change the configuration and with this in mind select "**OK**" by making sure it is highlighted in white and press Return. For Help **Telephone (0860) 325144**

STEP(4)

Your computer will now ask you if you wish to start the floppy drive change line test, please see Figure(2)

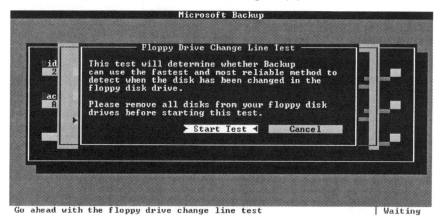

Figure (2)

Select "**Start Test**" by making sure that it is highlighted in white then press Return

The following screen will appear see Figure(3)

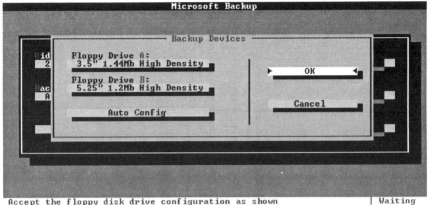

Figure (3)

STEP(5)

Press return again to start the test ensuring that "**OK**" is again highlighted.

Your computer will now carry out a processor and hard disk test on your machine and after a few seconds you will receive a further message see Figure(4)

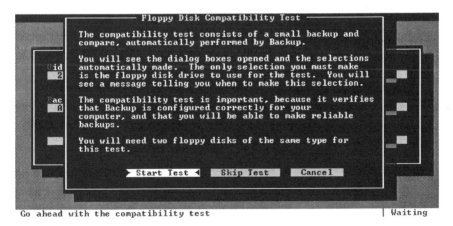

Figure (4)

STEP(6)

Select "**Start Test**" then press return

A full test will begin automatically.

Please note that an Alert box will appear telling you that your system will pause to allow you to select a drive.

Press return at the "**Continue**" Prompt

The following screen will appear see Figure(5)

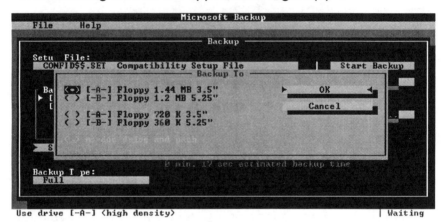

Figure (5)

STEP(7)

If you fully understand the various types Floppy Disks available and already know which disks you intend to use please continue to **STEP(9)** if you are at all confused continue to **STEP(8)**.

STEP(8)

At this point we should remind you that there are two types of floppy disk, "**High Density**" and "**Low Density**".

A 3½" high density disk will normally bear the letters HD on either the steel slide or on the top right hand side or the disk's plastic casing, you will also note that there are two square holes at the two bottom corners of the disk, a 5¼ Disk has an extra cut on the left hand side of the sleeve. See Figure(6) overleaf.

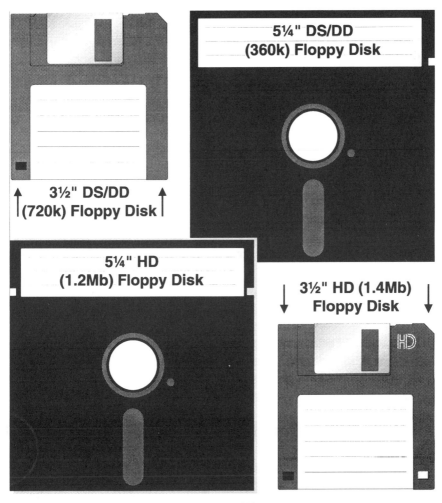

Figure (6)

A high Density disk simply means that the computer will use both sides of the disk to store information therefore holding twice as much information (1.44Mb instead of 720Kb, or 1.2Mb instead of 360Kb).

A Low Density disk will normally be totally blank. You can identify a low density disk immediately by noting that it only has one hole at the bottom left of the disk meaning that the computer can only access one side of the disk and therefore only hold half the amount of information. Please see Figure(6).

We recommend that you use High Density (1.4Mb) 3.5" Floppy Disks for all your backups as they can store twice as much information when compared to a standard density disk, thus saving you both time and money.

STEP(9)

You now need to use the arrow keys and the space bar to select either "**1.44Mb**" or "**720k**" when using 3½" Disks or "**1.2Mb**" or "**360k**" when using 5¼" disks. (1.44Mb Recommended)

When you have done this highlight "**OK**" and press return. Your computer will now start to perform the configuration test. If you have two clean disks ready proceed to **STEP(11)**,if you want to overwrite two already used disks proceed to **STEP(10)**.

STEP(10)

The computer will now prompt you to insert your first floppy disk into drive A: do so and press return. If you have inserted a used disk the computer will detect this and a screen similar to the following will appear, please see Figure(7).

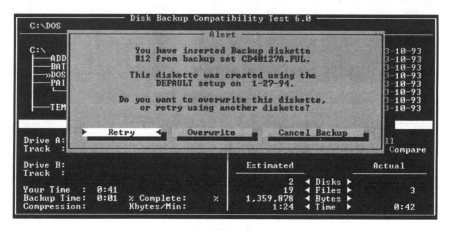

Figure (7)

If you are sure that you want to overwrite and completely wipe out any information on your disk then select the overwrite option and press return. The computer will now start to perform a test backup on to the first disk. After Backup has filled up the first disk it will ask you to insert the second disk. Remove the first and now insert the second, press return and proceed to **STEP(12)**

STEP(11)

The computer will now prompt you to insert your first floppy disk into drive A: do so and press return. The computer will now start to perform a test backup on to the first disk. After Backup has filled up the first disk it will ask you to insert the second disk, remove the first and insert the second, press return.

STEP(12)

A Backup Complete result screen will appear, press return for "**OK**". Now the computer will ask you to insert the first of your two backup disks. It does this so that it can compare the information stored on it to the information already held on the hard disk, this test also checks to see if the backup software is configured correctly for your computer.

Make sure that the first floppy backup disk is in the respective floppy drive and press return.

The computer will now begin to read the information from the floppy disk. When the computer asks insert the second disk. After a few seconds the compare complete table will show on your screen, press return and the following message will appear.

"**The compatibility test completed successfully**"

"**You can now make reliable disk backups.**"

Press return for "**OK**"

STEP(13)

The following screen will appear see Figure(8) with the "**Save**" option highlighted in order for you to save the newly created tailor made configuration. Press Return.

```
┌──────────────────────── Configure ────────────────────────┐
│  ideo and Mouse:                                           │
│    25 Lines, EGA/VGA Colors 1            ►     Save      ◄  │
│                                                            │
│  ackup Devices:                                            │
│    A: (1.44), B: (1.2)                        OK           │
│                                                            │
│        Compatibility Test...                 Cancel        │
└────────────────────────────────────────────────────────────┘
```

Save the configuration settings   │ Waiting

Figure (8)

You will now be left at the main Microsoft Backup menu. You can now backup your software safely. See Figure(1) in the next part of this section **"USING MS-DOS BACKUP"**.

USING MS-DOS BACKUP

STEP(1)

At the **"C:\"** prompt type **"Msbackup"** return, See Figure(1)

```
Microsoft Backup
File      Help
┌──────────────────── Microsoft Backup 6.0 ────────────────────┐
│                                                              │
│    ►      Backup      ◄              Restore                 │
│                                                              │
│           Compare                   Configure               │
│                                                              │
│                      Quit                                   │
│                                                              │
└──────────────────────────────────────────────────────────────┘
```

Back up your hard disks and network drives

Figure (1)

Ensure the **"Backup"** option is highlighted, then press return.

Now the computer will display another screen with a list of various options. Please see Figure(2)

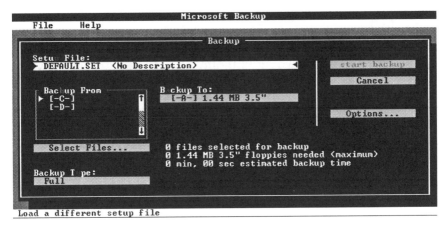

Figure (2)

STEP(2)

Use the down arrow (cursor) key to move the selected option on the screen to highlight your hard drive (usually [-C-]) in black.

Press Return and another screen similar to the one shown in Figure(3) below will appear, the "**Select Backup Files**" menu.

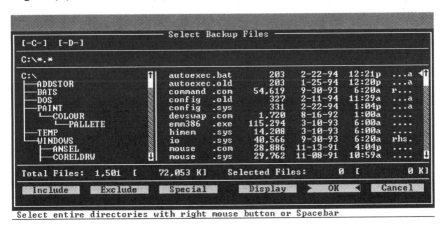

Figure (3)

To start with you will note that near the top left of the screen there is a statement line reading "**C:*.***" This line means that any file in the root directory of **Drive C:** (your hard drive) is selected for backing up. We recommend that you backup the whole of your hard disk to avoid any loss of your valuable data so proceed to **STEP (3)**. However you only want to backup part of your hard drive (i.e. personal files) then proceed to **STEP(4)**.

STEP(3)

You will note that in the "**Include**" option box shown at the bottom left hand side of your screen, the "**n**" letter within the word is highlighted in red. This means that whenever you use the Alt key in conjunction with "**n**" or any other highlighted letter in a word the relative menu will open, in this case the "**Include**" menu.

Press the "**Alt**" and "**n**" keys together to obtain the "**Include**" option listed at the bottom left of your screen. If you have a mouse simply move the pointer to the "**Include**" option box and click on the left mouse button. The "**Include files**" menu will now appear. Please see Figure(4).

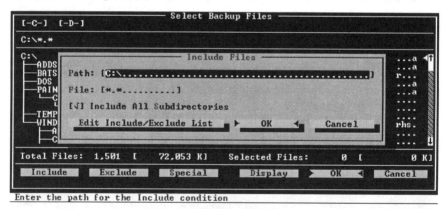

Figure (4)

Use the arrow keys to move the highlighted option to the "**OK**" box as the "**Include All Subdirectories**" option is automatically turned on. This means that all the files and directories on your hard disk will now be selected. Press Return and you will now move back to the "**Select Backup Files**" menu as seen earlier in Figure (3). You will now note that the total amount of files selected shown near the bottom of the screen has changed to show all the files on your hard disk, together with the number of disks that Microsoft Backup thinks that you will require for the entire Backup process. Press Return as the "**OK**" option is already selected. You will now be returned to the "Backup" screen shown earlier in Figure(2) Proceed to **STEP(5)**

STEP(4)

By using the up and down arrow keys you can view through all the directories on your hard disk. If you want to select an entire directory first highlight it (in black) then press the "**space bar**". All of the files shown on the right hand side of the screen will now be selected, you can see this by a tick mark appearing before all of the files. If you want to de-select a directory simply make sure it is still highlighted in black and press the "spacebar" again. Please see Figure(5) showing all the files in the "**C:\DOS**" directory being highlighted by ticks after pressing the "**spacebar**".

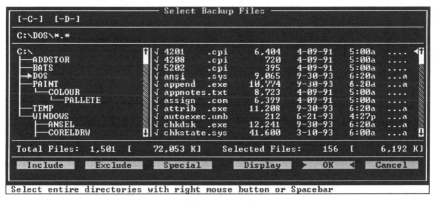

Figure (5)

If however you want to select specific files in a directory (not all of them), you can first move to the directory which holds the files you wish to backup, then use the right arrow (cursor) key to move the black box over to the right hand side of the screen. Now you can use the up and down arrow (cursor) keys to view through every file in the directory, selecting them one by one using the "**spacebar**". If you want to de-select a file simply press the "**spacebar**" again and it will be de-selected. Please see Figure(6) showing two picture files selected in the "**C:\paint**" directory.

```
┌─────────────────────── Select Backup Files ───────────────────────┐
│ [-C-] [-D-]                                                        │
│ C:\DOS\*.*                                                         │
│ C:\          ▲│√ 4201    .cpi    6,404   4-09-91   5:00a  ....  ▲  │
│  ├─ADDSTOR    │√ 4208    .cpi      720   4-09-91   5:00a  ....     │
│  ├─BATS       │√ 5202    .cpi      395   4-09-91   5:00a  ....     │
│  ├►DOS        │√ ansi    .sys    9,065   9-30-93   6:20a  ...a     │
│  ├─PAINT      │√ append  .exe   10,774   9-30-93   6:20a  ...a     │
│  │  └─COLOUR  │√ appnotes.txt    8,723   4-09-91   5:00a  ....     │
│  │     └─PALLETE│√ assign .com    6,399   4-09-91   5:00a  ....    │
│  ├─TEMP       │√ attrib  .exe   11,208   9-30-93   6:20a  ...a     │
│  └─WINDOWS    │√ autoexec.umb      212   6-21-93   4:27p  ...a     │
│     ├─ANSEL   │√ chkdsk  .exe   12,241   9-30-93   6:20a  ...a     │
│     ├─CORELDRW▼│√ chkstate.sys  41,600   3-10-93   6:00a  ...a  ▼  │
│ Total Files: 1,501 [  72,053 K]  Selected Files: 156 [  6,192 K]  │
│ ░Include░  ░Exclude░  ░Special░  ░Display░ ► ░OK░ ◄ ░Cancel░       │
├───────────────────────────────────────────────────────────────────┤
│ Select entire directories with right mouse button or Spacebar     │
└───────────────────────────────────────────────────────────────────┘
```

Figure (6)

You can now move back to the left hand side of the screen by using the left arrow (cursor) key. When you have finished selecting all the Files/Directories you wish to back up press return and the "**Backup**" screen will appear. The amount of files that you have currently selected is displayed near the bottom together with the approximate number of disks required. See Figure (2a)

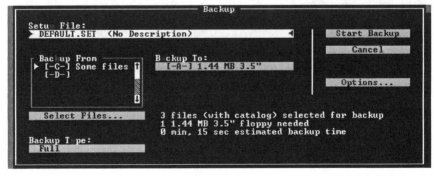

Figure (2a)

STEP(5)

Highlight the "**Backup To:**" Option box by using the right arrow key, when it is highlighted in white press return

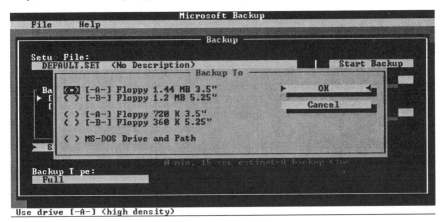

Figure (7)

STEP(6)

A "**Backup To:**" menu will appear as seen in Figure (7) above, showing the various options of floppy disks/drives that you can use on your computer. Select the highest capacity drive by first using the cursor (arrow) keys to move up and down the various options and then the space bar to select them. We recommend the "**[-A-] Floppy 1.44 Mb 3.5**" option.

If you have any difficulties in understanding the various drive options please refer back to "**RUNNING MS-DOS BACKUP (First time users) STEP(9)**" shown earlier in this section.

After you have selected your preferred type of floppy disk press return and you will be brought back to the "**Backup Menu**" as shown in Figure(2) or (2a).

STEP(7)

Move the highlighted box over to the "**Start backup**" option using the cursor (arrow) keys and press return.

You will now be prompted by an Alert signal asking you to Insert the first disk into drive A:. Make sure that the disk has been correctly labelled as **"Disk1"** and does not contain any important information on it. If you are at all unsure select the **"Cancel Backup"** option.

STEP(8)

If you have used a clean disk proceed to **STEP(9)**

If you have used a disk which has information on it the computer will prompt you with the following message, See Figure(8).

Figure (8)

If you are sure that no information on your floppy disk is of use to you then select the **"Overwrite"** option. If you are not sure then place another disk in to the floppy drive and select **"Retry"**. If this disk has no important files on it then choose the **"Overwrite"** option, but remember you can still exit the Backup procedure at any time by selecting the **"Cancel Backup"** option.

STEP(9)

Your computer will now start to backup all of the files/directories that you have selected on to the various numbered disks which you labelled earlier, prompting you with various messages and beeps telling you when to take out the first disk and put in the second, then when to take out the second disk and put in the third, etc. This will continue until all of the disks required have been inserted.

STEP(10)

After the backup is complete the computer will display a "**Backup Complete**" menu showing you how many disks you have used, the time it took to make the backup and the overall size of the files/directories you have backed up etc. Please see Figure (9) showing an example of a Backup Complete message after we selected three files for backing up.

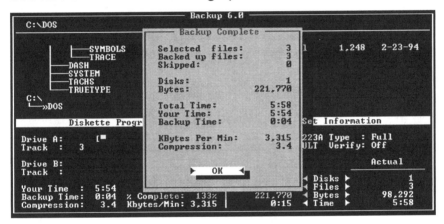

Figure (9)

Press Return for "**OK**".

You will now be left at the initial "**Microsoft Backup**" screen.

To Exit or Quit out of the program use the cursor (arrow) keys to move the highlighted option box to "**Quit**" and press return, alternatively you can press the "**Alt**" and "**Q**" keys simultaneously.

STEP(11)

We recommend that you store your new set of backup disks in a safe place away from the computer, preferably in a completely different location for the ultimate in security. This will prevent all data being lost in the event of fire or theft.

If your information is of extreme importance, then make another set of backup disks "**a great grandfather copy**" and put them in an altogether different location. This should certainly stamp out any risk of you losing information due to a set of disks being stolen or damaged.

NON COMPRESSION BACKUP'S

USING MS-DOS 3.3 TO MS-DOS 5.

When using a Non Compression backup your data stays the same size and is not compressed. If you wish to backup your entire machine quickly having not that much work on your hard disk, then please proceed to **STEP(1)**, if however you wish to back up a single directory i.e. your personal directory please go to **STEP(4)**.

STEP(1)

At the "**C:**" prompt type "**Backup C: A:*.*/s**" press return

STEP(2)

You will then be prompted to insert a blank disk labelled "**Disk1**" into Drive A:, do so. If the data (information) that you want to backup is too big to fit onto your floppy disk, then MS-DOS will ask you to insert a second labelled "**Disk2**" and so on. This will mean that your data will now be segmented across several disks until all of it has been backed up..

Please note you must always label your backup disks in the correct order in exactly the same order as they were used i.e. the first disk used would be labelled "**Disk1**", the second disk would be labelled "**Disk2**" and so on. You will need to know the correct order when you come to restore your data at a later date.

STEP(3)

When your computer has backed up all of the data it will simply state that the backup is complete, and will then ask you if you want to backup more data, type "**n**" for no, then return.

STEP(4)
BACKING UP A SINGLE DIRECTORY

At the "**C:**" prompt type "**Backup C:\directory name*.* A:/s**" return i.e. if you wanted to backup the directory of C:\DOS to your floppy drive A: you would type "**Backup C:\Dos*.* A:/s**" return. It is important to make a note of the above command on the first of your backup disks so that you are to safely restore your files at a later date.

Steps(2&3) now apply.

You have now completed all that we feel you need to know about backing up your hard drive.

If you require any more information on this section please telephone (0860) 325144.

RESTORING FILES TO YOUR YOUR HARD DISK
(MS-DOS)

Whilst we sincerely hope this never happens we would like you to picture the following set of circumstances.

You get up in the morning having worked most of the night and indeed for the last three months on a project that is so important to you that words cannot describe it. You turn on your machine eager to finish off your work only to hear a couple of beeps, you see a message saying:

"DRIVE NOT READY ERROR"

"Insert BOOT diskette in A:"

"Press any key when ready"

Your stomach churns, you experience a kind of red hot sensation around the ears and quickly remember you had a boot disk somewhere. Finding it, you insert it and press return.

Still nothing happens!

The alarms ringing inside your head start to become intolerable, as you remember that with all the intensity of your work you have neglected the paramount function of backing up your work on a regular basis.

Please, Please, Please, Please, never allow yourself to be in the above position. Believe us it's no fun. However there are ways in the above case to rectify the situation but they can take both time and a lot of brain power.

If the above applies to you and you are lost without hope please telephone (0860) 325144.

But hoorah, you have purchased "**The Book**"and learned how to backup your system, and are in proud possession of a set of numbered backup disks, and you know exactly where to find them. Quite a remarkable person really, aren't you. So how do we restore these files?

It's quite easy to restore files that you have backed up using the MS-DOS backup program, but what is meant by restoring files? Well, restoring files transfers the files from a backup format to a location you specify, in other words from your floppy disks to your hard disk.

If your hard disk fails, it's a good idea to restore the files to their original location as both you and the DOS commander will have become familiar with the overall location of everything. However you can restore files to an alternative location. I.e. You could restore your data to a completely different computer, provided of course it possessed certain basic factors such as a DOS 6 operating system, adequate Ram and a hard disk with enough room left to accept the data.

Before you are able to restore the files that you have backed up, you will need to be certain that your computer still possesses a version of the Disk Operating System (Commander) in this case DOS 6. You will soon know if it hasn't as the computer will not Boot (Start). If this happens please refer to "**INSTALLING MS-DOS**" shown earlier in this book and follow the procedures.

To restore your numbered backup disk(s) you need to carry out the following steps. Please do not vary from these steps as it could have serious consequences.

STEP(1)

At the MS-DOS "**C:**" prompt type "**Msbackup**" return

STEP(2)

If you have already configured the Microsoft Backup/Restore program (Msbackup) proceed to **STEP(13)**. If you have re-installed MS-DOS from scratch you must first configure the backup/restore program (Msbackup) in order to successfully restore your files, proceed to **STEP(3)**.

STEP(3)

Make sure that you have two spare floppy disks ensuring that there is nothing on them of importance and that all floppy disks have been removed from your floppy disk drives.

STEP(4)

A message will appear with a box headed "**Alert**" another message below will say:

"**Backup requires configuration for this computer**"

Underneath which will be an option to either:

"**Start Configuration**" or "**Quit**" out of the program.

You can select either option by using your left or right arrow keys, the option you have selected will be highlighted in and white the option you have not selected will remain grey.

Highlight the "**Start Configuration**" option and press return.

STEP(5)

A new screen will appear please see Figure(1)

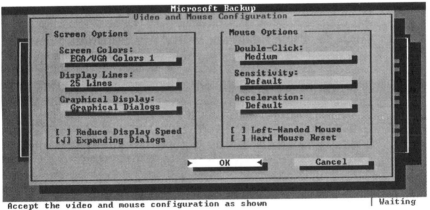

Figure (1)

Check to see that the options shown on the screen are correct. If you need to change any of these options, you can do so by using the arrow keys to move around the various option boxes using Return to change them.

Normally it is not necessary to change the configuration and with this in mind select "**OK**" by making sure it is highlighted in white and press Return. For Help **Telephone (0860) 325144**

STEP(6)

You computer will now ask you if you wish to start the floppy drive change line test, please see Figure(2)

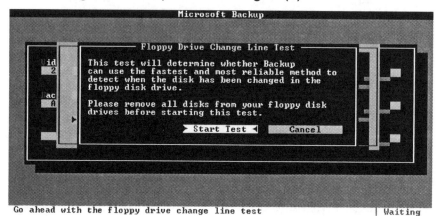

Figure (2)

Select "**Start Test**" by making sure that it is highlighted in white then press return. The following screen will appear see Figure(3)

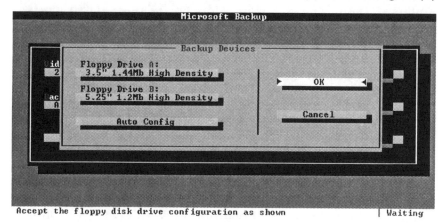

Figure (3)

STEP(7)

Press return again to start the test ensuring that "**OK**" is again highlighted.

Your computer will now carry out a processor and hard disk test on your machine and after a few seconds you will receive a further message see Figure(4)

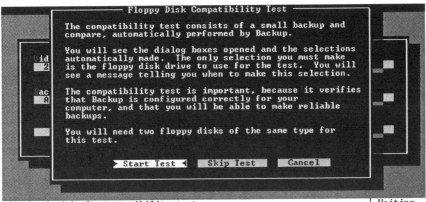

Figure (4)

STEP(8)

Select "**Start Test**" then press return. A full test will begin automatically. Please note that an Alert box will appear telling you that your system will pause to allow you to select a drive.

Press return at the "**Continue**" Prompt

A further "Back up" screen will now appear.

STEP(9)

You now need to use the arrow keys and the space bar to select either "**1.44Mb**" or "**720k**" when using 3½" Disks or "**1.2Mb**" or "**360k**" when using 5¼" disks. (1.44Mb Recommended)

When you have done this highlight "**OK**" and press return. Your computer will now start to perform the configuration test. If you have two clean disks ready proceed to **STEP(11)**,if you want to overwrite two already used disks proceed to **STEP(10)**.

STEP(10)

The computer will now prompt you to insert your first floppy disk into drive A: do so and press return. If you have inserted a used disk the computer will detect this and a screen similar to the following will appear, please see Figure(5).

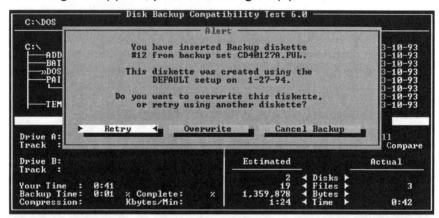

Figure (5)

If you are sure that you want to overwrite and completely wipe out any information on your disk then select the overwrite option and press return. The computer will now start to perform a test backup on to the first disk. After Backup has filled up the first disk it will ask you to insert the second disk. Remove the first and now insert the second, press return and proceed to **STEP(12)**

STEP(11)

The computer will now prompt you to insert your first floppy disk into drive A: do so and press return. The computer will now start to perform a test backup on to the first disk. After Backup has filled up the first disk it will ask you to insert the second disk, remove the first and insert the second, press return.

STEP(12)

A Backup Complete result screen will appear, press return for **"OK"**. Now the computer will ask you to insert the first of your two backup disks, it does this so that it can compare the information stored on it to the information already held on the hard disk. This test also checks to see if the backup software is configured correctly for your computer.

Make sure that the first floppy backup disk is in the respective floppy drive and press return.

The computer will now begin to read the information from the floppy disk. When the computer asks insert the second disk. After a few seconds the compare complete table will show on your screen, press return and the following message will appear.

"The compatibility test completed successfully"

"You can now make reliable disk backups."

Press return for "**OK**"

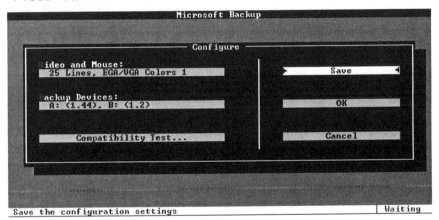

Figure (6)

The screen shown above will appear see Figure(6) with the "**Save**" option highlighted in order for you to save the newly created tailor made configuration. Press Return.

You will now be left at the main "**Microsoft Backup**" menu shown in Figure(7) overleaf, and you can now restore your files safely.

Proceed to **STEP(13)**

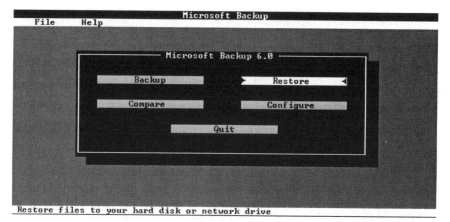

Figure (7)

STEP(13)

Choose the Restore button in the dialogue box by using your arrow (cursor) key to make the box white. Press Return.

The following screen will appear please see Figure(8)

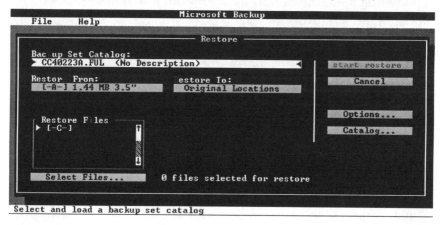

Figure (8)

STEP(14)

If you are restoring your files onto another computer or are completely starting from scratch after completely reinstalling the **MS-DOS** system including the "**Msbackup**" program proceed to the next step. If MS-DOS has not crashed and is fully intact i.e. you want to re-insert previously unwanted files back on to the hard disk proceed to **STEP(20)**.

STEP(15)

If your computer has crashed completely or you are loading your backup disks onto another computer or you simply want to restore a set of backup disks onto your computer, the backup program will not know where to find anything. It needs a method in order to identify which set of backup disks you wish to restore, and where you want them restored to. To do this it requires you to supply it with a catalogue reference, just as when you purchase anything from a club book, you must first of all locate the products by looking through the club book catalogue and then give the necessary code (catalogue numbers) numbers for each item to the club (computer).

STEP(16)

The word catalogue appears throughout the restore procedure. Highlight the "**Catalogue**" option box by using the arrow (cursor) keys, press return.

The "**Select Catalogue**" menu will now appear See Figure(9)

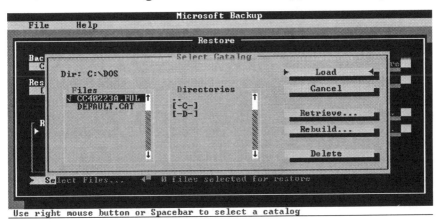

Figure (9)

STEP(17)

Use the arrow keys to highlight the **"Retrieve"** option box and press return. Now select the type of floppy drive your disks were saved on, normally "[-A-] Floppy Drive", Press Return

STEP(18)

You will now be prompted to insert the last disk (the disk with the highest number on it) of your set of backup disks into the respective floppy drive. Insert the disk and press return.

A message will appear saying **"Searching for catalogue on Drive A"**, then a further message will appear similar to this:

"Alert", **"Backup Catalogue has been retrieved"**

"CC40223B.FUL has been placed in C:\DOS".

Press Return

STEP(19)

Make sure your catalogue is selected. A tick will appear to the left of the Catalogue number, which you can select by using the arrow key to move up or down. Use the spacebar to either select or de-select the Catalogue number. When you are sure that the correct Catalogue is selected press return. You should now be at the restore screen. See Figure(10).

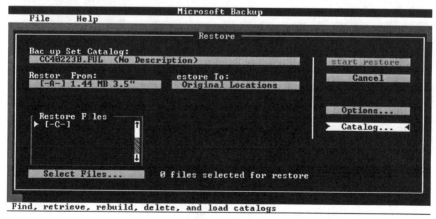

Figure (10)

STEP(20)

Make sure that below the **"Backup Set Catalogue:"** message on the top left of the screen there is a filename (for example: CC40223B.FUL) (See Figure10). If a filename is there then use the arrow (cursor) keys to highlight the option **"Select Files"**. Press return. A screen similar to Figure(11) will appear.

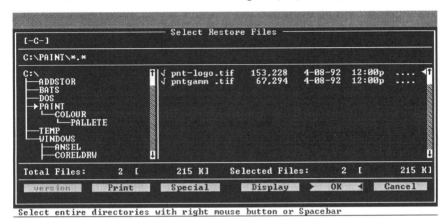

Figure (11)

STEP(21)

Now use the up and down arrow (cursor) keys in conjunction with the space bar to select the directories you want to restore. If you want to select or de-select certain files in a directory you can move across the page by using the right arrow key and then select the individual files you wish to restore.

In our example two files have been selected in the **"C:\Paint"** directory. See Figure(11).

When you have finished press return and you will be left back at the main **"Restore"** screen.

STEP(22)

You will note that the **"Start Restore"** option box will have now become available as an option. Highlight it and press return.

STEP(23)

An alert screen will now appear asking you to insert the first disk of your set of backup disks. Do so, then press return if **"Continue"** is highlighted. Now the computer will start to restore your files back onto your hard disk asking you at first to remove the first disk and insert the second, then to remove the second and insert the third, and so on until all of your backup disks have been inserted. When restore has finished it will prompt you with a screen similar to the following. See Figure(12)

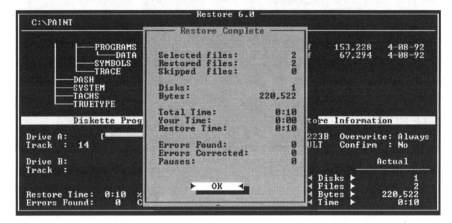

Figure (7)

STEP(24)

Press Return

You will now be left at the initial **"Microsoft Backup"** screen. Exit the program by highlighting the option box marked **"Quit"** then press return or press the "**Alt**" and "**Q**" keys simultaneously.

Now re-Start your machine, and if you were suffering from a hard disk crash or a severe delete problem, all of the files you have just selected will now be safely back on your hard disk.

If you have any problems please telephone (0860) 325144

NON COMPRESSION RESTORE (MS-DOS 3.3 TO DOS 5)

Non Compression means the data stays the same size and is not compressed. If you wish to restore the data on your hard disk from a previous Non Compression backup, then proceed to **STEP(1)**, if however you wish to restore a single directory specified on your backup disk(s) i.e. your personal directory please go to **STEP(4)**.

STEP(1)

At the "**C:**" prompt type "**Restore A: C:*.*/s**" press return

STEP(2)

You will then be prompted to insert a blank disk labelled "Disk1" into Drive A:. Do so, and after MS-DOS has finished copying the data from your first floppy disk back onto to your hard disk MS-DOS will ask you to insert the labelled Disk2 and so on.

STEP(3)

When your computer has restored all of the data it will simply state that the restore is complete.

STEP(4)

RESTORING A SINGLE DIRECTORY

At the "**C:**" prompt type "**Restore A: C:\Directory Name*.*/s**" return. I.e. if you wanted to restore the "**C:\DOS**" directory from your floppy drive A: you would type "**Restore A: C:\DOS*.*/s**" return. If you can't remember the name of the directory you initially backed up, look on the label of the first backup disk and if you have followed our instructions correctly before, the name of the directory should be marked on it.

STEPS(2&3) now apply.

Great stuff this, isn't it.

You now know as much as we feel you need to about restoring files back onto your hard disk.

If you are one of the unlucky ones who has just deleted a file by mistake and doesn't know how to get it back, then help is here, because unless the disk that the file used to be kept on has been written over you will more than likely be able to get it back.

How? You ask, well all you have to do is first of all make sure that you have exited any programs that you are running, then make sure that you are in the directory that used to contain the deleted file and type **"Undelete"** return. The rest is simple. Please see the STEPS below first showing the directory of **"C:\Paint\Files"**, then showing it after deleting a file, and finally using the undelete command to get it back.

STEP(1)

Here is an example of a directory which might have some files in it namely **"C:\Paint\Files"**. Please see Figure(1)

```
C:\>cd paint

C:\PAINT>cd files

C:\PAINT\FILES>dir

 Volume in drive C is SCAN-TECH
 Volume Serial Number is 1C59-A1CF
 Directory of C:\PAINT\FILES

.            <DIR>        05-06-94    2:16p
..           <DIR>        05-06-94    2:16p
GAMMA    TIF      7,444  08-14-93    2:00a
MONALISH TIF     70,003  06-05-94    1:01p
PICTURE  TIF     67,294  04-08-92   12:00p
PNT-LOGO TIF    153,228  04-08-92   12:00p
        6 file(s)       318,048 bytes
                     17,784,832 bytes free

C:\PAINT\FILES>_
```

Figure (1)

STEP(2)

As you can see there are several picture files in the directory. Right, let's accidentally delete one of them. Please see Figure(2).

```
..             <DIR>        05-06-94   2:16p
GAMMA     TIF      7,444 08-14-93    2:00a
MONALISA TIF     90,082 05-05-94    1:01p
PICTURE   TIF     67,294 04-08-92   12:00p
PNT-LOGO TIF    153,228 04-08-92   12:00p
        6 file(s)       318,048 bytes
                     17,784,832 bytes free

C:\PAINT\FILES>del monalisa.tif

C:\PAINT\FILES>dir

 Volume in drive C is SCAN-TECH
 Volume Serial Number is 1C59-A1CF
 Directory of C:\PAINT\FILES

.              <DIR>        05-06-94   2:16p
..             <DIR>        05-06-94   2:16p
GAMMA     TIF      7,444 08-14-93    2:00a
PICTURE   TIF     67,294 04-08-92   12:00p
PNT-LOGO TIF    153,228 04-08-92   12:00p
        5 file(s)       227,966 bytes
                     17,874,944 bytes free

C:\PAINT\FILES>_
```

Figure (2)

STEP(3)

As you can see the file "**Monalisa.tif**" has been deleted, now to get it back. We will now type the following "**Undelete**" return.

As shown in Figure(3) below we were asked by undelete first whether we want to undelete the file, to which we typed "**Y**" for yes, after which we were asked to type in the first character of the deleted file which is now shown as "**?onalisa.tif**", to which we typed "**M**" to complete the filename "**Monalisa.tif**".

```
UNDELETE -- A delete protection facility
Copyright (C) 1987-1993 Central Point Software, Inc.
All rights reserved.

Directory: C:\PAINT\FILES
File Specifications: *.*

     Delete Sentry control file not found.

     Deletion-tracking file not found.

     MS-DOS directory contains    1 deleted files.
     Of these,    1 files may be recovered.

Using the MS-DOS directory method.

     ?ONALISA TIF    90082  5-05-94  1:01p  ...A  Undelete (Y/N)?y
     Please type the first character for ?ONALISA.TIF: m

File successfully undeleted.

C:\PAINT\FILES>
```

Figure (3)

STEP(4)

The Monalisa.tif file will have now been completely restored because no files were written over it's hard disk space during the time it was left deleted.

Just to prove it here's the DOS screen after we typed "**dir**" return to view the directory. Please see Figure(4)

```
Using the MS-DOS directory method.

      ?ONALISA TIF     90082  5-05-94  1:01p  ...A  Undelete (Y/N)?y
      Please type the first character for ?ONALISA.TIF: m

File successfully undeleted.


C:\PAINT\FILES>dir

  Volume in drive C is SCAN-TECH
  Volume Serial Number is 1C59-A1CF
  Directory of C:\PAINT\FILES

.             <DIR>           05-06-94   2:16p
..            <DIR>           05-06-94   2:16p
GAMMA    TIF          7,444  08-14-93   2:00a
MONALISA TIF         90,082  05-05-94   1:01p
PICTURE  TIF         67,294  04-08-92  12:00p
PNT-LOGO TIF        153,228  04-08-92  12:00p
       6 file(s)        318,048 bytes
                     17,784,832 bytes free

C:\PAINT\FILES>
```

Figure (4)

Always remember that in order to safely restore any mistakenly deleted file in dos you must quickly stop whatever you are doing, exit out of any programs currently being run and use the "**Undelete**" command as quickly as possible.

We do not recommend trying this process out on any of your important files, as un-deleting files can be a risky business and is definitely not %100 guaranteed in successfully restoring your files.

If you have any problems please telephone (0860) 325144

USING ANTI-VIRUS PROGRAMS (MS-DOS)

WHAT IS A COMPUTER VIRUS?

A computer virus is a program designed to become a replica of another program and spread sometimes without indicating that it actually exists. Put more simply a virus looks at another program and because it has no identity itself, it tries to clone itself to be the same but without really knowing how to do it. Therefore it can impair your computer's functions.

Some viruses multiply without causing obvious changes, but the key factor is they can multiply relatively fast. For example a virus is rather like a flu virus being passed on throughout the community. Initially someone comes in from out of town with a runny nose, which unbeknown to him is really a flu virus. Because of the multiplication of the virus the person ends up with temperatures and all sorts of other symptoms which can lead in some rare cases to death unless he is properly treated. One day the man infected by the virus accidentally sneezes in a public place, and all of a sudden the flu virus is spread.

The spread of a flu virus is virtually the same as that of a computer virus, you cannot get a virus unless you have been in direct contact with one, i.e. being connected to a network, using a modem to link to another computer or receiving infected information from a floppy disk.

Some viruses are more dangerous than others, these strains of computer virus are sometimes capable of issuing random sounds or presenting you with unexpected screen messages. In extreme cases a destructive computer virus can damage files or even completely wipe out your hard disk. A computer virus is classified by how it actually affects a system.

Fortunately there are virus detector programs available that are specially written to understand the different virus classifications. They can do this by having all the known virus detector sequences located within them. Like a doctor they have a set of prescriptions and preventive medicines that can both prevent a virus from entering your computer system or if you unfortunately already have one, they are usually more than capable of exterminating it.

An Anti-Virus program protects your data by first having the ability to recognise more than eight hundred different viruses and then having the further ability of removing them from the affected areas in your computer, Microsoft's DOS 6 and 6.2 has two versions of anti-virus programs in it. One is **Anti-Virus** for **MS-DOS** and the other is **Anti-Virus** for **Windows 3.1**. MS-DOS6 and 6.2 also includes a program called **Vsafe** which is a memory resident program that constantly monitors your computer and warns of any changes that may be caused by a virus, rather like a weather system that warns the population of any change in the weather reporting the information by way of the media.

If a destructive virus infects your computer, you could well need a start-up disk to restart it as some viruses infect and sometimes delete the essential boot-up files needed to start your computer. It is important to make a start-up disk before your computer becomes infected. Please see the Section earlier in this book **"MAKING A BOOT-UP DISK"**, if you remember back in this earlier section, we asked you in **STEP(3)** to **"Copy C:\dos\msav*.* A:\"** return, this would have copied MS-DOS 6 or 6.2's antivirus programs to your floppy disk just in case they were needed at a later date. Right now let us explain why you copied the anti-virus programs over to your boot-up floppy disk.

A **"boot sector"** virus is held in a proportion of your hard disk that controls your operating system when your computer starts. A boot sector virus replaces the disk's original start-up procedure and loads its own virus into the memory. By creating a **Boot-Up** disk with the **AntiVirus** files on it before you are infected, any known virus can be destroyed when it loads itself or attempts to load itself into the boot sector of your hard disk.

A **"file infector"** virus adds a virus code to the files that run programs so that the virus becomes active whenever you run that program. Once the virus is active it can spread to other program files, and the creation of a new boot disk using the msav command has within it the ability to destroy a file infector virus and then to re-boot. The major problem and the **"big daddy"** of all viruses is the **"Trojan Horse"** virus which disguises itself as a legitimate program. If you run a program infected with a Trojan horse virus your computer may well become damaged, rather like the actual Trojan horse it is full of computer soldiers capable of wreaking havoc once within the confines of the city (your computer). The Trojan horse viruses are much more likely to destroy disks and destroy files than any other virus. The Trojan Horse virus may not actually be removable without completely re-formatting the computer's hard disk, however your Boot-Up disks will have the necessary files in it to give it a go by both identifying and then destroying the virus.

LOOKING FOR VIRUSES

The anti-virus program supplied with DOS 6+ can protect your computer by searching your computer's memory and disk drives. It uses several methods of recognising computer viruses.

1.) It scans for viruses and is capable of displaying information about each of the viruses it finds. This method does not automatically remove the problem from your computer.

2.) It scans for viruses, finds them and immediately removes them.

If you are using Microsofts Anti-virus for MS-DOS 6+ please follow the procedures listed next under **"USING ANTI VIRUS FOR MS-DOS"** below if you are using Micosofts Anti-virus for Microsoft's Windows 3.1 please refer to the Windows section in this book.

At the "**C:**" prompt type "**msav**" return (Alternatively if you used your Boot-up disk to start your computer, type "msav" return.)

The following screen will appear please see Figure(1)

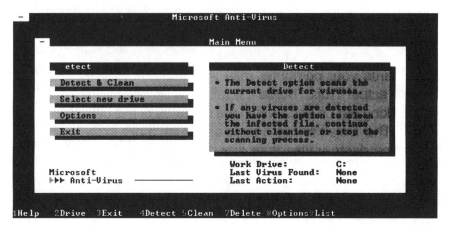

Figure (1)

You will note on the left hand side of the screen 5 boxes namely "**Detect**" "**Detect & Clean**" "**Select new drive**" "**Options**" and "**Exit**", each time you highlight one of the options by using your up and down arrow (cursor) keys the option (box) selected highlights in blue with the box on the right hand side of the screen showing you more information about the option.

Select one of the five options highlighting the preferred option in blue then press return and the virus program will do the rest. We recommend that you select the "**Detect & Clean**" option, if you are running **MSAV** from a Boot-Up disk use the "**Select new drive**" option before selecting the "**Detect and Clean**" option.

Having tested the program "**Vsafe**" for MS-DOS 6+ it is our considered opinion that although it could be useful, you are probably better off giving your computer a regular monthly checkup with the Microsoft Anti-Virus program shown above.

If you have any problems please telephone (0860) 325144

USING BATCH FILES TO RUN YOUR PROGRAMS

If you can imagine an army parade being governed by a sergeant major, every time the sergeant shouts out a command, the soldiers immediately carry out his orders. In the same way a batch file is a list of commands which can tell the computers to run various specific tasks, and the batch file could easily be termed as the sergeant major of the computer. A list of commands in a batch file can tell the computer to do a whole range of things, just like the sergeant major telling the parade to turn left, right, present arms etc. The parade already understands the commands given by the sergeant, because MS-DOS has already been written in a language the computer understands, so all you have to do is to learn the computer's language.

USING THE MS-DOS EDITOR

To show you how to create batch files using the "**edit**" command we have produced the following steps, first showing you around the MS-DOS editor program, then using it to create a menu and then the various batch files which will run from it.

STEP(1)

Start the editor program by typing "**edit**" return at the Dos prompt,

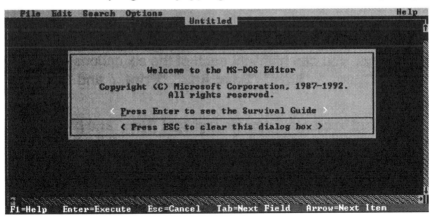

Figure (1)

A screen will appear similar to Figure (1). If you have a colour monitor the screen will be blue with grey borders. At the bottom of the screen will be a grey sliding scale with two arrows pointing left and right, and up the right hand side of the screen you will find another sliding scale with two arrows pointing up and down. Also you will note a **"Welcome to the MS-DOS Editor"** message in the centre of the screen. If you choose the option saying **"Press Enter to see the survival guide"** by pressing **"enter"** it will put you onto a comprehensive Help utility already contained in the editor program, and to exit out of the help utility simply press the **"escape"** key.

STEP(2)

When you edit a batch file it's name appears in the centre of the grey title bar at the top of the screen, together with the words **"File"**, **"Edit"**, **"Search"** and **"Options"**, and with the word **"Help"** on the right hand side of the screen. You will also note there are some numbers at the bottom right hand corner of the screen and **"<F1=Help>"**, **"Press ALT to activate menus"** on the left.

STEP(3)

Running through the sub-menus will prove informative. So let's access the **"File"** menu; If you press the **"ALT"** and **"F"** keys together you will note the word **"File"** turns black and a drop down menu will appear with various options on it. The first, which is **"New"**, is also highlighted in black, and by using the up and down arrow keys you can highlight each of the six options available, **"New"**, **"Open..."**, **"Save"**, **"Save As..."**, **"Print..."** and **"Exit"**.

STEP(4)

If you want to create a new file highlight **"New"** and press enter. The screen will clear with the top bar showing "Untitled".

STEP(5)

If you want to open an old file you should press the **"ALT"** and **"F"** keys and move the black box to **"Open"** and press enter. Then select the files you wish to open and press return for **"OK"**.

STEP(6)

If you want to save a file, you should press the "**ALT**" and "**F**" keys together and move the black box to "**Save**". Press enter, and the file will then be automatically saved. However if you have just created the file then you will be asked to type in a filename and then press return.

STEP(7)

If you wish to Save an existing file to another name, i.e. you have been editing "**autoexec.bat**" and wanted to rename it to "**autoexec.bak**" you should press the "**ALT**" and "**F**" keys. Then move the black box to the "**Save As...**" option and press enter. You should type in the new name for the file and press return.

STEP(8)

If you want to print your file you should press the "**ALT**" and "**F**" keys together then move the black box to the "**Print...**" option and press return.

STEP(9)

If you want to exit out of the editor program you should press the "**ALT**" and "**F**" keys together then move the black box to the "**Exit**" option and then press return. Please see Figure (2)

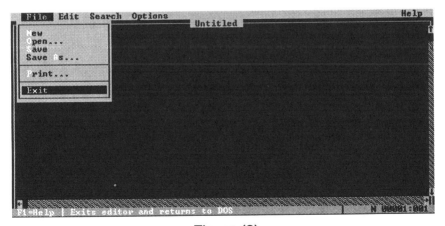

Figure (2)

STEP(10)

Now let's look at the "**Edit**" menu, You can do this by either pressing the "**ALT**" and "**F**" keys together and then pressing the right arrow key to access the edit menu, or you can press the "**ALT**" and "**E**" keys together which acess the edit menu direct. The Edit menu will be highlighted in black, and another drop down menu (sub-menu) will appear with the following options: "**Cut**", "**Copy**", "**Paste**" and "**Clear**". To access any of these options simply use the up and down arrow keys and then press return when the option you want is highlighted in black.

STEP(11)

You will note that there are various short cut key commands which can actually allow you to perform each of the tasks in the edit menu without actually having to access the edit menu. For instance: Pressing the "**Shift**" and "**Del**" keys together will "**Cut**" any highlighted text.

Pressing the "**Ctrl**" and "**Insert**" keys together will "**Copy**" all highlighted text,

Pressing the "**Shift**" and "**Insert**" keys will paste any copied text into the document.

Finally pressing the "**Delete**" key will delete any highlighted text or delete the next character to the right of the cursor's position.

STEP(12)

The next main option is "**Search**". This enables you to use the editor to search through a document and find or change certain words in it that you specify. To use search you can either press the "**ALT**" and "**F**" keys together and then press the right or left arrow keys until it is selected, or you can press the "**ALT**" and "**S**" keys together. The Search option will then be highlighted in black with a drop down menu below it containing these options:- "**Find...**", "**Repeat Last Find   F3**" and "**Change**". To run each of these options simply highlight them in black and press return.

STEP(13)

You can access the "**Options**" Menu in much the same was as you would the others by either pressing the "**ALT**" and "**F**" keys together and then using the arrow keys to select it, or by pressing the "**ALT**" and "**O**" keys together. Again a sub-menu will appear with the options "**Display**" and "**Help Path...**".The display option is particularly useful if you are currently using a black and white lap top computer as it allows you to change the background and foreground colours that the editor program uses.

STEP(14)

Finally, to highlight the "**Help**" option you can either press the "**ALT**" and "**F**" keys together and then use the left or right arrows to choose help, or press the "**ALT**" and "**H**" keys together, or simply press the "**F1**" key for the help survival guide. The help option can be used in virtually the same way as previously described earlier in the book. Please see "**USING MS-DOS HELP**".

MAKING A MENU

Let's create a menu to start the programs in your computer.

Wouldn't it be nice to create a start up box of your own allowing you to simply press one letter or number to immediately access you favourite or important programs, instead of typing several command's to do the same thing? This is a bit like using a telephone with a memory which allows you to press just one number to make a telephone call. Before you do this it is wise to create your own personal menu, which can be automatically read from your autoexec.bat file when your computer starts. A suitable name for your menu is "**menu.txt**". A file with a "**.txt**" extension is recognised by the computer as a text file and because it differs from a batch file it can be displayed after your computer has started. This will show you a permanent list of programs with their corresponding numbers/letters that will be easily recognisable. It is quite a good idea to separate different areas of your menu so that they correspond to the different areas of your computer's programs. This will also help to make the menu look as nice as possible, since you will see it every time your computer is turned on. Please see Figure(3) showing a typical **"menu.txt"** file.

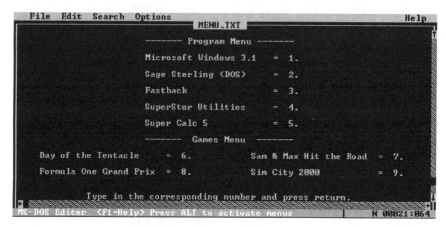

Figure (3)

To create your **"menu.txt"** file you should follow these steps.

STEP(1)

At the "C:\" prompt type **"Edit menu.txt"**

STEP(2)

Now simply make a screen similar to the one shown above in Figure(3), which shows your various programs on your hard disk with the corresponding numbers next to them. These numbers will be the names of your batch files which we will create next.

STEP(3)

Type **"ALT"** and **"F"** simultaneously then press **"S"** to save.

STEP(4)

Type **"ALT"** and **"X"** simultaneously to exit the editor program.

Your menu file will have now been created, to test what it will look like in DOS type the following: **"Type menu.txt"** return.

MAKING A BATCH FILE

To create a batch file which can start up one of the programs available on your hard disk, you should use an editor style program. For our needs and ease of use we will again use the MS-DOS editor program.

To demonstrate how to create a batch file, we have listed the necessary steps below to first create a **"menu.bat"** file which will automatically display the **"menu.txt"** file, (the one you have just created) whenever you type **"menu"** return.

STEP(1)

At the **"C:\"** prompt type **"Edit menu.bat"** return

STEP(2)

Type **"C:"** return

Type **"cd \"** return

Type **"Type menu.txt"** return

STEP(3)

Your screen should now look like Figure(4) below.

File Edit Search Options   Help
═══════════════════════════ MENU.BAT ═══════════════════════════
C:
cd \
Type menu.txt

Figure (4)

STEP(4)

Type **"ALT"** and **"F"** simultaneously then press **"S"** to save.

STEP(5)

Type **"ALT"** and **"X"** simultaneously to exit the editor program.

Your menu.bat file will have now been created, and you can test to see if it works by typing **"menu"** return.

Right then. Now that you have created your **"menu.bat"** file you need to create all of the separate batch files needed to run the various programs listed in your **"menu.txt"** file see Figure(3).

To do this you need to know where each of the programs are located on your hard disk. For instance:- Microsoft Windows is usually located in the "**C:\WINDOWS**" Directory of your hard disk, and Super Calc 5 can usually be found in the "**C:\SC5**" directory of your hard disk.

To give you an idea of what your batch file should look like we have given you three example of different batch files needed to run three of the programs listed in Figure(3). These are "**Microsoft Windows**", "**Super Calc 5**" and "**Day Of The Tentacle**". We have presumed that all of these programs have been installed on drive C, but if they are installed on a different drive you can simply change the first line of the batch file to the different drive letter, i.e. "**D:**" as opposed to "**C:**".

Making a batch file called "**1.BAT**" which will run Microsoft Windows every time you type "**1**" return.

STEP(1)

At the "**C:**" prompt type "**Edit 1.bat**" return

STEP(2)

Type "**C:**" return

Type "**cd windows**" return

Type "**win**" return

Type "**cd **" return

Type "**cls**" return

Type "**menu**" return

STEP(3)

Your screen should now look like Figure(5) below.

Figure (5)

STEP(4)

Type "**ALT**" and "**F**" simultaneously then press "**S**" to save.

STEP(5)

Type "**ALT**" and "**X**" simultaneously to exit the editor program.

Making a batch file called "**5.BAT**" which will run Super Calc 5 every time you type "**5**" return.

STEP(1)

At the "**C:**" prompt type "**Edit 5.bat**" return

STEP(2)

Type "**C:**" return

Type "**cd sc5**" return

Type "**lh mouse**" return (loads mouse driver into high memory)

Type "**sc5**" return

Type "**cd **" return

Type "**cls**" return

Type "**menu**" return

STEP(3)

Your screen should now look like Figure(6) below.

Figure (5)

STEP(4)

Type "**ALT**" and "**F**" simultaneously then press "**S**" to save.

STEP(5)

Type "**ALT**" and "**X**" simultaneously to exit the editor program.

Making a batch file called "**6.BAT**" which will run Super Calc 5 every time your type "**6**" return.

STEP(1)

At the "**C:**" prompt type "**Edit 6.bat**" return

STEP(2)

Type "**C:**" return

Type "**cd dott**" return

Type "**lh mouse**" return (loads mouse driver into high memory)

Type "**dott**" return

Type "**cd **" return

Type "**cls**" return

Type "**menu**" return

STEP(3)

Your screen should now look like Figure(7) below.

```
  File   Edit   Search   Options                              Help
                                    6.BAT
 C:
 cd dott
 lh mouse
 dott
 cd \
 cls
 menu
```

Figure (7)

STEP(4)

Type "**ALT**" and "**F**" simultaneously then press "**S**" to save.

STEP(5)

Type "**ALT**" and "**X**" simultaneously to exit the editor program.

When you have finished creating all of the relevant batch files to run your programs listed in the "**menu.txt**" file, you can insert the "**menu.bat**" command into your "**autoexec.bat**" file. This will tell your computer to display your "**menu.txt**" file whenever the computer is turned on. Please use the following steps:

STEP(1)

At the **"C:\"** prompt type "**Edit autoexec.bat**" return; a screen similar to the following will appear. Please see Figure(8).

Figure (8)

STEP(2)

Move your cursor to make a new line at the end of the file.

Type "**Type menu.txt**" return. Your screen should now look similar to Figure(9) shown below.

Figure (9)

STEP(3)

Type "**ALT**" and "**F**" simultaneously then press "**S**" to save.

Type "**ALT**" and "**X**" simultaneously to exit the editor program.

Now whenever your computer starts, your front end menu will be displayed. All you have to do is type in the corresponding number/letter then "**return**" to start any of the programs listed on the screen in the "**menu.txt**" file. That is, provided that you have mad₌ ˙˙ ʳᵃlevant batch file to go with the programs, i.e. "**1.bat**" for Wⁱⁿ⸱ˡows, "2.bat" for Sage and so on. Remember from now on you ₌.ᵢ call up and run your menu.bat file from anywhere on your hard disk, by simply typing "**menu**" return.

If you have any problems please telephone (0860) 325144

INSTALLING A MOUSE (MS-DOS)

If you have a mouse with your computer it will normally be connected to a port on the back of your computer normally "**COM1**".
This stands for communication port 1. Generally there are two
communication ports, the other being labelled "**COM2**". Please
see Figure(1) showing you how to recognise the two Com ports
on the back of your computer.

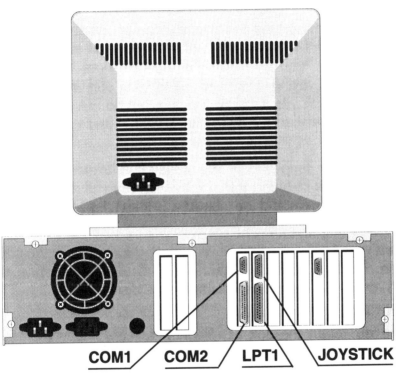

COM1 / COM2 / LPT1 \ JOYSTICK

Figure (1)

Your mouse will require a mouse driver (program) to make it
work. if you have purchased your machine already configured
with a mouse driver installed, then please ignore this section.
If you wish to install a mouse then follow these simple steps:

STEP(1)

Remove your mouse from it's packaging. Note that there is usually a small manual, a software disk and a mouse. It is advisable to carefully look at the rubber ball underneath the mouse as there is normally some foam packing to prevent the mouse ball from moving and causing damage during transit. If there is some packing remove it now. You will probably have to click open a plastic plate on the bottom of the mouse to do so.

STEP(2)

Exit out of any programs and ensure that your computer is turned off. Now connect your mouse to the "**COM1**" port at the rear of your computer. You can't miss this port because it should be clearly labelled, failing which it will be the only port or socket that the mouse will fit into anyway. Tighten, but do not over-tighten the holding screws that hold the connector in place.

STEP(3)

Insert the disk supplied with the mouse and follow the installation procedures included with the mouse's purchase. However, if you do not understand the instructions then follow these steps.

STEP(3a)

Insert your floppy disk into Drive A: or B: depending on the size of the disk and Type "**A:**" return, or "**B:**" return depending on which drive you have inserted the mouse disk in.

STEP(3b)

Type "**dir**" return and look for a filename with the extension ".**exe**" or ".**bat**". Note the filename and type it, the name may differ but it will probably be called "**install.exe**", type it and press return.

STEP(3c)

You should now follow the procedures given by the installation program on the screen. Please note that different mouse suppliers usually use different installation programs and drivers.

STEP(3d)

If you have any problems such as there is no disk included with your mouse, or you do not understand the installation procedure, then please **phone (0860) 325144** quoting your personal reference number. We will then advise you on ways of getting around this problem.

FORMATTING A 3½" 1.44Mb FLOPPY DISK

Insert a blank or unwanted 1.44mb disk into your floppy disk drive usually marked A:. Make sure that if you have any important files on the floppy disk you have safely copied them somewhere safe, as when you format a disk all information on the disk is completely erased.

STEP(1)

At the DOS prompt type the following

"Format A:" return, this message will now appear:-

"Insert new diskette for drive A:"

"and press ENTER when ready..."

STEP(2)

Make sure that the disk you have inserted into drive A has no important files on it, or is empty. If so, press the **"return/enter"** key and proceed to **STEP(3)**. If you are not sure then press the **"CTRL"** and **"C"** keys simultaneously, and only repeat **STEP(1)** after you have safely copied all of your important files either on to another disk or have found another clean or empty disk.

STEP(3)

The drive will now start to click as it slowly formats your disk.

Please Note:-If you are using DOS 5.0 or above you can speed the process up by typing:

"Format A:\ /q" instead of **"Format A:"**. The extra parameter tells DOS 5.0 or higher to quick format the disk if the disk has previously been formatted. This improves formatting times on average by about 300% or more.

STEP(4)

When the computer has finished formatting the floppy disk it will display a message similar to this:-

"Format Complete"

"Volume label (11 characters, ENTER for none)?"

Either type in a name or press enter at this point. The computer will now ask you if you want to **"Format another ? (Y/N)"**. If you want to format another disk take out the current disk in drive A:\ and put in another blank or empty disk, then type **"Y"**. If you do not need to format another disk, type **"N"**.

FORMATTING A 3½" 720k FLOPPY DISK

Insert a blank or unwanted 720k disk into your floppy disk drive usually marked A:. Make sure that if you have any important files on the floppy disk you have safely copied them somewhere safe, as when you format a disk all information on the disk is completely erased.

STEP(1)

At the DOS prompt type the following

"Format A: /f:720" return, this message will now appear:-

"Insert new diskette for drive A:"

"and press ENTER when ready..."

STEP(2)

Make sure that the disk you have inserted into drive A has no important files on it or is empty. If so, press the **"return/enter"** key and proceed to **STEP(3)**. If you are not sure then press the **"CTRL"** and **"C"** keys simultaneously and only repeat **STEP(1)** after you have safely copied all of your important files either on to another disk or have found another clean or empty disk.

STEP(3)

The drive will now start to click as it slowly formats your disk.

Please Note:-If you are using DOS 5.0 or above you can speed the process up by typing:

"Format A:\ /f:720 /q" instead of **"Format A: /f:720"**. The extra parameter tells DOS 5.0 or higher to quick format the disk if the disk has previously been formatted. This improves formatting times on average by about 300% or more.)

STEP(4)

When the computer has finished formatting the floppy disk it will display a message similar to this:-

"Format Complete"

"Volume label (11 characters, ENTER for none)?"

Either type in a name or press enter at this point. The computer will now ask you if you want to **"Format another ? (Y/N)"**. If you want to format another disk take out the current disk in drive A:\ and put in another blank or empty disk then type **"Y"**. If you do not need to format another disk, type **"N"**.

FORMATTING A 5¼" 1.2Mb FLOPPY DISK

Insert a blank or unwanted 1.2mb disk into your high density floppy disk drive usually marked B:. Make sure that if you have any important files on the floppy disk you have safely copied them somewhere safe as when you format a disk all information on the disk is completely erased.

STEP(1)

At the DOS prompt type the following

"Format B: /F:1.2" return, this message will now appear:-

"Insert new diskette for drive A:"

"and press ENTER when ready..."

STEP(2)

Make sure that the disk you have inserted into drive A has no important files on it or is empty. If so, press the **"return/enter"** key and proceed to **STEP(3).** If you are not sure then press the **"CTRL"** and **"C"** keys simultaneously and only repeat **STEP(1)** after you have safely copied all of your important files either on to another disk or have found another clean or empty disk.

STEP(3)

The drive will now start to click as it slowly formats your disk.

Please Note:-If you are using DOS 5.0 or above you can speed the process up by typing:

"Format B:\ /F:1.2 /q" instead of **"Format B: /F:1.2"** the extra parameter tells DOS 5.0 or higher to quick format the disk if the disk has previously been formatted. This improves formatting times on average by about 300% or more.)

STEP(4)

When the computer has finished formatting the floppy disk it will display a message similar to this:-

"Format Complete"

"Volume label (11 characters, ENTER for none)?"

Either type in a name or press enter at this point. The computer will now ask you if you want to **"Format another ? (Y/N)"**. If you want to format another disk take out the current disk in drive B:\ and put in another blank or empty disk, then type **"Y"**. If you do not need to format another disk, type **"N"**.

FORMATTING A 5¼" 320k FLOPPY DISK

Insert a blank or unwanted 320k disk into your high density floppy disk drive usually marked B:. Make sure that if you have any important files on the floppy disk you have safely copied them somewhere safe, as when you format a disk all information on the disk is completely erased.

STEP(1)

At the DOS prompt type the following

"Format B: /4" return,

The following message will now appear:-

"Insert new diskette for drive A:"

"and press ENTER when ready..."

STEP(2)

Make sure that the disk you have inserted into drive A has no important files on it or is empty. If so, press the **"return/enter"** key and proceed to **STEP(3)**. If you are not sure then press the "**CTRL**" and "**C**" keys simultaneously and only repeat **STEP(1)** after you have safely copied all of your important files either on to another disk or have found another clean or empty disk.

STEP(3)

The drive will now start to click as it slowly formats your disk.

Please Note:-If you are using DOS 5.0 or above you can speed the process up by typing:

"**Format B:\ /4 /q**" instead of "**Format B: /4**" the extra parameter tells DOS 5.0 or higher to quick format the disk if the disk has previously been formatted. This improves formatting times on average by about 300% or more.)

STEP(4)

When the computer has finished formatting the floppy disk it will display a message similar to this:-

"**Format Complete**"

"**Volume label (11 characters, ENTER for none)?**"

Either type in a name or press enter at this point. The computer will now ask you if you want to "**Format another ? (Y/N)**", if you want to format another disk take out the current disk in drive B:\ and put in another blank or empty disk then type "**Y**". If you do not need to format another disk, type "**N**".

If you have any problems please telephone (0860) 325144

MICROSOFT MS-DOS SHELL

Your computer's disk operating system has within it a system called "**MS-DOS SHELL**", which actually provides a visual alternative to the standard MS-DOS command prompts. It is capable of displaying files, directories and the applications that are available on your hard disk.

However when producing "**The Book**" it was generally felt that the "**MS-DOS SHELL**" was simply an inferior environment when compared to "**Microsoft Windows**", and therefore we have omitted it from the book; however should you wish to know more about the "**MS-DOS SHELL**" in a language that you can understand, we will be producing inserts in the near future which will cover the various parts and workings of MS DOS SHELL.

To order please telephone (0860) 325144.

If your newly installed game comes up with one of the following messages i.e.

"Cannot Load"

"Not enough conventional memory"

"Not enough expanded memory"

"Not enough extended memory"

or your system stops, then you need a Game Boot-up disk.

A Game boot-up disk can be left in your computer when you first turn it on. Either re-boot it or press the reset button. It will start the computer with the maximum amount of extended or expanded memory depending on which your games require.

Usually the game will tell you which type of memory it requires upon loading, by displaying a message similar to those we have just mentioned. If you are completely confused by expanded or extended memory, the safe option is to make two Game Boot-up disks. Configure one for **"extended memory"**. This will also give you the maximum amount of conventional memory. The other should be configured for **"expanded memory"**. This should ensure that if one doesn't work, the other will.

Before continuing make a note of how much conventional memory your computer currently has. You can do this by typing **"MEM"** return, from the DOS prompt.

For further information about expanded and extended memory please refer to the corresponding sections marked expanded and extended memory in the index, or **telephone (0860) 325145.**

GAME BOOT-UP DISK (EXTENDED MEMORY)

TO GIVE THE MOST AMOUNT OF CONVENTIONAL AND EXTENDED MEMORY AVAILABLE (IN DOS).

Insert a blank or unneeded 1.44mb disk into your floppy disk drive marked A:. Make sure that if you have any important files on the floppy disk you have safely copied them somewhere safe, as when you make a games disk all information on the disk is completely erased.

STEP(1)

At the DOS prompt type the following:-

"Format A:\ /s" return (the /s command informs the computer to copy the system boot-up files needed in order for it to run.)

The following message will now appear.

"Insert new diskette for drive A:"

"and press ENTER when ready..."

Again make sure that the disk you have inserted in drive A has no important files on it or is empty. If so, press enter. If you are not sure, type "**CTRL**" and "**C**" simultaneously and only repeat STEP(1) after you have safely copied all of your important files either on to another disk or have found a clean or empty disk.

If you pressed enter at the prompted question the computer will start clicking away as it slowly formats your disk.

Please Note:- If you are using DOS 5.0 or above you can speed the process up by typing:-

"Format A:\ /q/s" return instead of "**Format A: /s**" return, the extra parameter tells DOS 5.0 or higher to quick format the disk if the disk has previously been formatted. This improves formatting times on average by about 300% or more.)

When the computer has finished formatting the floppy disk it will display a message similar to this:-

"Format Complete"

"System transferred"

The system files are the computer's own **"Hidden"** boot-up files and they are vital. If you do not inform the computer to copy them it will not boot from your floppy drive A; in this case your Game Boot-up disk.

After the system files have been copied the computer will display a message similar to this:-

"Volume label (11 characters, ENTER for none)?"

Either type in a name or press enter at this point.

The computer will now ask you if you want to:-•

"Format another ? (Y/N)"

If you want to make another Boot-up disk take out the current disk in drive A:\. Put in another blank or empty disk then type "**Y**", if you do not need to make another Boot-up disk type "**N**".

STEP(2a)

Now you can test to see whether your computer can load from your newly created Boot-up disk. To do this leave the disk in drive A: and reset the computer by either pressing the main "**RESET**" button normally situated on the front panel of your computer or by preferably holding down the "**CTRL**", "**ALT**" and "**DELETE**" keys simultaneously. Your computer will now restart, and after a short while you will be left with a message similar to this:-

"Enter new date (mm-dd-yy):"

Do not bother to enter anything, just simply press enter twice and you will now be left at the "**A:**" prompt.

Please Note that you have so far only created a Boot-up Disk not a Game Boot-up disk. You have yet to maximise your disk for extended / expanded memory performance.

STEP(2b)

At the DOS prompt type "**MEM**" to see how much conventional memory you have left, and make a note of this figure for future reference.

STEP(3)

The next step is to copy your configuration files and the necessary drivers needed to Boot-up you computer normally.

Now type the following:-

"**Copy C:*.sys A:**" return

"**Copy C:\autoexec.bat A:**" return

"**Copy C:\dos*.sys A:**" return

"**Copy C:\dos\emm386.exe A:**" return

"**Copy C:*.* A:**" return

Please note that if you are prompted by the computer at any time to overwrite a file, type "**N**". Even if you cannot fit all of your Root directory (**C:*.***) onto your Boot-up disk you should be safe.

STEP(4a)

Type "**Edit A:\config.sys**" return

A screen will now appear looking something like this:-

DEVICE=C:\DOS\SETVER.EXE

DEVICE=C:\HIMEM.SYS

DEVICE=C:\EMM386.EXE

DOS=HIGH

FILES=40

BUFFERS=10

COUNTRY=044,437,C:\DOS\COUNTRY.SYS

DEVICE=C:\DOS\DISPLAY.SYS

If you have any problems please telephone (0860) 325144

Now try changing it to look like the example shown below:-

DEVICE=**A:**\HIMEM.SYS

DEVICE=**A:**\EMM386.EXE **NOEMS**

DOS=HIGH,UMB

COUNTRY=044,437,C:\DOS\COUNTRY.SYS

FILES=**30**

DEVICE**HIGH**=C:\DOS\DISPLAY.SYS

STEP(4b)

If the first two lines of the above example were not already in your config.sys file, add them now as they are crucial in achieving extended or expanded memory.

Also please note wherever you see a "**DEVICE=** "command in a line, as long as it is after the "**device=emm386.exe noems**" line you can change it to "**DEVICEHIGH=**". This will cause the device driver to load into higher memory, thus freeing up more conventional memory, for instance:-

Before changing the line to DEVICEHIGH= the line would look something like this:-

"**DEVICE=C:\DOS\DISPLAY.SYS**"

After modification it would look something like this:-

"**DEVICEHIGH=C:\DOS\DISPLAY.SYS**"

STEP(4c)

Also note that if a line in your config.sys file reads "**DOS=HIGH**" you can change it to "**DOS=HIGH,UMB**". (see example above) This again causes DOS to load more of itself into higher memory saving you an extra **55k** of conventional memory. If however the line wasn't in the file at all and you are using MS-DOS 5.0 or above you can insert it as shown above immediately after the "**DEVICEHIGH=A:\EMM386.EXE NOEMS**" line. This will immediately increase the computer's conventional memory pool by about **101k** of conventional memory.

STEP(4d)

Another trick in maximising your Game Boot-up disk is to tell DOS to skip some of your drivers completely. A safe bet is to tell your computer to skip the **"country.sys"** and **"display.sys"** drivers when the computer Boots-up on drive A:. You can do this by inserting a **"REM"** statement in front of each unwanted line i.e.

Before inserting Rem Statements

DEVICE=A:\HIMEM.SYS

DEVICE=A:\EMM386.EXE NOEMS

DOS=HIGH,UMB

COUNTRY=044,437,C:\DOS\COUNTRY.SYS

DEVICEHIGH=C:\DOS\DISPLAY.SYS

After inserting Rem Statements

DEVICE=A:\HIMEM.SYS

DEVICE=EMM386.exe NOEMS

DOS=HIGH,UMB

REM COUNTRY=044,437,C:\DOS\COUNTRY.SYS

REM DEVICEHIGH=C:\DOS\DISPLAY.SYS

STEP(5a)

To test whether your computer's new Game Boot-up disk still works properly after changing the **"A:\config.sys"** file you must first save and exit the file editor. Leave the Games Boot-up disk in drive A:\ whilst you **"RESET"** the machine or press the **"CTRL"**, **"ALT"** and **"DELETE"** keys simultaneously. **DO NOT REBOOT your machine until you have completed STEP(5b).**

STEP(5b)

To quickly save the **"A:\config.sys"** and exit the file editor press the **"ALT"** and **"F"** keys simultaneously, and then press **"X"**. At the **"Save file on exit?"** **"<YES> <NO>"** prompt type **"Y"**. The computer will now exit the editor program after saving your **"A:\config.sys"** file and will leave you at the DOS prompt.

Now you can safely reboot your machine as explained earlier in STEPS (2) and (5a).

STEP(6)

If your computer boots correctly proceed to STEP(8). If it fails to boot proceed to STEP(7)

STEP(7)

If your computer does not boot correctly reset the machine again without the Game-Boot-up Disk in drive A:\

At the DOS Prompt type "**EDIT A:\CONFIG.SYS**". This time try removing the REM Statements which you earlier put in front of the "**COUNTRY.SYS**" and "**DISPLAY.SYS**" lines. Now save your file and exit the editor program again as explained in STEP(5b). If your computer still does not boot up **telephone (0860) 325144.**

STEP(8)

Now that you have successfully optimised your "**CONFIG.SYS**" file, you can now edit and optimise your "**AUTOEXEC.BAT**" file. This will again increase the available conventional memory.

At the Dos prompt type edit "**A:\autoexec.bat**"

The Following screen will appear looking something like this:-

C:\DOS\SMARTDRV.EXE

@ECHO OFF

Prompt pg

PATH=C:\DOS;C:\;C:\WINDOWS;C:\TEMP;C:\MOUSE;

SET TEMP=C:\TEMP

C:\DOS\SHARE.EXE

MOUSE

Now try changing it to look like the example below:-
LOADHIGH C:\DOS\SHARE.EXE
@ECHO OFF
Prompt pg
PATH=A:\;C:\DOS;C:\;C:\WINDOWS;C:\TEMP;C:\MOUSE;
SET TEMP=C:\TEMP
LOADHIGH MOUSE

As you can see the **"smartdrv.exe"** program has been loaded into higher memory as has the **"mouse"** driver; share has also been taken out. If you are using a specialist driver for instance for a CD-ROM drive you can also load it into higher memory by again typing **"LOADHIGH"** in front of it.

STEP(9a)

Now save and exit the editor program by again typing "**ALT**" and "**F**" simultaneously then press "**X**". The computer will again prompt you with the following message "**Save file on exit?**" "**<YES> <NO>**". Type "**Y**" and the editor program will save your file and exit leaving you at the DOS prompt.

STEP(9b)

RESET your Machine with your Game Boot-up disk in drive A and type "**mem**" to see how much extra conventional and extended memory you have gained.

STEP(10)

You can now re-try running the game that initially prompted you with one of the following messages:- "

"Cannot load"

"Not enough conventional memory"

"lack of extended memory"

or statements to that effect.

If you have any problems please telephone (0860) 325144

GAME BOOT-UP DISK (EXPANDED MEMORY)

TO GIVE THE MOST AMOUNT OF EXPANDED MEMORY (IN DOS)

Insert a blank or unneeded 1.44mb disk into your floppy disk drive marked A:. Make sure that if you have any important files on the floppy disk you have safely copied them somewhere safe as when you make a games disk all information on the disk is completely erased.

STEP(1)

At the DOS prompt type the following:-

"Format A:\ /s" return. (the /s command informs the computer to copy the system boot-up files needed in order for it to run.)

The following message will now appear.

"Insert new diskette for drive A:"

"and press ENTER when ready..."

Again make sure that the disk you have inserted in drive A has no important files on it or is empty. If so, press enter. If you are not sure then type **"CTRL"** and **"C"** simultaneously and only re-peat STEP(1) after you have safely copied all of your important files either on to another disk or have found a clean or empty disk.

If you pressed enter at the prompted question the computer will start clicking away as it slowly formats your disk.

Please Note:- If you are using DOS 5.0 or above you can speed the process up by typing:-

"Format A:\ /q/s" return instead of **"Format A: /s"** return. The extra parameter tells DOS 5.0 or higher to quick format the disk if the disk has previously been formatted. This improves format-ting times on average by about 300% or more.)

When the computer has finished formatting the floppy disk it will display a message similar to this:-

"Format Complete"

"System transferred"

The system files are the computer's own **"Hidden"** boot-up files and they are vital. If you do not inform the computer to copy them it will not boot from your floppy drive A; in this case your Game Boot-up disk.

After the system files have been copied the computer will display a message similar to this:-

"Volume label (11 characters, ENTER for none)?"

Either type in a name or press enter at this point.

The computer will now ask you if you want to:-•

"Format another ? (Y/N)"

If you want to make another Boot-up disk take out the current disk in drive A:\. Put in another blank or empty disk, then type **"Y"**. If you do not need to make another Boot-up disk type **"N"**.

STEP(2a)

Now you can test to see whether your computer can load from your newly created Boot-up disk. To do this leave the disk in drive A:. Reset the computer by either pressing the main **"RESET"** button normally situated on the front panel of your computer or by preferably holding down the **"CTRL"**, **"ALT"** and **"DELETE"** keys simultaneously. Your computer will now restart, and after a short while you will be left with a message similar to this:-

"Enter new date (mm-dd-yy):"

Do not bother to enter anything, just simply press enter twice and you will now be left at the **"A:\"** prompt.

Please Note that you have so far only created a Boot-up Disk not a Game Boot-up disk, so you have yet to maximise your disk for extended / expanded memory performance.

STEP(2b)

At the DOS prompt type **"MEM"** to see how much conventional memory you have left, and make a note of this figure for future reference.

STEP(3)

The next step is to copy your configuration files and the necessary drivers needed to Boot-up you computer normally.

Now type the following:-

"**Copy C:*.sys A:**" return

"**Copy C:\autoexec.bat A:**" return

"**Copy C:\dos*.sys A:**" return

"**Copy C:\dos\emm386.exe A:**" return

"**Copy C:*.* A:**" return

Please note that if you are prompted by the computer at any time to overwrite a file, type "**N**". Even if you cannot fit all of your Root directory (**C:*.***) onto your Boot-up disk you should be safe.

STEP(4a)

Type "**Edit A:\config.sys**" return

A screen will now appear looking something like this:-

DEVICE=C:\DOS\SETVER.EXE

DEVICE=C:\HIMEM.SYS

DEVICE=C:\EMM386.EXE NOEMS

DOS=HIGH

FILES=40

BUFFERS=10

COUNTRY=044,437,C:\DOS\COUNTRY.SYS

DEVICE=C:\DOS\DISPLAY.SYS

If you have any problems please telephone (0860) 325144

Now try changing it to look like the example shown below:-

DEVICE=**A:**\HIMEM.SYS

DEVICE=**A:**\EMM386.EXE

DOS=HIGH,UMB

FILES=40

BUFFERS=10

COUNTRY=044,437,C:\DOS\COUNTRY.SYS

DEVICE=C:\DOS\DISPLAY.SYS

STEP(4b)

Please note that the line "**device=emm386.exe noems**" has been changed to allow emm386.exe to use expanded memory. If the first two lines were not already in your "**config.sys**" file add them now as they are crucial to achieving expanded or extended memory.

STEP(4c)

Also note that if the line in your "**config.sys**" file reading "**DOS=HIGH**" was not initially included you should add it as it will save you an extra "**46k**" of conventional memory.

STEP(4d)

Another trick in maximising your Game Boot-up disk is to tell DOS to skip some of your drivers completely. A safe bet is to tell your computer to skip the "**country.sys**" and "**display.sys**" drivers when the computer Boots-up on drive A:. You can do this by inserting a REM statement in front of each unnecessary line i.e.

Before inserting Rem Statements

DEVICE=A:\HIMEM.SYS

DEVICE=A:\EMM386.EXE NOEMS

DOS=HIGH,UMB

COUNTRY=044,437,C:\DOS\COUNTRY.SYS

DEVICEHIGH=C:\DOS\DISPLAY.SYS

After inserting Rem Statements
DEVICE=A:\HIMEM.SYS
DEVICE=EMM386.EXE NOEMS
DOS=HIGH,UMB
REM COUNTRY=044,437,C:\DOS\COUNTRY.SYS
REM DEVICEHIGH=C:\DOS\DISPLAY.SYS

STEP(5a)

To test whether your computer's new Game Boot-up disk still works properly after changing the "**A:\config.sys**" file you must first save and exit the file editor. Leave the Games Boot-up disk in drive A:\ whilst you "**RESET**" the machine or press the "**CTRL**", "**ALT**" and "**DELETE**" keys simultaneously. **DO NOT REBOOT your machine until you have completed STEP(5b).**

STEP(5b)

To quickly save the "**A:\config.sys**" and exit the file editor press the "**ALT**" and "**F**" keys simultaneously, and then press "**X**". At the "**Save file on exit?**" "**<YES> <NO>**" prompt type "**Y**". The computer will now exit the editor program after saving your "**A:\config.sys**" file and will leave you at the DOS prompt.

Now you can safely reboot your machine as explained earlier in STEPS (2) and (5a)

STEP(6)

If your computer boots correctly proceed to STEP(8) if it fails to boot proceed to STEP(7)

STEP(7)

If your computer does not boot correctly reset the machine again without the Game-Boot-up Disk in drive A:\

At the DOS Prompt type "**EDIT A:\CONFIG.SYS**". This time try removing the REM Statements which you earlier put in front of the "**COUNTRY.SYS**" and "**DISPLAY.SYS**" lines, then save your file and exit the editor program again as explained in STEP(5b).

If your computer still does not boot up **telephone (0860) 325144.**

STEP(8)

Now that you have successfully optimised your "**CONFIG.SYS**" file, you can now edit and optimise your "**AUTOEXEC.BAT**" file. This will again increase your computer's available conventional memory.

At the DOS prompt type edit "**A:\autoexec.bat**" return.

The Following screen will appear looking something like this:-

```
File   Edit   Search   Options                              Help
                          AUTOEXEC.BAT
C:\DOS\smartdrv.exe
@ECHO OFF
PROMPT $p$g
PATH C:\DOS;C:\;C:\WINDOWS;C:\TEMP;C:\MOUSE;
SET TEMP=C:\TEMP
C:\DOS\SHARE.EXE
mouse
```

C:\DOS\SMARTDRV.EXE

@ECHO OFF

Prompt pg

PATH=C:\DOS;C:\;C:\WINDOWS;C:\TEMP;C:\MOUSE;

SET TEMP=C:\TEMP

C:\DOS\SHARE.EXE

MOUSE

Now try changing it to look like the example below:-

@ECHO OFF

Prompt pg

PATH=A:\;C:\DOS;C:\;C:\WINDOWS;C:\TEMP;C:\MOUSE;

SET TEMP=C:\TEMP

MOUSE

As you can see the "**smartdrv.exe**" and "**share.exe**" programs have been completely removed freeing up an extra 32k of conventional memory. If you are using a specialist driver for instance for a CD-ROM drive you should leave it in to enable CD-ROM games to play.

STEP(9a)

Now save and exit the editor program by again typing "**ALT**" and "**F**" simultaneously. Then press "**X**", and the computer will again prompt you with the following message "**Save file on exit?**" "**<YES> <NO>**". Type "**Y**" and the editor program will save your file and exit leaving you at the DOS prompt.

STEP(9b)

RESET your Machine with your Game Boot-up disk in drive A and type "**mem**" to see how much extra conventional and expanded memory you have gained.

STEP(10)

You can now re-try running the game that initially prompted you with one of the following messages:-

"**Cannot load**"

"**Not enough conventional memory**"

"**Lack of expanded memory**"

or words to that effect.

If you have any problems please telephone (0860) 325144

WHAT TO DO IN CASE OF AN EMERGENCY
(Problem Solving)

We are about to try and cover some of the problems that could occur whilst running MS-DOS and it's various programs.

The first important topic is obviously fault finding during the setup of (MS-DOS). Whilst it is unlikely you will encounter any major problems, there are several common faults you may come across so please refer to the relative sections below.

PROBLEMS DURING MS-DOS SETUP

One of the most likely problems you could incur during setup is that your computer will give you a message stating that you do not have enough space to install MS-DOS. If this happens you must make more room. Whilst we have already covered this, it was commonly felt that to run through the procedures again would be helpful to you. This is how you should create more free space on your hard disk.

STEP(1)

First of all find out how much disk space you need to free up, you can do this by pressing "F3" twice before you quit setup.

STEP(2)

After exiting setup type **"A:\chkdsk C:"**. The check disk command shows a line similar to this: **"3,561,472 Bytes available on disk"**. The number tells you how much free space you have on your C: drive in this case **3.5Mb**.

STEP(3)

Delete all the files you no longer wish to use by using the delete command (del filename.extension). Remember all filenames are eight letters in length or less with a dot then a three letter extension, once you have freed up enough space the amount of disk space you have created should be more than the amount of disk space shown in STEP(1).

Whilst writing this passage, we felt that a picture could be worth a thousand words. So we have created a diagram for you.

Please see Figure(1)

Free Hard Disk Space (3.5Mb)

```
  104,820,736 bytes total disk space
   16,173,056 bytes in 3 hidden files
      100,352 bytes in 26 directories
   84,936,704 bytes in 1,748 user files
    3,561,472 bytes available on disk

        2,048 bytes in each allocation unit
       51,182 total allocation units on disk
        1,739 available allocation units on disk

      655,360 total bytes memory
      623,504 bytes free

Instead of using CHKDSK, try using SCANDISK. SCANDISK can reliably detect
and fix a much wider range of disk problems. For more information,
type HELP SCANDISK from the command prompt.

A:\>
```

Figure (1)

STEP(4)

If you now have more free hard disk space than the amount shown above in Figure(1), you are free to run SETUP again.

COPYING SETUP FILES ACROSS TO YOUR HARD DISK

It is possible to copy single files from your MS-DOS Setup disks directly to your computer. This will be useful if you have accidentally lost or deleted some of the MS-DOS system files.

The files on the Setup disks are compressed, therefore you cannot use them until they have been decompressed. When you run "MS-DOS SETUP" the files are automatically decompressed as they are copied to your hard disk, but if you wish to copy single files without using a setup disk you will obviously need to use a different procedure.

An underscore symbol "_" at the end of a file's extension tells you that it is a compressed file. I.e. "**himem.sy_**" would be a compressed file.

If you decompress a compressed file YOU MUST TELL THE COMPUTER THE FULL EXTENSION OF THE FILE INCLUDING THE UNDERSCORE. YOU MUST ALSO TELL THE COMPUTER TO COPY THE FILE FROM THE FLOPPY DISK TO HARD DRIVE, IN THIS CASE THE DIRECTORY "**C:\DOS**".

These are the steps you should take to expand the file "**A:\Himem.sy_**" to "**C:\DOS\Himem.sys**":

STEP(1)

Make sure that the file "**expand.exe**" is on your hard disk. "**Expand.exe**" is usually found in the directory that contains your version of MS-DOS, i.e. in the directory of "**C:\DOS**". If it's already there then proceed to STEP(3), If you can't find it don't panic! All you have to do is to simply copy it over to your hard disk. Please proceed to STEP2.

STEP(2)

Make sure the "**MS-DOS setup Disk1**" is in drive A:

At the "**C:**" prompt type "**cd dos**" return

Type "**copy A:\expand.exe C:\dos**" return

STEP(3)

Now type "**Expand A:\himem.sy_ C:\DOS\himem.sys**" return

If you require more information about the correct extension names for all the MS-DOS setup disk files, you can use the MS-DOS EDITOR to read the "**packing.lst**" file on the first MS-DOS setup disk. This file contains a list of all the files on each of the MS-DOS setup disks.

Alternatively we have compiled a packing.lst table for MS-DOS6 Please see Figures(2,3 &4).

If you have any problems please telephone (0860) 325144

Microsoft MS-DOS 6 Packing List for 1.44Mb disks.
Contents of MS-DOS Setup Disk 1

8514.VI_	8514.VID	HIMEM.SY_	HIMEM.SYS
ANSI.SY_	ANSI.SYS	IO.SYS	IO.SYS
ATTRIB.EXE	ATTRIB.EXE	KEYB.COM	KEYB.COM
AUTOEXEC.BAT	AUTOEXEC.BAT	KEYBOARD.SYS	KEYBOARD.SYS
BUSETUP.EXE	BUSETUP.EXE	MEM.EX_	MEM.EXE
CGA.GR_	CGA.GRB	MODE.CO_	MODE.COM
CGA.IN_	CGA.INI	MONO.GR_	MONO.GRB
CGA.VI_	CGA.VID	MONO.IN_	MONO.INI
CHKDSK.EXE	CHKDSK.EXE	MORE.COM	MORE.COM
CHOICE.COM	CHOICE.COM	MOVE.EX_	MOVE.EXE
COMMAND.COM	COMMAND.COM	MSD.EXE	MSD.EXE
CONFIG.SYS	CONFIG.SYS	MSDOS.SYS	MSDOS.SYS
COUNTRY.SYS	COUNTRY.SYS	NETWORKS.TXT	NETWORKS.TXT
DBLSPACE.BIN	DBLSPACE.BIN	NLSFUNC.EXE	NLSFUNC.EXE
DEBUG.EXE	DEBUG.EXE	OS2.TXT	OS2.TXT
DEFRAG.EXE	DEFRAG.EXE	PACKING.LST	PACKING.LST
DEFRAG.HL_	DEFRAG.HLP	QBASIC.EXE	QBASIC.EXE
DELTREE.EX_	DELTREE.EXE	RAMDRIVE.SY_	RAMDRIVE.SYS
DOSSETUP.INI	DOSSETUP.INI	README.TXT	README.TXT
DOSSWAP.EX_	DOSSWAP.EXE	RESTORE.EX_	RESTORE.EXE
EDIT.COM	EDIT.COM	SETUP.EXE	SETUP.EXE
EGA.CP_	EGA.CPI	SETUP.MSG	SETUP.MSG
EGA.GR_	EGA.GRB	SMARTDRV.EX_	SMARTDRV.EXE
EGA.IN_	EGA.INI	SYS.COM	SYS.COM
EGA.SY_	EGA.SYS	UNFORMAT.COM	UNFORMAT.COM
EGA.VI_	EGA.VID	UNINSTAL.EXE	UNINSTAL.EXE
EGAMONO.GR_	EGAMONO.GRB	VGA.GR_	VGA.GRB
EXPAND.EXE	EXPAND.EXE	VGA.VI_	VGA.VID
FDISK.EXE	FDISK.EXE	VGAMONO.GR_	VGAMONO.GRB
FORMAT.COM	FORMAT.COM	WINA20.38_	WINA20.386
HERC.GR_	HERC.GRB	XCOPY.EX_	XCOPY.EXE
HERC.VI_	HERC.VID		

Figure (2)

Contents of MS-DOS Setup Disk 2

APPEND.EX_	APPEND.EXE	MWBACKUP.HL_	MWBACKUP.HLP
COUNTRY.IC_	COUNTRY.ICE	POWER.EX_	POWER.EXE
DELOLDOS.EX_	DELOLDOS.EXE	PRINT.EX_	PRINT.EXE
DISKCOMP.CO_	DISKCOMP.COM	QBASIC.HL_	QBASIC.HLP
DISKCOPY.CO_	DISKCOPY.COM	REPLACE.EX_	REPLACE.EXE
DISPLAY.SY_	DISPLAY.SYS	SETVER.EX_	SETVER.EXE
DMDRVR.BI_	DMDRVR.BIN	SHARE.EX_	SHARE.EXE
DOSHELP.HL_	DOSHELP.HLP	SMARTMON.EX_	SMARTMON.EXE
DOSKEY.CO_	DOSKEY.COM	SMARTMON.HL_	SMARTMON.HLP
DOSSHELL.CO_	DOSSHELL.COM	SORT.EX_	SORT.EXE
DOSSHELL.EX_	DOSSHELL.EXE	SSTOR.SY_	SSTOR.SYS
DRIVER.SY_	DRIVER.SYS	SUBST.EX_	SUBST.EXE
EDIT.HL_	EDIT.HLP	TREE.CO_	TREE.COM
EGA.IC_	EGA.ICE	VFINTD.38_	VFINTD.386
FASTHELP.EX_	FASTHELP.EXE	XBIOS.OV_	XBIOS.OVL
FASTOPEN.EX_	FASTOPEN.EXE		
FC.EX_	FC.EXE		
FIND.EX_	FIND.EXE		
GRAPHICS.CO_	GRAPHICS.COM		
GRAPHICS.PR_	GRAPHICS.PRO		
HELP.COM	HELP.COM		
HELP.HL_	HELP.HLP		
KEYBOARD.IC_	KEYBOARD.ICE		
I ABEL.EX_	LABEL.EXE		
LOADFIX.CO_	LOADFIX.COM		
MOUSE.CO_	MOUSE.COM		
MSBACKFB.OVL	MSBACKFB.OVL		
MSBACKFR.OVL	MSBACKFR.OVL		
MSBACKUP.EX_	MSBACKUP.EXE		
MSBACKUP.OVL	MSBACKUP.OVL		
MWBACKF.DL_	MWBACKF.DLL		
MWBACKR.DL_	MWBACKR.DLL		
MWBACKUP.EX_	MWBACKUP.EXE		

Figure (3)

Contents of MS-DOS Setup Disk 3

AV.GR_	AV.GRP	MWAVDLG.DL_	MWAVDLG.DLL
BK.GR_	BK.GRP	MWAVDOSL.DL_	MWAVDOSL.DLL
BKAV.GR_	BKAV.GRP	MWAVDRVL.DL_	MWAVDRVL.DLL
BKUD.GR_	BKUD.GRP	MWAVMGR.DL_	MWAVMGR.DLL
BKUDAV.GR_	BKUPAV.GRP	MWAVSCAN.DL_	MWAVSCAN.DLL
CHKSTATE.SY_	CHKSTATE.SYS	MWAVSOS.DL_	MWAVSOS.DLL
DBLSPACE.EX_	DBLSPACE.EXE	MWAVTSR.EX_	MWAVTSR.EXE
DBLSPACE.HL_	DBLSPACE.HLP	MWGRAFIC.DL_	MWGRAFIC.DLL
DBLSPACE.IN_	DBLSPACE.INF	MWUNDEL.EX_	MWUNDEL.EXE
DBLSPACE.SYS	DBLSPACE.SYS	MWUNDEL.HL_	MWUNDEL.HLP
DBLWIN.HL_	DBLWIN.HLP	SIZER.EX_	SIZER.EXE
DOSSHELL.HL_	DOSSHELL.HLP	SPATCH.BAT	SPATCH.BAT
EMM386.EX_	EMM386.EXE	UD.GR_	UD.GRP
INTERLNK.EX_	INTERLNK.EXE	UDAV.GR_	UDAV.GRP
INTERSVR.EX_	INTERSVR.EXE	UNDELETE.EXE	UNDELETE.EXE
MEMMAKER.EXE	MEMMAKER.EXE	VSAFE.CO_	VSAFE.COM
MEMMAKER.HL_	MEMMAKER.HLP	WNTOOLS.GR_	WNTOOLS.GRP
MEMMAKER.IN_	MEMMAKER.INF		
MONOUMB.38_	MONOUMB.386		
MSAV.EXE	MSAV.EXE		
MSAV.HL_	MSAV.HLP		
MSAVHELP.OV_	MSAVHELP.OVL		
MSAVIRUS.LS_	MSAVIRUS.LST		
MSBACKDB.OVL	MSBACKDB.OVL		
MSBACKDR.OVL	MSBACKDR.OVL		
MSBACKUP.HL_	MSBACKUP.HLP		
MSBCONFG.HL_	MSBCONFG.HLP		
MSBCONFG.OVL	MSBCONFG.OVL		
MSCDEX.EXE	MSCDEX.EXE		
MSTOOLS.DL_	MSTOOLS.DLL		
MWAV.EX_	MWAV.EXE		
MWAV.HL_	MWAV.HLP		
MWAVABSI.DL_	MWAVABSI.DLL		

Figure (4)

For your ease of use we have listed some of the major problems that could occur whilst running MS-DOS. For instance, if your computer suddenly stops running and repeatedly does the same even though you have tried to re-start it, this is what you should do.

Do you remember when you made your **"EMERGENCY BOOT-UP DISK"**? Well, if you can find it, you should be in luck because it should contain everything you require to fix your computer.

Simply turn off your computer, and wait for 30 seconds. Now insert your **"EMERGENCY BOOT-UP DISK"** or a **"GAME BOOT-UP DISK"** into Drive A: and turn on your computer. The computer should now load and run correctly from Drive A:. If you have any problems **please telephone (0860) 325144.**

To completely fix your hard disk so that it can re-boot and work correctly from drive C:, refer to **"USING YOUR EMERGENCY BOOT-UP DISK TO FIX YOUR HARD DRIVE"**, later on in this section.

If you haven't made an **"EMERGENCY BOOT-UP DISK"** or **"GAME BOOT-UP DISK"** smack your wrists now because you are in a lot of trouble. Now go and make yourself a cup of tea and come back in ten minutes whilst we figure out how to help you. Don't worry too much, just carefully follow these procedures.

STEP(1)

Make sure your computer is switched off.

If you are using MS-DOS 6+ proceed to STEP(6) if you are using MS-DOS 5 proceed to the next step.

STEP(2)

Find your MS-DOS installation disks, (don't worry, we're not about to re-install DOS) and insert the MS-DOS setup Disk1 into your boot-up floppy drive (Usually Drive A:)

STEP(3)

Turn on your computer and wait for a Blue Screen to appear welcoming you to Microsoft MS-DOS Setup. Now press the "F3" key to exit.

STEP(4)

Another message will appear warning you that you are exiting setup, asking you to make sure the floppy disk1 is in drive A: and to press the y key. Press the "y" key

(In DOS 6 the message would read MS-DOS is not installed press the F3 key again to exit.)

You will now exit the installation program and will be left at the "A:\" prompt.

STEP(5)

Now you need to access your hard disk. Do this by typing "C:" return, and you will be left at the "C:\" prompt. Proceed to STEP(8)

STEP(6)

Switch on your computer.

When your computer starts, MS-DOS displays the following message: "**Starting MS-DOS...**" When this message appears press the "F5" function key. Please remember to take your finger **off** and don't keep it pressed down. Carrying out this procedure will bypass the "**config.sys**" and "**autoexec.bat files**". The following screen will be displayed, please see Figure(5). If this does not work proceed back to Step(2) using your "**MS-DOS 6 setup Disk 1**" to start your computer instead of MS-DOS 5.

```
256KB CACHE MEMORY
Starting MS-DOS...

MS-DOS is bypassing your CONFIG.SYS and AUTOEXEC.BAT files.

MIcrosoft(R) MS-DOS(R) Version 6.20
           (c) Copyright Microsoft Corp 1981-1993
C:\>
```

Figure (5)

STEP(7)

You will now be left at the "**C:**" prompt and your computer will have been given a basic initial configuration, therefore some parts of your system may not work correctly, i.e "**Microsoft Windows**".

STEP(8)

Now type "**dir**" return. A list of the files contained in your root directory will appear on the screen. **Please note:-** If your hard disk does not display any files or you cannot access your hard disk **please telephone (0860) 325144.**

STEP(9)

Type "**rename config.syd config.sys**" return. This will make the old copy of your config.sys file "**config.syd**" become the new "**config.sys**" file, thus fixing any newly created errors. If this did not work try typing "**rename config.bak config.sys**" return, or "**rename config.old config.sys**" return.

If this did not work **please telephone (0860) 325144**

STEP(10)

Now type "**rename autoexec.syd autoexec.bat**". This will make the old copy of your autoexec.bat file "**autoexec.syd**" become the new "**autoexec.bat**" file, again hopefully fixing any newly created errors. If the above still did not work, try typing "**rename autoexec.bak autoexec.bat**" return, or now try typing "**rename autoexec.old autoexec.bat**" return.

If this still did not work, **please telephone (0860) 325144**

STEP(11)

Now remove all floppy disks from your computer and reboot by pressing the "**CTRL**", "**ALT**" and "**DELETE**" keys at the same time. Wait for 10-15 seconds and if nothing happens turn off your computer, wait for 30 seconds and then turn it on again.

Your computer should now re-boot correctly.

If it does not work, **please telephone (0860) 325144.**

USING YOUR EMERGENCY BOOT-UP DISK TO FIX YOUR HARD DRIVE

If your computer's hard disk does not boot-up or start correctly you should in most cases be able to use your **"EMERGENCY BOOT-UP DISK"** to initially act as a temporary BOOT-UP disk configured to run all of your programs correctly. Then go on to use it to fix the hard disk boot-up problem by copying all of the EMERGENCY DISKS files back onto the hard drive.

Please follow these procedures.

STEP(1)

Simply turn off your computer, wait for 30 seconds. Now insert your **"EMERGENCY BOOT-UP DISK"** or **"GAME BOOT-UP DISK"** into Drive A: and turn on your computer. The computer should now load correctly from drive A:, and should now work as if nothing had ever happened except that you will not be able to format any disk inserted in your floppy boot-up drive A:.

To attempt to make your hard disk drive C: boot-up correctly, proceed to STEP(2).

If you have any problems **please telephone (0860) 325144.**

STEP(2)

Copy all of the files from your **"EMERGENCY BOOT-UP DISK"** onto your hard disk. To do this type the following from the "**A:**" prompt.

Type "**Copy A:*.* c:**" return.

Type "**sys C:**" return. This will copy the hidden system files needed to boot-up MS-DOS from your hard drive.

STEP(3)

Now remove all floppy disks from your computer and reboot by pressing the "**CTRL**", "**ALT**" and "**DELETE**" keys at the same time. Wait for 10-15 seconds, if nothing happens turn off your computer, wait for 30 seconds and then turn it on again.

STEP(4)

Your computer will now reboot correctly from your hard disk.

If you have any problems, **please telephone (0860) 325144.**

SUMMARY OF PROBLEM SOLVING

Whilst there are many other problems that could occur, after due consideration we have agreed that many of the solutions are difficult to follow and require verbal assistance. Therefore, if you experience problems with your computer that you are not able to solve, please ring **(0860) 325144** and we will endeavour to assist you.

We are about to list and briefly describe most of the commands you will need to use when using MS-DOS 5 or above.

If you use MS-DOS HELP, you will find more detailed information about each of the commands.

If you do not understand how to use MS-DOS HELP please refer to the relevant section in this book (USING MS-DOS HELP).

MS-DOS 3,5, 6 and 6.2 COMMANDS

We have already stated that to use any version of DOS lower than DOS 5 is not advisable as you will not be able to use your computer to it's full potential.

Most of the following commands apply to "**DOS 3, 5, 6 and 6.2**", however there are a few that only apply when using DOS 5,6 and 6.2 or only DOS 6 and 6.2. For ease of use all the DOS commands that you would type at the "C:\" prompt are in bold, and if the command requires DOS 6 or above, they are labelled accordingly. Please see the following tables.

COMMANDS	EXPLANATIONS
attrib	Displays all the pieces of information belonging to the file.
break	Turns off and on the option of pressing Ctrl+C to exit out of a program.
buffers	Allocates memory for a required number of disk buffers when your computer boots.
call	Calls one batch program from another without making the first batch file stop.
cd	Displays the name of a current directory or changes to another when a suitable name of a directory is typed after it (cd dos).
chdir	Check the directory for disk errors.
chkdsk	Checks a disk for disk errors. When the "**Chkdsk /f**" command is used it corrects the errors for you. Do not use the /f option if you are running inside windows.
cls	Clears the screen.
command	Re runs command.com (the MS-DOS command interpreter)
copy	Copies one or more files to a location that you specify (copy autoexec.bat C:\dos)
date	Displays the date and lets you change it.

COMMANDS	EXPLANATIONS
dblspace	Starts the Doublespace (disk compression) program. DOS 6+
defrag	Starts the defragmentation program DOS 6+.
del	Deletes files that you specify i.e."**del test.txt**".
deltree	Deletes all files and sub directories of the current directory.
device	Loads the device driver you specify into memory.
devicehigh	Loads the device driver you specify into upper memory.
dir	Displays a list of files and sub-directories in the current directory.
diskcomp	Compares the contents of two floppy disks.
diskcopy	Copies the entire contents of one disk to another (Both the disks must be the same format).
dosshell	Starts MS-DOS SHELL.
edit	Starts the MS_DOS EDITOR program.
emm386	Enables or disables emulation 386 expanded or extended memory support on a 386 or above computer.

COMMANDS	EXPLANATIONS
emm386.exe	Provides access to upper memory areas and uses extended to simulate expanded memory.
exit	Quits the MS-DOS interpreter.
fdisk	Starts the F-DISK program used to configure hard disks.
find	Looks for a specific string of text in a file or number of files.
format	Formats a disk so that it can be used by MS-DOS.
help	Starts MS-DOS HELP program, also when it can be used to immediately display information about a dos command or query by typing the subject you wish to receive help on after it i.e. Type "**help format**" return
install	Loads a program into your computer's system.
loadhigh or lh	Loads a program into upper memory
md	Makes a directory.
mem	Displays the amount of used or free memory on your computer.
memmaker	Start the MEMMAKER program for DOS 6+.
msbackup	Starts the MS-BACKUP program for DOS 6+.

COMMANDS	EXPLANATIONS
msd	Start the Microsoft Diagnostics program. This provides detailed information about your computer.
path	Indicates the directories that MS-DOS should search through when looking for a program that you have just typed in.
pause	Pauses the processing of a batch file/program until any key is pressed. You may only use this command in batch files/programs.
print	Prints a text file i.e Type **"print test.txt"** return.
rd	Removes a directory from the hard disk.
rem	Tells your computer not to look at anything in the current line of text acting as a reminder for yourself.
rename	Renames a file.
replace	Replaces a file in a specified directory with files from the source directory that have the same name.
restore	Restores files that were backed up by using MS-DOS **backup** program, **not** the DOS 6+ **msbackup** program.
ver	Displays the current version of DOS you are using.

COMMANDS | EXPLANATIONS

Command	Explanation
setver	Enables programs originally made for earlier versions of dos to run, by giving them the correct version number.
shell	Specifies the name and location of the command interpreter.
smartdrv	Speeds up your computer's hard disk by using extended memory to cache information written or read from the hard drive.
tree	Displays the structure of a current directory showing all the sub-directories held inside it.
type	Displays the contents of a text file onto the screen i.e. Type "**menu.txt**" return.
undelete	Undelete's previously deleted files.
unformat	Retrieves the original information held on a disk which was previously destroyed by using the format command. (Please note there are occasions when unformat will not work.)
vsafe	Continuously monitors your computer for Viruses and tells you if any are present.
xcopy	Copies the entire contents of a directory and it's sub-directories to another specified place.

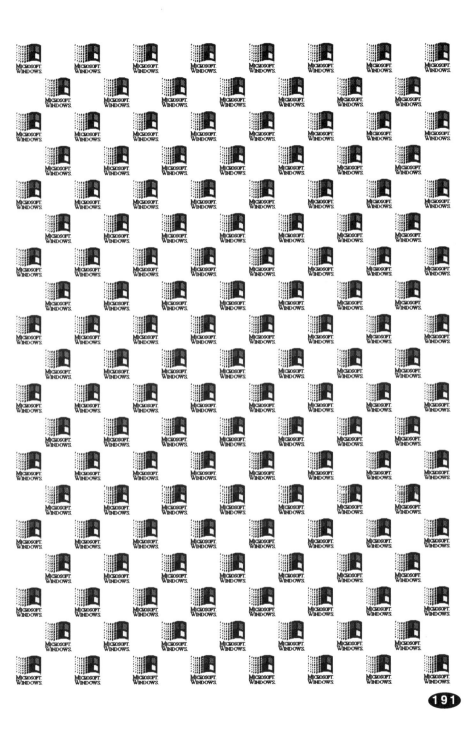

SETTING UP MICROSOFT WINDOWS 3.1

Setting up Microsoft Windows 3.1 on your computer is really very simple. You can choose between two methods, "**Express Setup**" and "**Custom Setup**". The "**Express Setup**" option means you simply install Windows in a preset way designed to be compatible with most machines. If you select the "**Custom Setup**" option you are given more options on how Windows is setup. We strongly recommend that you use "**Express Setup**" especially if you are not wholly conversant with your computer.

PRE-INSTALLATION GUIDE USING EXPRESS SET-UP

When you install Windows using the "**Express Setup**" option the setup program automatically identifies your hardware and software configurations so that Windows can run alongside your MS-DOS system. It also updates several important files and creates several new ones.

However all you will need to do is simply insert the disks into your floppy drive when your computer asks you to, and answer a few simple questions such as "**What is your name?**" and "**What sort of a printer do you have?**". If you already have any programs installed on your computer, "**Express Setup**" will recognise and configure them so they will run within Windows.

Please Note:- Windows will not be able to run some of the less commonly known applications unless you choose the "**Customise Setup**" option, or set them up later in the Windows environment.

Basically, to Setup Windows using the "**Express Setup**" method, you will need to know :

1.) What type of printer you have, if any.

2.) Which communication port your printer is connected to.

3.) Your Name and Company (These are not essential)

Remember when you tell your computer the printer that you are using it is important to locate the exact name in the list provided by Windows. However if your printer does not appear in the list you can almost always use the "**Generic / Text Only**", or "**IBM Graphics**" settings in the list. Also note that if you are using a bubblejet printer it will normally run on the "**HP Deskjet**" setting. This means that you won't have to find it's exact name, although it is better if you can!

Finally most computers are equipped with one or more Parallel Ports i.e."**LPT1**" & "**LPT2**", and one or more Serial Ports i.e."**COM1**" & "**COM2**". You can use these ports to connect your printer to the computer. However, you will be using "**LPT1**" for your printer and "**COM1**" for your Mouse.

INSTALLING WINDOWS 3.1 USING "EXPRESS SETUP"

Re-Boot your computer is the normal way and follow these steps.

Caution: Before you turn install MIcrosoft Windows 3.1 make sure that you have turned off any automatic service system such as "**Network**", "**Pop-Up Program**" or "**Printing Notification Systems that display directly to your screen**". This should only apply if you are using your computer in a commercial environment, but it is important to note that these systems must be turned off in order to run the Windows 3.1 Setup.

STEP(1)

Insert the "**Windows 3.1 Setup Disk1**" into your floppy drive.

STEP(2)

At the DOS prompt "**C:**" type "**A:**" return. This will take you to Drive A:

STEP(3)

At "**A:**" prompt type "**Setup**" return

STEP(4)

A Windows Setup Screen will appear reading:-

"Welcome to Setup"

There are three possible selections that you can make **"F1"**, **"Enter"** and **"F3"**.

"F1" allows you to learn more about Microsoft Windows.

"Enter" will take you into the main Setup program.

"F3" will quit the installation program.

Press "**Enter**"

STEP(5)

You will now be shown another Windows Setup screen which gives you two more possible selections. These are **"Express Setup"** which is recommended or **"Custom Setup"**

Select "**Express Setup**" then press return.

STEP(6)

If Setup finds a previous version of Microsoft Windows proceed to STEP(7). If you are installing Windows for the first time proceed to STEP(8)

STEP(7)

The Setup program will now display a screen telling you that it has found a previous version of windows. Press enter, and you will be prompted with another screen confirming that you have told Setup to upgrade Windows, then press enter again.

STEP(8)

Setup now checks your machine and starts the installation. You will note that there is a yellow line which slowly grows as the percentage of completed installation increases.

STEP(9)

After a short while setup will ask you to insert the next setup disk **"Microsoft Windows 3.1 Disk 2"**. Remove Disk 1 and insert Disk 2 then press return.

The bar will now continue to increase as the necessary files are copied to your hard disk. When the bar reaches 100% Windows will display a short message and then put you into the Windows Setup environment.

STEP(10)

You will now note that your mouse is working. Move your mouse and check that an arrow appears on the screen.

As you can see, there is a dialogue box with a Windows Setup message asking you to type in your name. Type in **"your name"** then press return. Now type in your company (if applicable), then press return or alternatively use the mouse to continue by moving the arrow over the **"Continue"** button, and then press the mouse button when you wish to proceed.

STEP(11)

You will now be presented with another Windows Setup message asking you to make sure that the information you have typed in is correct. If it is click your mouse on the **"Continue"** button or press return. If you want to change the name you can by clicking the mouse onto the **"Change"** button and you will then be left back at STEP(10).

STEP(12)

Windows will now almost immediately ask you for **"Disk 3"**, take out Disk 2 from your Floppy Disk Drive and insert Disk 3, Click your mouse on **"OK"** or press return.

You will now see a dialogue box with a blue bar that slowly increases as the rest of the Windows files are copied onto your hard disk. Remember you can Exit the Windows Setup program at any time by clicking your mouse on the **"Exit Setup"** Button or by simply pressing return for cancel.

STEP(13)

When the blue bar reaches 34% Windows Setup will ask you to insert the next disk. Take Disk 3 out of your Floppy Disk Drive and then insert "**Disk 4**" and either click on "**OK**" with your mouse or press return.

When the blue bar reaches 65% you will again be asked to insert the next disk. Do so, and then press return or click on "**OK**" with your mouse.

When the blue bar reaches 96%, Windows Setup will ask you to insert "**Disk 6**". Remove Disk 5, insert disk 6 and press return or click on "**OK**" with your mouse. If you are upgrading to Windows 3.1 from a previous version proceed to STEP(17)

STEP(14)

Windows Setup will now present you with a dialogue box labelled "**Printer Installation**". If you have or intend to use a printer with your Windows installation you will need to scroll through the list of printers using the "**up**" and "**down**" arrow keys or the mouse by clicking on the up and down arrows. If you have no printer at all select proceed to Step(17) after first selecting "**No Printer Attached**" at the top of the printer list, and then clicking on the "**Install**" button with your mouse or by pressing return.

Please note:- When selecting a printer the printer that is currently selected will be highlighted in blue. It is important to remember that there will be occasions when your printer does not appear in the list of available printers. Don't panic, as there are several ways to overcome this problem. For instance if you have a "**Bubblejet printer**" that does not appear on the list you can select "**HP Deskjet**" and it will almost certainly work. If you have an unlisted "**Laser printer**" the same will apply by selecting "**HP Laserjet**" or "**HP Laserjet Plus**". However this doesn't always work for dot matrix printers. If you can't find your printer on the list select "**IBM Graphics**" and your printer should work. Press return or click on "**Install**" to install the printer.

STEP(15)

Windows Setup will now present you with a further printer installation box asking you to select the port that you wish to use to connect the computer to your printer. If you are confused as to which one you should select please see Figure(1) showing the location of your various ports on the back of your computer.

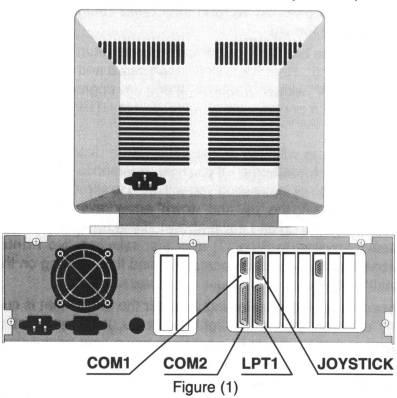

COM1   **COM2**   **LPT1**   **JOYSTICK**

Figure (1)

As you can see you need to know the printer ports that your particular printer uses to connect to the computer. It will either be a **"COM1"** or **"COM2"** port, or in nearly all cases the **"LPT1"** port. To check on this your printer will almost certainly have a manual with a section marked **"setting up your printer"**. In this section you will be told if your printer uses a parallel or serial cable to talk to your computer.

If your printer uses a serial cable to connect itself to your computer the end of the cable will look like one of those shown below, and will only connect to the "**COM1**" or "**COM2**" ports on the back of your computer. Please see Figure(2).

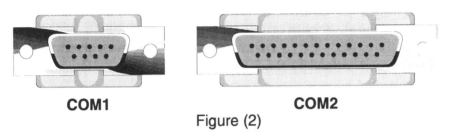

COM1   **COM2**

Figure (2)

If your printer uses a parallel cable to connect itself to your computer the cable will look like the one shown in Figure(3), and will connect to the "**LPT1**" port on the back of your computer.

LPT1

Figure (3)

Now select which port your printer will connect to, and then click on the Install button.

STEP(16)

A note will be now displayed telling you that Windows is setting up your printer(s). However Windows Setup might ask for another Windows disk with your printer driver on it. If so simply find the disk, (usually disk 6 or 7) insert it into your drive and then click on the "**OK**" button with your mouse.

STEP(17)

Windows Setup now builds up your desktop groups adding the various Windows and icons which you need to click on to run your programs in Windows.

After this, Windows Setup now scans your hard disk looking for any additional programs that can be run from inside Windows. We recommend you follow the suggested names given to the various applications by simply clicking on the **"OK"** button if asked.

STEP(18)

After Windows Setup has added all of the additional programs, you will then be presented with another dialogue box giving you the options to either:-

"Run Tutorial" (The Windows Teaching Program)

"Skip Tutorial" (Bypass The Teaching Program),

"Help" (Gives you further Help about this screen)

"Exit Setup" (Exits the Windows Installation).

If you are using Windows for the first time we recommend that you select **"Run Tutorial"** option. This tutorial program is extremely useful for the beginner, and we therefore totally recommend that you use it. If you have used Microsoft Windows before select the **"Skip Tutorial"** button.

STEP(19)

Windows will now display an **"Exit Windows Setup"** message giving you the options of either **"Re-Boot"** the machine or returning to **"MS-DOS"**. We recommend that you click on the **"Re-Boot"** button after taking any disks out of the machine.

STEP(20)

Windows is now Setup,

Type **"win"** return to start Windows.

WHAT IS MICROSOFT WINDOWS 3.1?

Microsoft Windows is basically an operating system which will transform the way you use your personal computer. It has the rare ability to run more than one program (application) at the same time, but before we get into greater depth it is a good idea to explain just exactly what Microsoft Windows is.

Imagine a large house with lots of windows, all of which are large enough for you to see precisely what is going on inside the house, provided the curtains are opened and the lights are switched on. Well, Microsoft Windows is capable of showing you exactly what is going on inside your computer. You can open the curtains on each window to view all the different programs available inside and then start the programs simply by clicking on them (switching on the light switch). Windows tries to use the full power of your computer, but instead of relying on complicated commands to start and run programs it uses a mouse with icons instead.

Now you're probably wondering what is a mouse and what is an icon. All will be revealed later on in this section.

WHAT CAN WINDOWS DO FOR YOU?

Well, it has a **"Program Manager"** which can help you organise the applications (programs) in your computer. It also has a **"File Manager"** which helps you manage the files and directories on your hard disk. There is also a **"Control Panel"** which is rather like the dashboard in a car, this allows you to change various Windows settings such as Screen Colours, Fonts (Typefaces), Printers etc. There is also a **"Print Manager"** which schedules and fulfils all of your print requests, but we will be explaining more about all the functions of Windows later on in this section.

Before you can install Windows 3.1 on your machine you must be in possession of a machine that at least has the following minimum configuration.

"**386**" machine or above with a minimum of "**2Mb**" of ram (4Mb or more recommended) and a "**40Mb**" Hard disk. (80Mb or more is recommended). Also a mouse is strongly recommended even though you can just about run Windows without one.

BASIC WINDOWS FUNCTIONS

If you have a new computer with Microsoft Windows already installed, or you have just loaded the Microsoft Windows operating system, most of the following will be very important in assisting you to get the best out of Microsoft Windows. If you have not installed Microsoft Windows please refer to the "**SETTING UP MICROSOFT WINDOWS**", section earlier in the book.

We have tried to explain the basic skills you need to work with Windows and therefore this section of The Book is likely to be the one you will use as a reference in the future.

The Windows program provides everything you need to allow you to manage your applications (programs) and files easily and effectively. If you have never seen Windows before it is important to explain the items that will appear on your screen. Windows essentially works with dialogue boxes and drop down menus. A dialogue box is really the basic Window that enables you to view programs (look into the house). Each dialogue box will have in the top left hand corner a small grey box with a line through it. We will now refer to this as a switch. At the top right hand corner of the box you will find two grey buttons, one with an arrow pointing down, the other with an arrow pointing up. These open and close the dialogue boxes like a curtain. You will also find that between the switch and the arrow buttons there is a long title bar with the name of the dialogue box you are currently looking at.

This box is initially coloured blue when you start windows for the first time, but you can change this and the other basic colours displayed in Windows. This will be explained later. Each Dialogue box has a small border normally coloured grey, and it is possible to enlarge the dialogue boxes (Windows) by clicking on and stretching the sides of the borders. Please see Figure(1)

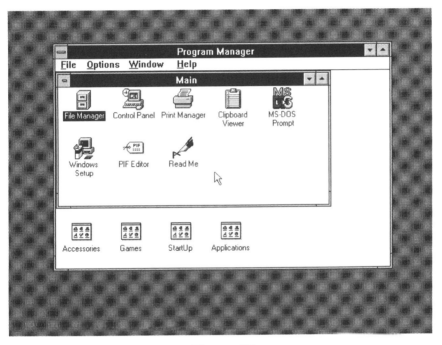

Figure (1)

As we mentioned earlier, Windows uses Icons to substitute keyboard commands. These Icons normally take the form of small pictures leaving no doubt as to what they are and do. For instance the Windows "**File Manager**" is represented by a picture of a filing cabinet and the Windows "**Paintbrush**" program is represented by a picture of a paint pallet. Icons also have the name of the program they represent beneath them.

Before you can effectively run Windows by using the Icons to run programs you must learn how to use a mouse.

A mouse basically has four major components. See Figure(2)

1.) A rubber ball that rolls along the desktop.

2.) Two or Three Switches.

3.) A long wire connecting it to your computer.

4.) A conveniently shaped case, to allow comfort during use.

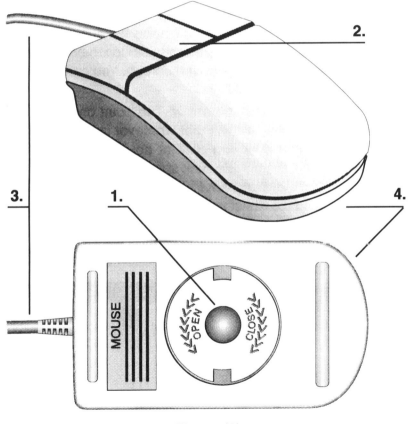

Figure (2)

You will find it strange when you first start to move the mouse around and we recommended that you practise moving the mouse around whilst looking at the corresponding arrow on the Windows screen "**What is this Arrow?**" you ask. Well, every time the ball moves it sends a signal to the computer which is then able to copy your movements from the desk to the screen, and it uses the arrow to show you where you are going. For instance, if you move the mouse to the right the arrow will move to the right, if you move the mouse to the left the mouse will move to the left, and so on.

It is important to make sure that the distance you move the mouse on the desktop is relative to the distance moved on the screen. In other words you should not be moving your mouse three centimetres to the left only on the desktop in order to move the arrow only one centimetre on the screen. You can adjust this by using the "**Control Panel**".

First of all let's talk about the arrow. The point on the arrow is called the hot spot. This means that whatever is underneath the tip will respond whenever you click or double click the mouse button; you can set the double click speed to your own personal preference in the "**Control Panel**". You will be using a lot of double clicks in the future whilst using Windows so it is important to get used to the double click speed. Please see Figure(3)

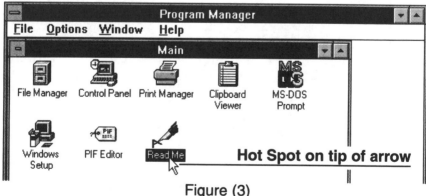

Figure (3)

We have just mentioned double and single clicking (sounds funny doesn't it?), well, it simply means that if you press the mouse button once you will highlight the Icon underneath the arrow point (hot spot). Please see Figure(3) showing a single click on the "**Read Me**" icon. If you click on an Icon twice in quick succession, you will run the Icons program. Please see Figure(4) showing the result of a double click on the "**Read Me**" icon.

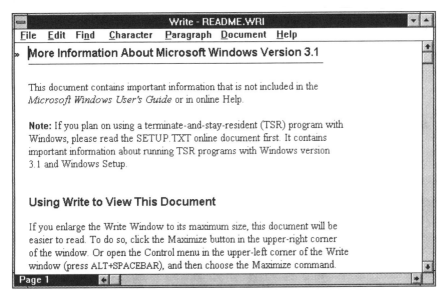

Figure (4)

To exit the "**readme.wri**" document press the "**Alt**" and "**F4**" keys together. We have found the Paintbrush program in Windows extremely useful in teaching you how to use and move a mouse, and we advise you to spend some time in this program simply using your mouse and noting the effects upon the screen. To run the Paintbrush program move the mouse arrow over the top of the small box labelled accessories. Please see Figure(5). Double click with your mouse and the **Accessories** windows will appear. Now move your mouse so that the arrow is over the Paint Palette Icon shown in Figure(6) and double click.

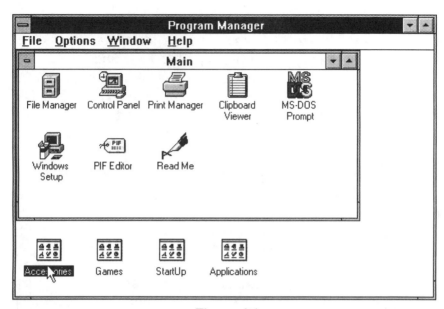

Figure (5)

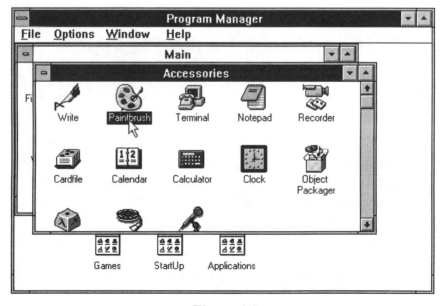

Figure (6)

If you don't manage to start the program straight away don't worry, just keep on double clicking until it works. (This means Click Click as in two clicks in quick succession).

Microsoft Windows will now present you with a program in a dialogue box with the title **"Paintbrush - [Untitled]"**. We will be describing how to use this program later on in this section, but for the time being move the hot spot of the arrow to the left hand side of the screen where you will see something that looks like a household paintbrush. Click on it once and the box will turn black. As you move your mouse to the middle of the screen, the arrow will turn into a dot. Now hold down the mouse button and then continue to move the mouse, and "hey presto" you will have produced a black line. Practice moving the mouse around the screen until you have become used to it. Remember when you press the mouse button down you will be able to draw, and when you take your finger off the mouse button you will stop drawing. Please see Figure(7) showing a quick doodle using **"Paintbrush"**.

Figure (7)

Now we've got this far, and you will have at least used your mouse for half an hour. You may have noticed that it doesn't respond the way you want it to, i.e. the double clicking is too fast or slow and the movement of the arrow / paintbrush is not to your liking. All is not lost, let's set the speed of your mouse.

First exit the paintbrush program by moving your mouse to the top left hand side of your paintbrush window. When it changes to an arrow, place the hot spot of the arrow over the centre of the grey switch and click the mouse button once. A drop down menu will appear, so move your arrow down and ensure the hot spot is over the word "**Close**" and click once. You will then be asked by Paintbrush if you want to save your picture (current changes). Move your arrow over the "**NO**" button and click for No, you will now exit Paintbrush, and Windows will now present you with the Program Manager. Now move your arrow so that it is on the Main dialogue box title bar. Please see Figure(8) below.

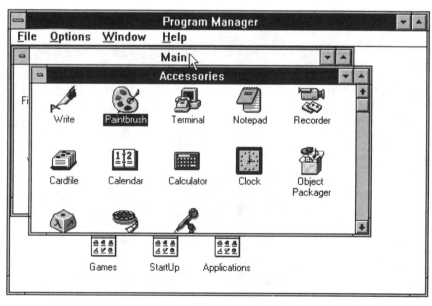

Figure (8)

Click on the title bar to bring the Main Program Group to the front, Please see Figure(9).

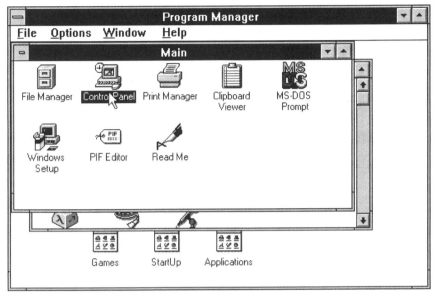

Figure (9)

Now move your mouse so that the arrow pointer is over the Icon showing a computer with a red, yellow and green screen labelled "**Control Panel**" . Double click onto the icon, a further Dialogue box will appear called "**Control Panel**" See Figure(10).

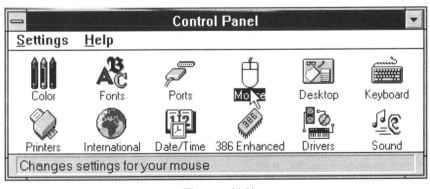

Figure (10)

Take the arrow to the Mouse Icon and double click on it and a further dialogue box will appear, labelled Mouse, See Figure(11).

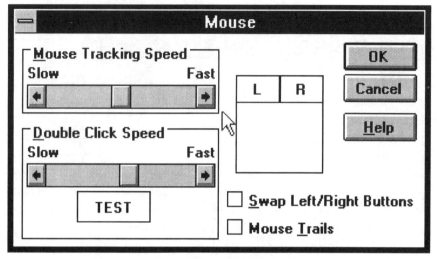

Figure (11)

You will note that inside the dialogue box are two main headings; "**Mouse Tracking Speed**" and "**Double Click Speed**" with two sets of arrows pointing left and right. The arrows pointing right have the word "**Fast**" above them and the arrows pointing to the left have the word "**Slow**" above them. There is also a smaller box with the word "**TEST**" in it together with a larger box representing the mouse with the letters "**L**" and "**R**" inside it.

Let's change the overall speed of the mouse (Mouse Tracking Speed). If you take your arrow hot spot over the left hand arrow marked "**Slow**" and click the mouse button, the grey sliding bar will start to flash and move towards slow. If you keep on clicking onto the "**Slow**" arrow the slide bar will move completely to the left, giving you the slowest possible setting for your mouse. Also, if you click on the arrow marked "**Fast**" the flashing slide will eventually stop at its fastest speed.

Try it out and set it to your personal preference. You will note the faster you set it the quicker the arrow moves around the screen and the slower you set it the slower the arrow moves around the screen. Microsoft Windows sets a default of midway between "**Fast**" and "**Slow**".

Now let's change the "**Double Click Speed**", Please remember that if you set the double clicking speed to its fastest setting, once you click on "**OK**" you will find it almost impossible to double click the mouse when activating an Icon. We had a competition to see who could click the fastest and it turned out to be the person with a severe nerve problem. We do not recommend becoming the champion, as you will need to be a virtual head-case to succeed. If you wish to adjust the double click speed you should set it midway, using the "**TEST**" button to check your settings. You can use it by double clicking on it's box, and if you have double clicked correctly it will turn black. If it does not, try adjusting your settings.

Finally you will note that there is a small box labelled "**Swap Left/Right Buttons**". If you click on this a cross will appear and your buttons will reverse. Note the change of the "**L**" and "**R**" in the Box above.

Once you are satisfied with your changes click on "**OK**" and you will return to the "**Control Panel**". Now click on the grey switch in the top left hand side of the Control Panel and click on Close, and you will revert back to your Program Manager.

Now just for a while go back to the "**Paintbrush**" program and practice with your new mouse settings. If it isn't right simply repeat the above procedure of changing your mouse settings and try again.

WHAT CAN WINDOWS DO FOR YOU?
(Applications/Basics)

Well, you're probably wondering "**What is the point of having a program that flashes up Windows and Icons, seemingly at this point for no purpose at all**". Let's for a moment look at your exact requirements for using your computer, and also study the ways in which you can make your tasks easier.

First of all Windows can offer a much faster speed in making your programs work for you. Let's find out why. To do this we need to look at all the things that would make your daily tasks easier and then find out whether or not Windows can provide a solution. Let's suppose you were working in an office which operated a book keeping system for several thousand clients, with each of those clients having a totally different business. Each of them would also have a requirement to use the office for a specific service, for instance:-

All the businesses products and services need a system for storing their financial data in order to find out how much they are making or losing, and all those businesses would also have the basic need to communicate with their clients or potential clients by advertising or phone and so on. In order for the office to provide these standard services it would need the ability to answer questions effectively about any one of their clients at any given time.

Well, the Windows environment essentially is the "**Main Office**" in charge of controlling the many different companies that it deals with. On top of this Windows is actually able to mimic any skill or service held in it's main office, like a jack of all trades. Unlike people, Windows is able to remember all the tasks it needs to do instantly and more importantly carry them out perfectly.

So let's look at what you would need in an office to run it correctly. Well you would need a **"Managing Director"** (**Program Manager**) who would be directly responsible for everything that runs within the company. You would also need a selection of people that would take care of the main tasks needed to run the office. First of all you would need an **"Company Co-ordinator"** (**File Manager**) in charge of making sure he and anyone else knows where everything is at any given time. Secondly you would need an **"Office Manager"** capable of changing the company's structure (**Control Panel**) . Thirdly you will need an area in the office where people can manage and receive everything that needs to go out of the company on paper (**Print Manager**) . Finally you would need somebody to take charge of distributing memo's around the company (**Clipboard Viewer**) . You would also need to be in contact with the basic shop-floor where all the routine work is done (**MS-DOS Prompt**) , and equally if the office were to move to a larger location or upgrade its current services, you would need someone to set that up (**Windows Setup**) .

As you can see, Windows covers all these areas, but it covers them at incredible speed (provided you have invested in the correct computer).

Now let's look more in depth at each of these main functional areas of the company (**Windows 3.1**).

In this section we will assume that you have never worked with Microsoft Windows at all, but we feel sure that those who have been involved with windows will also find the following section helpful. Some of the areas we will cover have been proven to save time whilst using the conventional sequences. Our preliminary look at windows is designed for mouse users only. If you do not have a mouse this section will still provide a good overview of windows, however you will need to learn keyboard procedures found later on in the section marked **"KEYBOARD SHOTCUTS"**.

If you are not used to using a mouse please refer to '**USING A MOUSE IN MICROSOFT WINDOWS 3.1**" found earlier in the "**WHAT IS MICROSOFT WINDOWS**" section. We have found it helpful for the first time to use "**Microsoft Windows Tutorial**" either during the initial setup procedures or by running the "**Wintutor.exe**" program. To run the Windows Tutorial program please follow these steps.

STEP(1)

Make sure that you are already in Windows, if you are not type "**Win**" return at the "**C:**" prompt. Now use your mouse to click on the "**File**" menu, as shown in Figure(1) below.

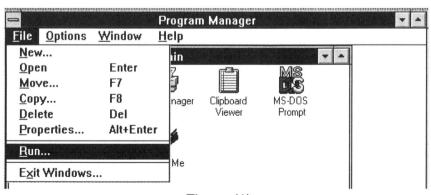

Figure (1)

STEP(2)

As shown in Figure(1) click onto the **"Run"** option and the following screen will appear. Please see Figure(2) below.

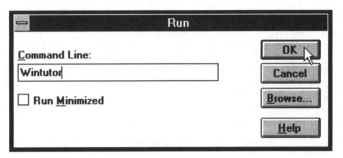

Figure (2)

STEP(3)

Now simply type in **"Wintutor"** and click onto the "**OK**" button. The Windows Tutorial program will now start. If you want to brush up on your mouse skills type "**M**", or if you want to find out more about Windows basics type "**W**". Please See Figure(3) below.

This Tutorial has two lessons.

- If you want to learn how to use the mouse, or if you need to brush up on your mouse skills, type **M** to begin the Mouse lesson.

- If you are already a skilled mouse user, type **W** to begin the Windows Basics lesson.

Or, if you want to run the Tutorial at another time:

- Press the **ESC** key to exit the Tutorial.

Figure (3)

The quick way to start **"Wintutor"** is to click onto the **"Help"** button on the main **"Program Manager"** screen and then click on the **"Wintutor"** option, it will start immediately as in Figure(3).

Right then, lets look at basic Windows. You will need to know a few terms that will become more and more familiar as you use windows. You will be working in oblong areas of the screen, called windows, Please see Figure(4) below.

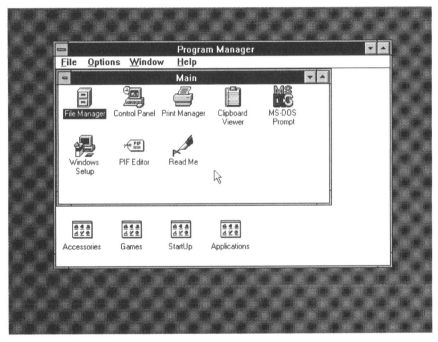

Figure (4)

These Windows appear on a background called **"THE DESK-TOP"**. When windows is setup for the first time **"THE DESKTOP"** will be grey, but it is possible to change your Desktop colour by using the Colour option in the **"Control Panel"**. Don't worry, all will be explained later. Each window has a **"Title Bar"** running from left to right which is usually coloured blue, unless you have again changed the colour. To the left-hand side of the bar is a grey switch, ▭ this can be used to close, minimise or maximise the size of your window. On the right-hand corner of the bar you will find two grey buttons, one with an arrow pointing down the other with an arrow pointing up ▾▴ . These can also minimize or maximize windows by clicking on the appropriate button.

Each time you wish to start a program inside the Windows environment such as a Word-processing, Spread-sheet or Drawing package, you will use small symbols called "**Icons**" to activate or start the necessary programs. You can do this by double clicking, using the mouse pointer on the screen. Please see Figure(5).

| Write | Paintbrush | Terminal | Notepad | Recorder |

| Cardfile | Calendar | Calculator | Clock | Object Packager |

| Character Map | Media Player | Sound Recorder |

Figure (5)

Now let's summarise on what we've learnt to date:- if you refer to Figure 6, we have clearly labelled each part of a Windows screen. We have done this so that you can learn each of the actual names for future reference. They are as follows:

(**A**) The Desktop background labelled, (**B**) A Window

(**C**) The grey on/off switch (**D**), A typical icon.

(**E**) The minimize and maximise buttons

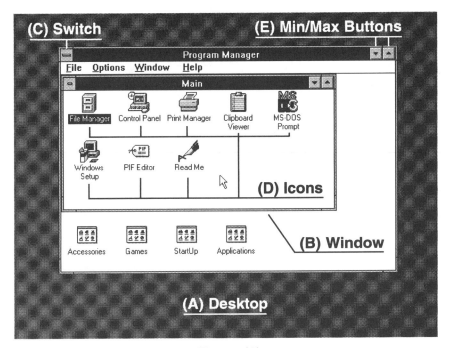

Figure (6)

Remember it is always a good idea to familiarise yourself with these terms as they will be repeated again and again throughout the book, but just in case you are not totally sure we have listed each item with a recognisable explanation.

(A) Desktop - means the table on which you work

(B) Window - means the T.V. you are viewing on the table

(C) The grey switch - is effectively the on/off button on the T.V.

(D) The Icons - these will change the channels

(E) The up/down arrows - move the T.V. on or off the table.

Briefly, if you can imagine a large house with lots of windows, with valuables inside. Unless someone turns the lights on or opens the curtains in each window you will not be able to see what's inside. So to find out in Windows what each window possesses you must first of all go to the window, then open the curtains and finally turn the light on. Only then will you be able to view the contents of a window, but you must remember to turn the light off before you leave. i.e. close Windows before turning off the computer.

Windows has the rare ability to allow you to open and view several windows at the same time. The advantages to this are obvious, in that you will be able to work with a word processing package and a spreadsheet package at the same time. This means the computer will carrying out complicated calculations together with standard wordprocessing all at the same time. You can also flip between the two instantly to cross reference any information you might need.

When you start windows for the first time a window called the "**Program Manager**" 🖼️ will appear and will continue to run as long as you are using windows.

The Program Manager window tells you the contents of the Main Group (a group is a collection of programs/applications that you can run in windows), with the icon names referring to the applications in the group. The Windows Program Manager also displays icons for other groups of applications, all of which run inside the Program Manager. If you like, the Program Manager is the basic building/machine in which both the employees and the applications work.

Please note, your Program Manager window contains another group of icons called Applications. During the Windows setup, you are asked whether you would like to enable Windows to run applications already installed on your computer from within it. The Applications group is where these application's corresponding icons are stored. In other words, if you are just installing Windows for the first time, many of the old programs that you are used to using can now be run in the Windows environment. I.e. if you have a favourite Word-processing program which you are familiar with, you can run it inside Windows whilst other programs are still running.

You can perform many important tasks by using your Program Manager. For instance you can start or organise your applications into groups, and of course you can stop using Windows by turning the light off. I.e. You can either Click onto the "**File**" menu then select "**Exit Windows**", or Click onto the "**Grey Switch**" at the top left of the Program Manager Window and then click "**Close**". Or you can simply press the"**Alt**" and "**F4**" keys together. After all these options you are asked to confirm that you are exiting Windows. Click onto "**OK**" or press "**return**" or "**spacebar**".

A CLOSER LOOK AT THE PROGRAM MANAGER

You will note that in the Program Manager window directly below the title bar are four options - **"File"**, **"Options"**, **"Windows"** and **"Help"**.

If you move your mouse arrow so that the point is over the **"File"** option and click once on your mouse, a drop down menu will appear. Please see Figure (1).

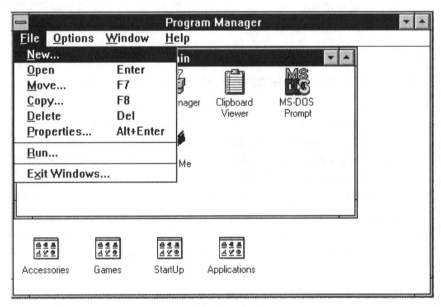

Figure (1)

If you take away your mouse arrow and click it anywhere in the Program Manager window the dropdown menu will disappear. Let's try it. Take the arrow to **"File"** and click once, and the menu appears. Now place the arrow anywhere on the white background and click, and the menu disappears. You will note that the **"File"** option has it's own drop down menu. This has the current option displayed in the same colour as the Program Manager title bar, the current option being **"New"** in the example displayed above. If you look closer at the list you will see that the **"N"** in **"New"** is underlined as are the rest of the options in the dropdown menu. The underlined letters represent the keyboard alternatives which you can press to choose your options, either as an alternative or a necessity if you are not using a mouse. The list of options displayed are as follows:-

"**New...**"   "**Open**"   "**Move**"   "**Copy**"
"**Delete**"   "**Properties...**"   "**Run**"   "**Exit Windows...**"

Do not forget that each underlined letter represents the keyboard alternative to using a mouse.

Let's run through the options in the "**File**" drop down menu. It is important to realise that if you take your arrow to any one of the options and keep the mouse button pressed, the coloured bar will move to the option that you have selected. For instance if the mouse arrow is placed over "**Delete**" and then the mouse button is clicked and held on then the blue bar will move to "**Delete**". You can then scroll through any of the options shown by moving your mouse up and down. Until you let go of the mouse button your selection will not be performed, however if you do not want to select any of the options, you can simply move the arrow to another area of the screen and then let go of the mouse button. This will cause the drop down menu to disappear.

Let's click on the "**New**" option. Click once on "**New**" and another smaller window will appear. Please see Figure(2) below.

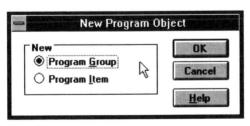

Figure (2)

As you can see the Window has a title, two option buttons and three grey confirmation buttons.

In the top lefthand corner is the familiar switch that allows you to switch off the current box. ⊟

Let's look around the "**New Program Object**" box. You will note that "**Program Group**" and "**Program Item**" options have a round circle in front of them. One circle is selected with a black dot in it the other is not. Take your mouse arrow to the "**Program Group**" circle, click once and the black dot will appear, having moved from the circle labelled "**Program Item**". This can be done vice versa.

Once you have decided whether you want a "**New Item**" (Application/Program) or "**Program Group**" to be added to your Windows environment, take your arrow over to the button marked "**OK**", and click once. In our first example we will be selecting the "**Program Item**" option.

You always have the option to use the cancel button if you are not sure or change your mind and do not wish to continue. Please remember that the online "**Help**" button is there if you should become puzzled. Don't forget that if you don't have a mouse you will have to use the corresponding keys which are underlined.

Right, use your mouse to select the "**Program Item**" option. Make sure that the circle next to it has a black dot and click on the "**OK**" button, and the dialogue box shown in Figure(3) will appear.

Program Item Properties	
Description:	OK
Command Line:	Cancel
Working Directory:	
Shortcut Key: None	Browse...
☐ Run Minimized	Change Icon...
	Help

Figure (3)

The dialogue box is headed **"Program Item Properties"**. You will need to select one or all of these four options.

"Description"   **"Command Line"**
"Working Directory"   **"Shortcut Key"**

It is important to find out from your new program the correct **"Description"**, **"Command Line"** and **"Working Directory"**. For instance if your program is held in a directory called **"BEGIN"**, then you should type the same directory name in the **"Working Directory"** dialogue box. I.e. **"C:\BEGIN"**, provided of course that your program is installed on Drive C:.

To type text into any of the text boxes provided simply take the cursor/text placement line to the box next to the **"Working Directory"** option and click on the mouse button. The cursor line will start to flash in that box, you can now begin to type.

If you usually type **"BEGIN"**, return to start your program. Then you should edit your **"Command Line"** dialogue box to have the word **"BEGIN"** in it, and so on.

The **"Description"** dialogue box simply asks you to give the program a name. This name will be displayed underneath the icon after the program has been added to your current Windows Group. Now simply enter the correct commands/text into each of the three main options.

If you cannot remember or do not know what your **"Program Item Properties"** are, you can take your arrow to the button marked **"Browse..."** and click once. A further dialogue box will now appear labelled browse, Please see Figure(4).

First of all you will find a small box in the bottom left hand corner labelled **"List Files of Type"**. To the right of it is a second box labelled **"Drives"**. The purpose of these boxes will become clear in moment, please note that there is a drop down option arrow, ⬇ to the right of each box. Please see Figure(4)

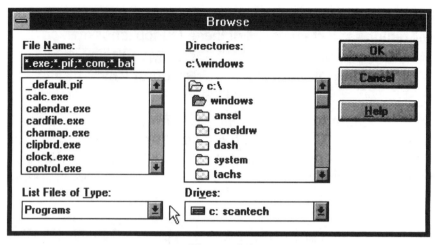

Figure (4)

If you take your arrow over the arrow in the **"List Files of Type:"** box and click your mouse button a drop down menu will appear, Please see Figure(5).

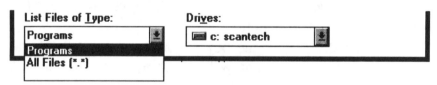

Figure (5)

If you click it once more it will disappear, and likewise if you take your mouse arrow over the drop down arrow in the **"Drives"** box and click it, another drop down menu will appear. See Figure(6).

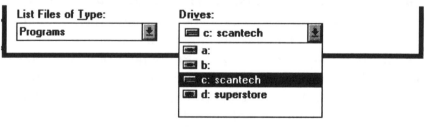

Figure (6)

Above the "**Drives**" drop down menu is a larger box labelled "**Directories**" showing yellow folders. The top one is marked "**C:**". If you take your mouse arrow to any of these yellow folders and click once a blue band will appear highlighting your selected folder. This effectively tells you that windows understands which directory you wish to browse through. If you double click on the blue band the contents of the directory will appear in the opposite dialogue box. Repeat this procedure throughout the yellow folders and you will be able to view all the executable files/programs in any of your chosen directories, (Simple isn't it).

However don't forget that the reason for you browsing through these directories is simply to select the correct directory/ filename which is needed to start your program. Once you have done this by selecting the necessary file from the list on the left hand side of the screen, click onto the "**OK**" button and you will revert back to the main "**Program Item Properties**" screen.

The "**Command Line**" box will have now changed to the correct filename and directory path needed to start your program. If you were to click on "**OK**" now the description for the program would be the same as the program name without the extention. I.e. "**Cardfile.exe**" would be named "**Cardfile**". Now simply click on the "**OK**" button and Windows will do the rest, by adding the new program Icon to your currently selected "**Program Group**", and leaving you back at the main Program Manager screen. If you have a problem there is a help button in each dialogue box, or alternatively you can **telephone (0860) 325145**.

The next option listed in the "**File**" drop down menu is "**Open**". This will have exactly the same result as pressing the "**Return/ Enter**" key, as in whatever Icon or Group that is currently highlighted will either open up or run. Let's try. Go down to the bottom of your Program Manager and click on one of the four program groups. They will be labelled "**Accessories**", "**Games**" "**StartUp**", "**Applications**" and "**Main**" if you have minimised it.

Now go to the "**File**" option and click. The File Sub menu will now appear, so click onto "**Open**". The Program group will immediately open up. Please see Figure(7) showing the result of initially highlighting the "**Accesories**" program group and then clicking onto "**Open**" in the "**File**" Sub-Menu.

Please note:- the easiest way to open Program Groups or Run programs, is to Double Click on them.

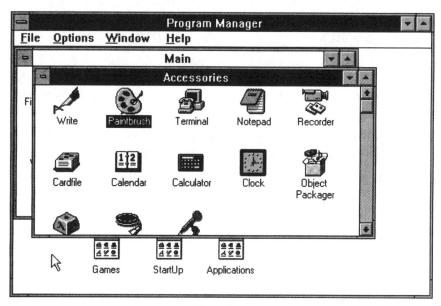

Figure (7)

The "**Delete**" option in the drop down box will delete whatever program group or Icon that you have selected, but exercise extreme caution. Once you use this function the Icon or Program Group will be deleted for GOOD, unless of course you want to recreate the Icon or Program Group using the "**File**" - "**New**" option again.

Further on in the "**File**" drop down menu you will notice the word "**Properties**" appearing. You can use this to change the properties of a Program Group or Application.

The rest of the dropdown menu is self explanatory. **"Move"** will move an Icon/Application from one Program Group to another, **"Copy"** will copy an Icon/Application from one Program Group to another, and **"Run"** will start a program that you name. **"Exit"** will of course tell Windows to close taking you out of the Windows environment and back into DOS.

The next Submenu shown on the Program Manager's main windows is **"Options"**, so lets look at it. Take your arrow to **"Options"** on the Program Manager screen and click, and a dropdown menu will appear. A handy option listed is **"Auto Arrange"**. Click on it and a tick will appear together with all of your icons being automatically arranged for you, all with equal spacing. Please see Figure(8) below showing the **"Options"** sub menu.

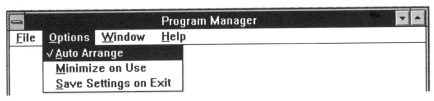

Figure (8)

Now click on the **"Windows"** option and Figure(9) will appear, showing various ways of arranging your Icons/Program Groups. Numbers 1 to 5 represent the Program Groups installed in Windows, the one with the tick being the currently highlighted group.

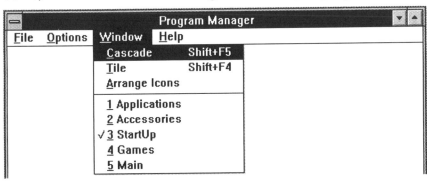

Figure (9)

Finally the Help option is always there on any main Window and is self explanatory. Please see Figure(10).

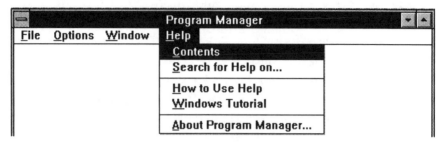

Figure (10)

Before we leave the Program Manager, remember that this is the window that runs everything else. It is therefore important to check the settings on your Program Manager each time you start or exit Windows. This is not only a good habit to get into but it also helps you to understand how the Program Manager works.

If you have any problems please telephone (0860) 325144

Windows File Manager ▤ is a quick and powerful tool that can help you organise your file and directories on your hard disk. You can use your File Manager to look at all your files and directories and then build a directory system that makes sense to you, rather than having to puzzle out what is meant by the default range of directories. In short you can use File Manager to tailor make your system for your own personal needs.

You can use File Manger to move and copy files, start programs, connect to networks, print files and organise the information held on your Hard Drive(s) or Floppy disks.

When you use File Manager you work inside various Window and Dialogue boxes showing the various directories and their contents held on your computer's hard or floppy drives. A directory window graphically displays the structure of the directories on your hard or floppy disks rather like a family tree and is in fact called a directory tree. Please see Figure(1)

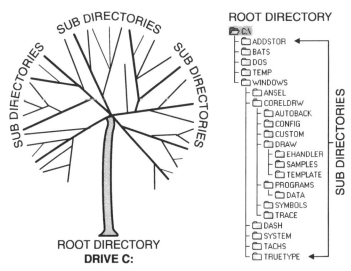

Figure (1)

To start the File Manager you must first of all choose the File Manager Icon 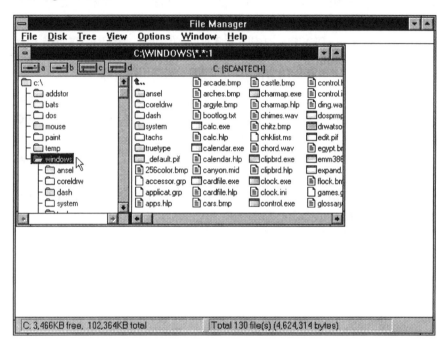 which can be found in the Main window dialogue box. Use your mouse to move your arrow over the top of the Icon and double click to start. Figure(2) shows the initial File Manager screen.

Figure (2)

When you first start the File Manager a directory windows box will appear showing you what is in the current drive or floppy disk. The directory window is split in half, the left half displays the directory tree with the currently viewed directory being highlighted in blue, the right half lists the files in the currently highlighted directory. At the top of the directory window is a title bar stating again the current directory being viewed.

CHANGING DRIVES IN FILE MANAGER

You will note there are some buttons showing the available disk drives labelled 🖴a and 🖴c . If you have more than two drives they will also appear as 🖴b , 🖴d etc. To activate a particular drive simply use the mouse to put the arrow over the drive you want to use and click.

UNDERSTANDING THE DIRECTORY TREE

The directory tree shows the structure of the directories held on a disk. The disk structure begins at the upper left hand corner of the window with the Root Directory. As you know the Root Directory is the base of any disk where all other directories grow from. It is represented graphically by a small icon representing a File with the name of the Drive next to it like this 📁 c:\ See Figure(3) Below the root directory there are Sub-Directories shown graphically by more iconic Files with their respective names next to them. These sub-directories are always connected to the root directory, just as a son is connected to his father, who in turn is connected to his fathers (The son's grandfather)

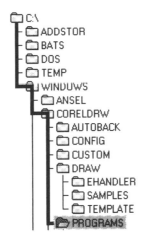

PATH=C:\WINDOWS\CORELDRW\PROGRAMS

Figure (3)

235

SELECTING FILES AND DIRECTORIES

Before you can work with a file or directory you must first of all select it. You can select a single file/directory or several, selecting more than one item is called an extended selection.

When a file or directory is selected, its name and icon are highlighted in the directory window.

To select a file or directory, use your mouse to move over the top of its icon and relative name and then simply click on it using the mouse button.

In the contents list of a directory on the right hand side, you can select more than one file or directory at a time. This allows you to work with several files at once. Perhaps you want to select several files and move them to another directory, or select a group of files or directories. In order to do this you can use the mouse or keyboard but we strongly recommend that you restrict your activities to the mouse as it is much easier.

SELECTING FILES THAT ARE LISTED IN ORDER

STEP(1)

Place your arrow over the first file that you want to select, then click the mouse button. (in our example "**_default.pif**")

STEP(2)

Press and hold the "**shift**" key. Now move your mouse arrow down or up until it is over the last of the files that you wish to select and click on it whilst still holding the shift key in. In our example "**calc.hlp**", all of the files in the middle of the two selected will be selected as well. You can use this method to select all of the files in a directory if you wish by first clicking on the first file at the top of the window, then by keeping the shift key held down, click on the last file in the directory, and all the files in the directory will be selected. Please see Figure(4)

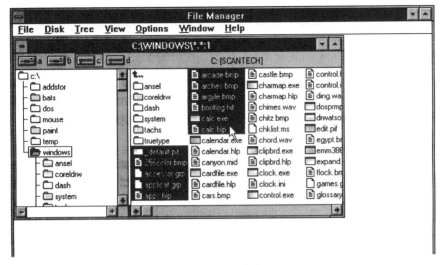

Figure (4)

SELECTING RANDOMLY PLACED FILES

Simply Press and hold down the **"Ctrl"** key whilst you click on each item. Please see Figure(5)

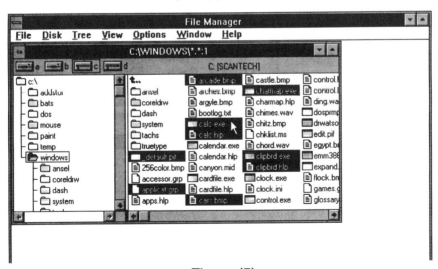

Figure (5)

I.e. the same extension or file name "***.exe**", "**letter*.***" etc.

STEP(1)

Using your mouse to select and click on the "**File**" option, a Drop-down menu will appear. Now click on the option "**Select Files**" and the Select Files dialogue box will appear.

STEP(2)

In the file box type in the name of the file or extension that you want to select. You can use wild cards to select everything with the same name or extension. For instance, if you wanted to select everything that had the file extension "**.exe**" you would type "***.exe**", or if you wanted to select everything which had the first three letters "**let**" you would type "**let*.***",to select every file in the directory you could type "***.***" See Figure(6).

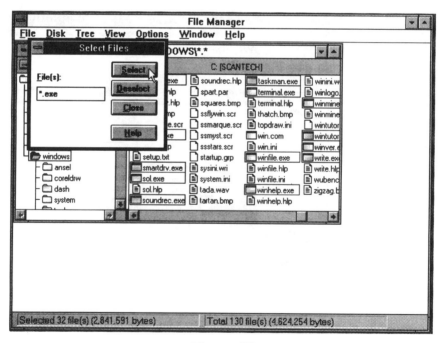

Figure (6)

STEP(3)

When you have made your selection use your mouse to click on the "**Select**" button, the dialogue box will disappear and the files will be selected. You can also use the "**de-select**" button at any time to cancel your selection. **Please note:-** you can also select all the files in a directory at any time by pressing the "**Ctrl**" and "**/**" keys together. Click on the "**Close**" button to finish.

CANCELLING A SELECTION

To de-select files after selecting them, do this:-

If you wish to cancel a selection for instance after using the "**Ctrl**"+"**/**" command hold down the "**Ctrl**" key again and simply use the mouse to click on the files you want to de-select. If you want to de-select all of the files in the directory, press the "**Ctrl**" and "****" keys simultaneously or simply click once on the top left hand side corner of the right hand dialogue box. See Figure(7).

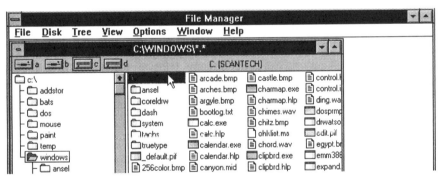

Figure (7)

CANCELLING A GROUP OF SELECTED FILES

STEP(1)

Click on the "**File**" option and from the drop down menu click on "**Select Files**" Please See Figure(6).

STEP(2)

In the files box type the name of the selected file/s that you wish to cancel. You can use wild-cards to select a group of files or all the files that are selected in a directory i.e "**calendar*.***".

STEP(3)

Click on the "**De-Select**" button.

STEP(4)

Repeat STEPS(2) and (3) until you have completed de-selecting your files.

STEP(5)

When you have finished de-selecting, click on the "**Close**" button to confirm. **Please note:-** you can cancel all selections by pressing the "**Ctrl**" and "****" keys at the same time or by clicking on the top left hand side corner icon in the right hand window as shown earlier in Figure(7).

CHANGING WHAT YOU SEE IN YOUR FILE MANAGER

When you run your File Manager, the directory window and the dialogue boxes display the directory tree of your current drive and the contents of your current directory. By using the commands on the "**View**" menu found along the top menu bar, you can choose to display only directory tree or only the contents of the current directory. This is how you should do it:

TO ONLY DISPLAY THE DIRECTORY TREE

STEP(1)

Move your arrow to the "**View**" option and click

STEP(2)

From the drop down menu click on the "**Tree Only**" option, this is what you will see. Please see Figure(8).

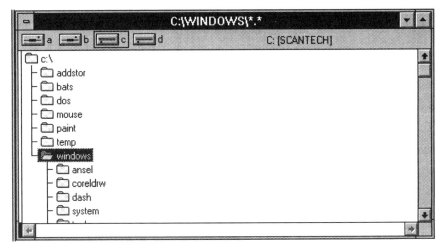

Figure (8)

TO ONLY DISPLAY THE CONTENTS OF A DIRECTORY

Move your arrow to the **"View"** option and click, now click on the **"Directory Only"** option, this is what you will see. Please see Figure(9).

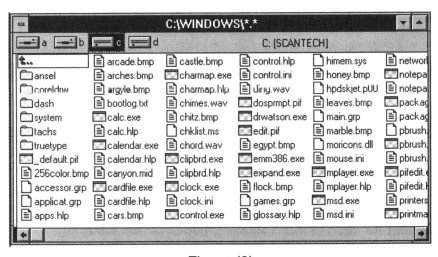

Figure (9)

TO DISPLAY BOTH THE DIRECTORY TREE AND THE CONTENTS OF A DIRECTORY

STEP(1)

Move your arrow to the **"View"** option and click

STEP(2)

Click on the **"Tree and Directory"** option, and this is what you will see. Please see Figure(10).

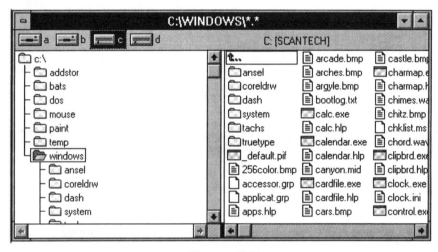

Figure (10)

GENERAL OVERVIEW OF THE FILE MANAGER

Well we hope by now you will have realised how easy Windows is to use (simplicity itself). Each window has a title bar telling you what program you are in and a menu bar listing the different options available in the program. Each option has a drop down menu facility telling you what they are capable of doing.

If you click on the various options i.e. **"File"**, **"Disk"**, **"Tree"**, **"View"**, **"Options"**, **"Window"** and **"Help"** a drop down menu will appear for each of them allowing you to do the following.

Please see Figure(11)

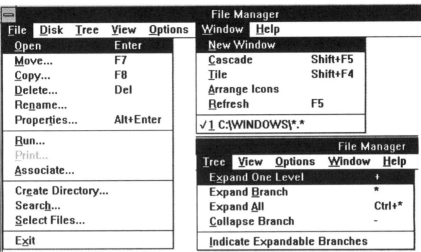

File Manager					
File	**Disk**	**Tree**	**View**	**Options**	**Window** **Help**

Open	Enter
Move...	F7
Copy...	F8
Delete...	Del
Rename...	
Properties...	Alt+Enter

Run...
Print...
Associate...

Create Directory...
Search...
Select Files...

Exit

New Window	
Cascade	Shift+F5
Tile	Shift+F4
Arrange Icons	
Refresh	F5

√ 1 C:\WINDOWS*.*

File Manager

Tree	**View**	**Options**	**Window**	**Help**

Expand One Level	+
Expand Branch	*
Expand All	Ctrl+*
Collapse Branch	-

Indicate Expandable Branches

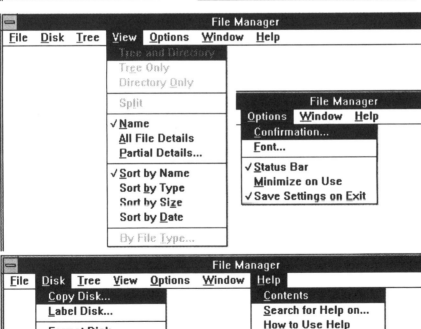

File Manager					
File	**Disk**	**Tree**	**View**	**Options**	**Window** **Help**

Tree and Directory
Tree Only
Directory Only

Split

√ Name
All File Details
Partial Details...

√ Sort by Name
Sort by Type
Sort by Size
Sort by Date

By File Type...

File Manager

Options	**Window**	**Help**

Confirmation...
Font...

√ Status Bar
Minimize on Use
√ Save Settings on Exit

File Manager					
File	**Disk**	**Tree**	**View**	**Options**	**Window** **Help**

Copy Disk...
Label Disk...

Format Disk...
Make System Disk...

Select Drive...

Contents
Search for Help on...
How to Use Help

About File Manager...

Figure (11)

243

From here on in Windows will become much more versatile as you will begin to realise that each program runs in exactly the same way. All that is different are the actual functions within each drop down menu and title bar. Because of this we intend to simplify each program that you have in Windows. In short we will use fewer words and more pictures.

OPENING MORE WINDOWS IN FILE MANAGER

In the File Manager it is possible to open more than one window at the same time. For instance, if you wanted to work with drives "C:" and "A:" at the same time it would be helpful if you could view the contents of each drive at the same time to perhaps move selected files from one to the other, or delete similar items in each drive. You can open an additional window in the following way:- Take your arrow to a drive icon, these are the buttons labelled a and c now double click on the "A" button, a new window will appear. Please see Figure(12).

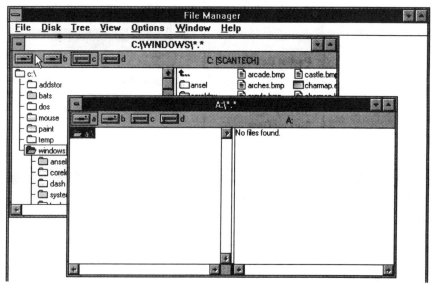

Figure (12)

COPYING FILES IN FILE MANAGER

Sometimes you will want to copy files from one drive to another, with File Manager this procedure is so simple a child can do it. This is what you should do:-

STEP(1)

Take your arrow to a file in the file list on drive "**C:**"on the right hand side of your dialogue box and grab it by holding down your mouse button, rather like a holding a piece of metal. If you let go of the button you will drop the file (metal), so to move it keep your finger held firmly on the mouse button.

STEP(2)

Move your mouse down to the window displaying drive "**A:**" and let go of your button when the arrow is in the dialogue box. Please note you will see a small icon representing the file attached to the arrow when you move it, and when you let go of the file it will automatically be copied to (in this case) drive "**A:**", and the small icon will disappear.

WORKING WITH FILES AND DIRECTORIES

You can use the file manager to work with files and directories individually or in groups. If you look at a list of files in the file manager window, you will note there are several different icons, these represent the directories and different types of files held on your disk.

If you see an icon representing a file folder ▢ windows (usually yellow) with a corresponding name, it means that it represents a directory. (These are usually listed in alphabetical order).

If you see an icon looking like a grey rectangle with a green line across the top ▨ autoexec.bat it represents a program or batch file that can be run. Their default file name extensions are either "**.exe**", "**.com**",. "**.pif**" or "**.bat**", and if you double click on this type of icon, it will try to start the corresponding application.

If you see an icon looking like a piece of paper with writing on it, 📄 pbrush.hlp just as if it was a letter with the right hand corner folded over, it represents a document file. These files are always connected to an application. When you open one of these files by double clicking it the program it is connected to will automatically start and the file will appear on the screen just as if you had opened it up in the relative program. In Figure(13) below we have shown what happens when you double click on in this case the 📄 pbrush.hlp file.

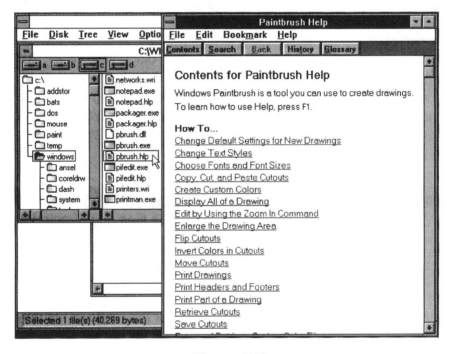

Figure (13)

If you see an icon with a piece of paper with a red exclamation mark on it 🗋 msdos.sys it denotes a system or hidden file. These files contain your system files or hidden attributes **AND SHOULD NOT BE TAMPERED WITH**, or you could regret it.

If you see an icon showing a blank piece of paper, ▯ config.sys this simply denotes all other types of files.

Please note that many of the File Manager tasks involve the naming or renaming of files and directories, Windows has been designed to handle files in exactly the same way as MS-DOS , only it's a lot more user friendly.

VALID NAMES FOR FILES AND DIRECTORIES

As we have mentioned in MS-DOS all directories and file names are made up from a name of no more than eight letters and an optional extension of no more than three letters. The two parts are always separated by a dot for example:- **"Ourfile.txt"** (Ourfile is a valid filename and .txt is a valid extension). Please note that the names must start with either a letter or a number, and contain either upper or lower-case characters, but they must not contain any of the following symbols. Please see the list below:-

" . "   " / "   " \ "   " ! "   " ["   "] "   " : "

" ; "   " | "   " = "   " , "

If you use any of the above characters, you could well be faced with serious problems so don't do it. Also the name cannot contain any spaces or be called any of the following names reserved for MS-DOS. These are **"Con"**, **"Aux"**, **"Com1"**, **"Com2"**, **"Com3"**, **"Com4"**, **"Lpt1"**, **"Lpt2"**, **"Lpt3"**, **"Prn"** and **"Null"**.

If you wish to know any other information on naming files please refer back to the **NAMING FILES AND DIRECTORIES** Section in MS-DOS or **phone (0860) 325144.**

CREATING A DIRECTORY

You can create a directory by using the **"Create Directory"** option in the **"File"** drop down menu seen at the top left corner of the main File Manager window. This is how you should do it:-

STEP(1)

Click on the directory that you want to make a new directory in, Please see Figure(14).

STEP(2)

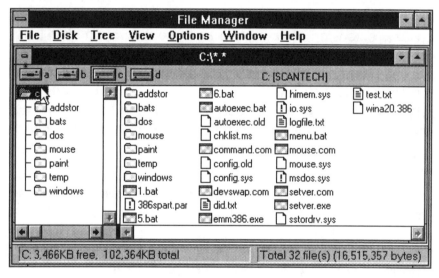

Figure (14)

Click on the **"File"** option and a drop down menu will appear, now move your arrow down to **"Create Directory"** and click.

STEP(3)

A dialogue box will appear showing the current directory that you are in, this is the directory that you are about to make a new directory in. If the directory is not the correct one you can cancel the whole operation by clicking on the cancel button.

If the directory is the correct one start typing the name of your new directory in the text box provided. For ease of use we will use "**test**" as a name for the new directory, and when you have finished click on the "**OK**" button and the new directory will appear on the left hand side of the screen. Please see Figure(15)

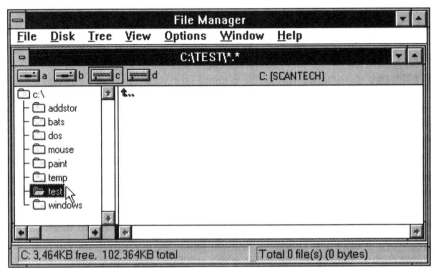

Figure (15)

DELETING A DIRECTORY

Before you delete a directory you must make sure that none of the files or directories held within it are needed, because when you delete a directory all the information held within it is completely destroyed and un-retrievable. Use the following STEPS with great care.

STEP(1)

Using your mouse click onto the directory you wish to delete.

STEP(2)

Press the delete key on your keyboard and the following message will appear. Please see Figure(16)

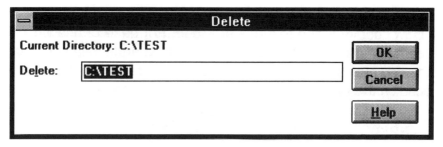

Figure (16)

STEP(3)

If you are sure that you want to delete the directory and its entire contents, click on **"OK"**, if you are at all not sure click on **"Cancel"**.

USING FILE MANAGER TO PRINT FILES

You can use the File Manager to print a file and print files that are associated with applications. You can also use the print command or if you are using a mouse you can simply pick up the file and drag it into the minimised Print Manager icon. 🖨

It is a good idea to remember that some applications do not support printing through the file manager. If this is the case or if a file is not associated with an application, you must always open the application first and then print the file from there.

PRINTING A FILE BY DRAGGING THE FILE ICON

First of all you must make sure that the Print Manager is started and has been reduced to a small icon. To do this you must follow these steps:

STEP(1)

Minimise the **"File Manager"** by clicking on the down arrow in the top right hand side of the File Manager window.

STEP(2)

Now double click on the **"Print Manager"** icon to activate Print Manager and then minimise the **"Print Manager"** by clicking on the down arrow in the top right hand side of the Print Manager window. Now, reactivate the **"File Manager"** by double clicking on the File Manager icon in the bottom left hand side of the screen.

STEP(3)

Now you need to shrink the File Manager's main window by moving your mouse to the bottom of the screen until it is on the outer border of the File Manager Window. The arrow will now change to an up and down re-sizing arrow. Now push the mouse button down and keep it in whilst you move the arrow up and shrink the File Manager window. Let go of the button when the border has moved about 30% up the screen. The File Manager Window will have now been re-sized. Please See Figure(17)

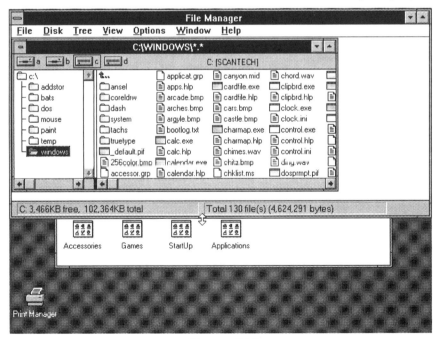

Figure (17)

STEP(4)

Now select a printable file (an icon with lines on it) 📄 pbrush.hlp. Click and hold down the mouse key whilst you drag the file to the Print Manager Icon. Let go when the file icon is directly over the Print Manager and Windows will do the rest. **Please Note:-** make sure that your printer is turned on.

STARTING A PROGRAM FROM THE FILE MANAGER

It is possible to use the File Manager to start an application, if you remember we have already explained about ".Exe" files, ".Com" files, ".Pif" files and ".Bat" files, all these files are represented by this icon ▨ and all you have to do is to double click on this icon to start the respective program.

Some programs run through DOS these are called DOS based programs. If you start a program through Windows that is DOS based, Windows will automatically switch back to DOS in order to run the program.

PLEASE NOTE THAT IF YOU ARE ABOUT TO START A GRAPHICAL DOS BASED PROGRAM i.e. A GAME OR ART PROGRAM IT IS ALWAYS BETTER TO EXIT WINDOWS AND START THE PROGRAM THROUGH DOS AS YOU WILL EXPERIENCE A DISTINCT LACK OF SPEED IF YOU RUN IT THROUGH WINDOWS.

Remember we have said all the way through this passage that Windows is particularly easy to use. In-fact it is so easy that many of the functions that Microsoft list in their manuals are really not required as they are self explanatory. When you use Windows they tend to be learned more easily as text tends to puzzle the beginner. We therefore strongly recommend that you spend time simply clicking and running through both the menu bars and the drop down menus in each program to discover what they do. It really is easy!

However, Windows has several important functions, some of which can be found in **"File Manager"**. Although these functions can all be performed in DOS, Windows allows you to perform them more easily I.e. **"Formatting a disk"**, **"Making a system disk"**, **"Copying a disk"** and **"Labelling a disk"** all become pathetically easy, and once you've learned them they will become part of your daily routine.

FORMATTING A FLOPPY DISK.

We have explained in the DOS section that formatting prepares a floppy disk so that information can be stored on it and read back at a later date. When a floppy disk is formatted File Manager destroys all the information that was on it in the beginning by creating a new Root Directory, File Manager then checks for unusable portions or areas of the disk that cannot be used. These are called Bad Sectors.To Format a floppy disk follow these steps:

STEP(1)

Insert a disk into your floppy disk drive. Use your mouse to click on the **"Disk"** option in the menu bar. A drop down menu will now appear.

STEP(2)

Use your mouse to select the **"Format Disk"** option by clicking on it, a dialogue box will now appear. See Figure(18)

Figure (16)

STEP(3)

You will note that there are several options in the box. The first thing you have to do is to make sure that the disk you have just inserted in your floppy drive corresponds to the "**Disk in**" box. If you only have one floppy drive it will always read as "**Drive A:**", if you have inserted a floppy disk into "**Drive B:**", you should change the option accordingly.

Now check the "**Capacity**" of your disk. If you are using a "**High Density**" disk then you will have noted before you inserted the disk that the letters "HD" were marked on it. This automatically means that the disk has a "**1.44Mb**" capacity and you should check that "**1.44Mb**" is displayed in the capacity box. If you are using a "**Low Density disk**", (easily checked by it having only one square hole in the bottom left hand corner), then you need to select "**720k**" option in the capacity box as this is the maximum capacity for that type of disk.

You can select the different capacities for your disk by simply clicking on the small down arrow next to each option box and then clicking on the preferred option.

If you want to give your disk a name you can label it by first clicking on to the Label Dialogue Box and then type in your preferred name for the disk.

If you are using a previously formatted disk then you can select the "**Quick Format**" option by clicking on the square box next to it. When you have done so a cross will appear in the box to confirm that this option has been selected. This speeds up the overall formatting time by at least "**300%**".

If you want to make a system disk simply click on the "**Make System Disk**" option box, and a small cross will appear in the box to confirm that this option has been selected.

Please note that you can make a "**system disk**" and use the "**quick format**" option at the same time, just as we explained earlier in the DOS section.

STEP(4)

To start formatting your floppy disk click on the "**OK**" option button, and the following message will appear. Please see Figure(19)

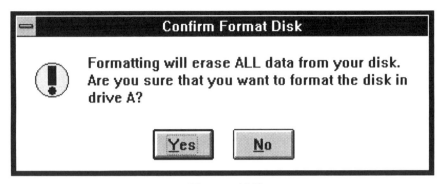

Figure (19)

If you are sure you want to proceed then click on the "**YES**" button and all the information on your disk will be deleted whilst File Manager formats your floppy disk. When File Manager has finished formatting your disk, you will receive another message similar to the one shown in Figure(20). If you wish to format another disk click on the "**Yes**" button if you do not wish to click on "**No**". **Please Note:-** If the disk is already formatted you can use the "**Label Disk**" and "**Make System Disk**" options immediately.

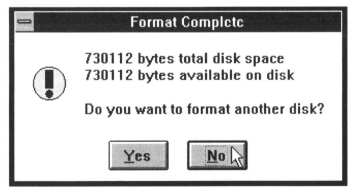

Figure (20)

WINDOWS CONTROL PANEL

Windows has a Control Panel that allows you to visually change the configuration of your system whilst you use your Windows operating system. The "**Control Panel**" stores the changes in a file called "**Win.ini**", so that it will be setup in exactly the same way the next time you start Windows.

Let's look at some of the functions that the Control Panel has within its Window. First of all double click the Control Panel Icon with your mouse to start the Control Panel see Figure(1)

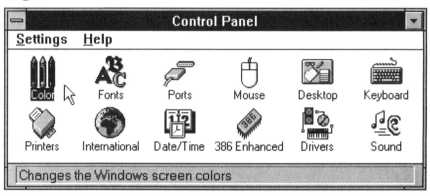

Figure (1)

The Icons in Figure(1) represent the various settings that you can change by using the Control Panel windows. The following list explains what each of the icons represent and do. Please remember that to start any of the options shown you must first double click on them with the mouse.

This changes the overall colour of your desktop to what ever you select in the options provided. (Simply Click and Play)

Fonts This allows you to add or remove the windows True Type fonts, please see "**Installing True Type Fonts**" later in this book.

Ports This allows to change the overall setting for your Communication Ports (You don't normally need to touch this)

Mouse Sets up your mouse to meet your personal requirement (Please refer back to "**Using a Mouse**" in the section marked "**What is Windows**" earlier on in this book)

Desktop This option just allows you to play around, adjusting silly things you don't really need. We all think it's a bit pointless apart from adjusting the Icon Spacing.

Keyboard This sets your keyboard to your own personal requirements. However, unless you are a skilled typist it is best to leave it alone.

Printers This allows you to install and configure printers that you want to use with Windows, and also allows you to turn the Print Manager off. On some machines if you turn the Print Manager off it will allow you to print more quickly, however when doing so it prevents you from Multi-tasking. This option is described later on in The Book in more detail, please see "**Installing Printers**".

International This allows you to re-configure the language on your computer, or adjust the **"Date"**, **"Time"**, **"Currency"** and **"Number formats"**. Many people complain that they can't type a "£" sign when using Windows. This is because when you first install Windows your computer will be configured for an American keyboard and therefore show "$" (Dollars) not "£" (Pounds). When you change the settings, remember that Windows will ask you to insert one of the Windows installation disks holding the specific countries file, so please have them ready.

Date/Time This one's really easy. All you need is the correct time and date, then you simply type either the correct date/time in or click on the up and down arrows to set the overall Windows Time.

386 Enhanced This option will only appear when you are using a 386 or above computer in the special Windows 386 enhanced mode. If it doesn't appear and you are using a 386 or above computer try exiting Windows then restarting it by typing "**win/3**". This forces Windows into using the 386 Enhanced mode. The 386 Enhanced mode can adjust your Windows **"Permanent/Temporary Swap File"** and turn on **"32Bit access to the hard disk"** for added hard disk performance. This option is described in more detail later on in The Book, please see **"386 Enhanced"**.

Drivers This option allows you to install a sound card driver for Windows. This is required in order for you to listen to or create sounds via information received from your sound card, or **"midi"** information from a synthesizer or instrument connected to it.

You do not need to know too much about this function other than you will need a software driver to load in the correct software for your sound card. To explain, we have shown you how to install a sound card driver below.

STEP(1)

Click on the driver's icon, a window will appear headed Drivers, please see Figure (2).

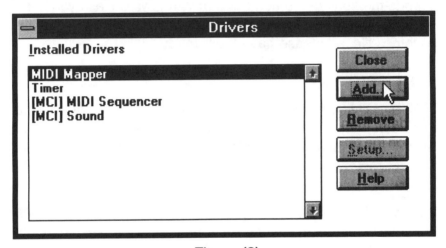

Figure (2)

You will note that there are several installed drivers already present from your original Windows setup. These drivers are simply standard drivers that will allow you to perform equally standard tasks. However, if you wish to install a new driver for a new sound card perhaps, you will note a button in the driver's dialogue box marked "**Add**"

STEP(2)

Click on "**Add**" and the Add dialogue box will appear as shown in Figure(3) overleaf. Let's suppose that you wanted to install an "**Ad Lib**" Sound card driver, being the driver required in the handbook of your newly acquired sound card.

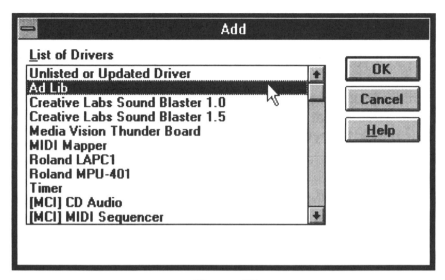

Figure (3)

Select "**Ad Lib**" with your mouse arrow and click on "**OK**". You will then be presented with an "**Install Driver**" dialogue box as shown in Figure (4), requesting for a Windows Disk to be inserted into Drive A.

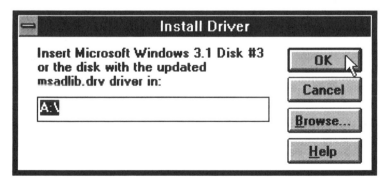

Figure (3)

STEP(3)

Insert the appropriate disc and click "**OK**", your driver will then be added to your system.

Should you wish to remove a driver from the dialogue box, click on the **"Remove"** button. A remove dialogue box will appear asking you if you are sure that you wish to remove the driver that you have highlighted. If yes click **"Yes"**, if no click **"No"**, but remember your first shot is your last shot!, i.e. **Never remove any of the drivers that are first installed with windows. If you do your Windows system will not run.**

This icon assigns sounds to system and application events. You must have correctly installed sound driver before this sequence will work. If you double click on the icon a sound dialogue box will appear as shown in Figure(4) below, but unless you have already installed a sound card and it's appropriate driver it will normally be left blank as no midi mapper/ sound driver is present on a standard Windows setup.

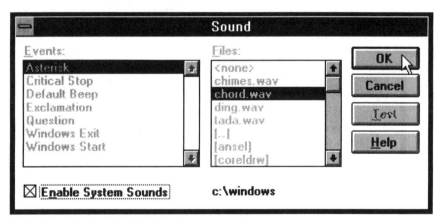

Figure (4)

If you have any problems please telephone (0860) 325144

So let's summarise this section. We now know that the "**Control Panel**" provides you with a visual way of changing the Windows configuration whilst you are using Windows.

When you change an option by using the "**Control Panel**", the change is always stored in a file called "**WIN.INI**" so that it will always be there each time the machine is turned on. We will be mentioning "**WIN.INI**" file later on in The Book, but for the meantime good luck with the use of your Control Panel.

Although we have briefly explained the formation of a window, we thought it important to create a section that leaves no doubt as to the capabilities of the Windows environment.

This section sets out to describe the different parts of a Window that effectively become the tools that you will work with whilst using your applications or documents.

You should realise that all windows are alike in certain areas and possess the same functions such as title bars and menus. They are only alike in their basic functions so don't be caught out by thinking what you can do with one window can be done with another. The parts of a window that you need to know are shown in Figure(1) below.

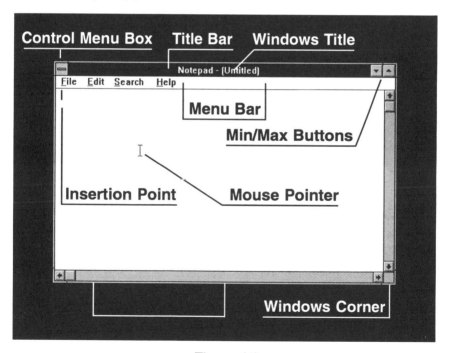

Figure (1)

1. CONTROL MENU BOX

We have for your ease inserted Figure (2), and identified where the different elements are. So let's start with the **"Control Menu Box"** ⊟ . We have previously called it a Switch in the past but Microsoft call it the Control Menu Box for their own reasons.

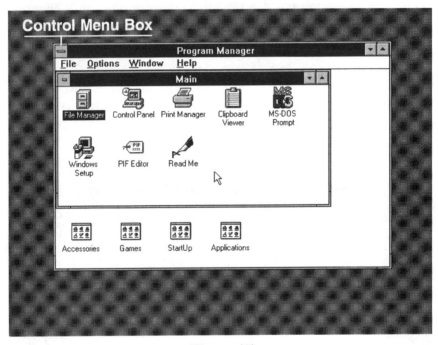

Figure (2)

The **"Control Menu Box"** ⊟ is in the upper left-hand corner of every window, you can use the associated keyboard commands in the Control Menu Box to **"Re-Size"**, **"Move"**, **"Maximise"**, **"Minimise"**, and **"Close"** Windows as well as switch between the different Windows using the **"Next"** command.

However, if you use a mouse these tasks are performed much more quickly by clicking and dragging for each specific function.

Please remember back to the section labelled **"USING A MOUSE IN MICROSOFT WINDOWS 3.1"** when we explained how to drag a component from one place to another by holding your mouse button down when over the component and letting go of it after relocating the element. Rather like picking up a bucket, walking down a pathway and putting the bucket somewhere else i.e. your hand is the mouse switch, the bucket is the element, the pathway is the Windows environment.

2. THE TITLE BAR

The "**Title Bar**" shows the name of the application or document that you are currently working on. Please see Figure(3).

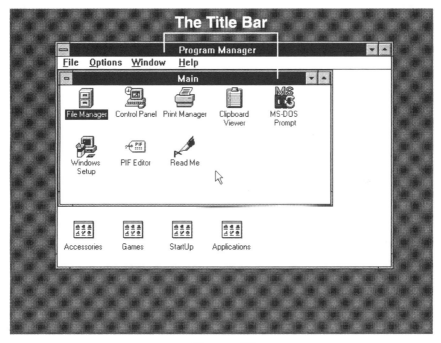

Figure (3)

However, if more than one window is open the Title Bar for the Window that you are working on will be coloured and the one underneath will not.

Let us explain, each time you take your mouse arrow to a title bar and click it, Windows tells you that it understands which one you are using by changing (is active), making sure that the colour of the bar that you have just clicked is the brightest and any other title bars underneath either have no colour or are a tint of their previous or normal colour, please see Figure(4).

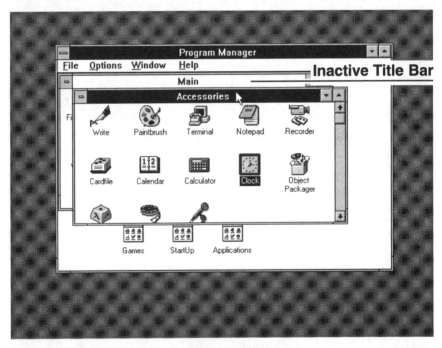

Figure (4)

If you are in default Windows setup mode, that is you have not changed the colours, a non-active window title bar will be white, and an active Window title Bar will be blue.

3. THE WINDOW TITLE

Depending upon the type of Window that you are working with the title can represent the name of an application, the name of a document, the name of a group, directory, file or a personal name that you have given for you own recognition. If you have not yet saved a document, windows tells you by marking the Title Bar **"Untitled"**. Please see Figure(5) below.

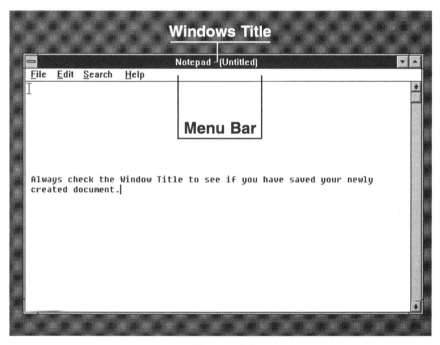

Figure (5)

4. THE MENU BAR

The **"Menu Bar"** lists the available option menus or things that you can do in that particular Window. A Menu contains a list of commands or actions that have been preprogrammed as a part of the program, most applications have a File Menu, an Edit Menu and a Help Menu, but there will be other headings unique to different applications. Please See Figure(5).

5. SCROLL BARS

By using **"Scroll Bars"** you can move different parts of work into view if the entire document is too big to fit inside your Window. There are two scroll bars, one horizontal and one vertical and if you click onto the respective arrows, **"Up"** ,**"Down"** , **"Left"** or **"Right"** , your window will start to scroll or move across the page to a desired position.

Please see Figure(6) showing an image which does not fit into a Window.

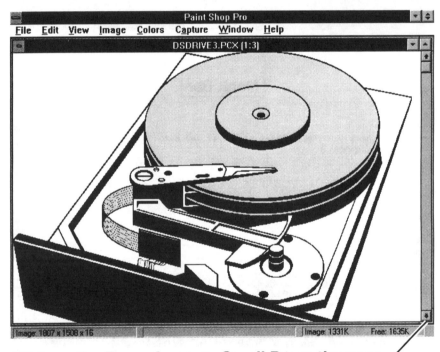

Click on the Down Arrow to Scroll Down the page

Figure (6)

Now please see Figure(7) showing the rest of the image after using the "Down" button to scroll down the page.

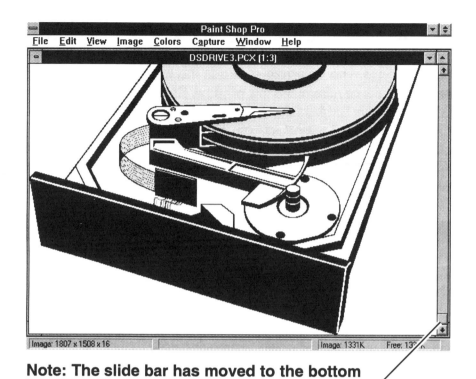

Note: The slide bar has moved to the bottom

Figure (7)

You can also use the scroll bar to view unseen parts or lists of information that will not fit into a window, such as a "**Readme.txt**" file in "**Windows Write**" or "**Notepad**".

We strongly recommend that you open up a file in Notepad, click onto the scroll bar arrows and watch what Windows is doing. If you click the up arrow and hold it down a slide flashes and moves up and if you click the down arrow a slide flashes and moves down. If you click a left-hand side arrow the slide flashes and moves to the left, if you click a right hand arrow the slide flashes and moves to the right.

You can also click onto the slide bar or the slide itself to scan through pages more quickly.

6. MAXIMISE AND MINIMISE BUTTONS

You will note in the top right-hand side of your Window two small buttons ▼▲. The up arrow enlarges the window and the down arrow shrinks or minimises the window. So remember ▲ is BIG-GER, and ▼ is SMALLER, this will apply to every Window. If you have just enlarged a window from its standard size to fill the complete screen another small arrow will replace the ▲ arrow, with this button ⬍ called the Restore button, when clicked on the Window will change back to its original size.

7. THE WINDOW BORDER

The "**Window Border**" is the outside edge of your Window, a thin grey frame, (rather like a picture frame); You can lengthen or shorten it by moving your mouse arrow to the border, your mouse arrow will then change into a double headed arrow, then you will be able to hold your mouse button down and move the border to the left or right / up and down, by moving your mouse. When the border is in the desired position you should release the button and the size will automatically change. Please See Figure(8) showing the "**Windows File Manager**" before changing it's size.

Figure (8)

Now please see Figure(9) showing the change after using the mouse to drag first the File Manager window down and then using it to grab the right hand corner of the **"C:\Windows"** to proportionally enlarge it so that more files can be viewed.

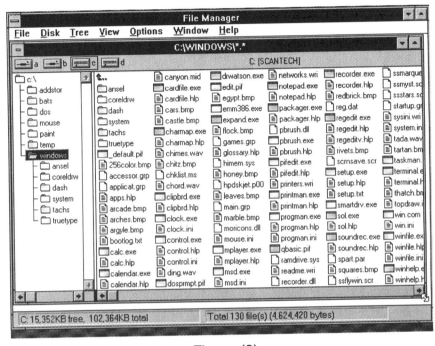

Figure (9)

8. THE WINDOW CORNER

As briefly explained above the **"Window Corner"** can be used to lengthen or shorten the two adjoining sides at the same time. If you look carefully at the corner of your window frame you will see that there are corner pieces rather like the pieces that you would fit to a picture frame to prevent damage. If you take your mouse arrow to the corner position hold the button and move the mouse towards the centre of your window the effect will be self explanatory. Again please see Figure(9) above showing a Window being re-sized after moving the **"Window Corner"**.

9.) INSERTION POINT

The "**Insertion point**" is a flashing cursor that indicates the position at which text or graphics can be inserted. It also tells you where you are in a particular document, but be careful as some windows applications have different insertion points although they always flash off and on. Please See Figure(10) showing an insertion point in a Notepad document.

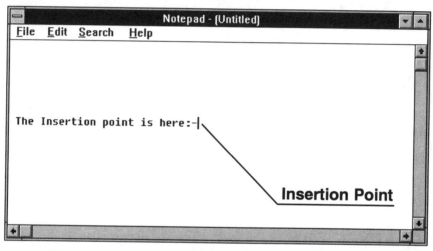

Figure (9)

If you can imagine marking your place in a hand written document with a pencil line the insertion point works in exactly the same way.

10.) MOUSE POINTER OR ARROW

The mouse pointer or arrow ⊾ will only move across your screen if a mouse is installed into your hardware. Please refer to the section "**USING A MOUSE IN MICROSOFT WINDOWS 3.1**" which will explain precisely how useful your mouse will be to you.

As you work in windows two types of windows appear on your desktop called "**Application Windows**" and "**Windows**" within the "**Application Windows**". Please see Figure (1).

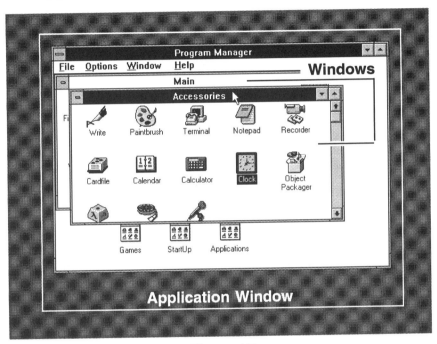

Figure (1)

An application window is really the factory where the work takes place. The Window containing the applications is the people or machines that do the job. But another Window will sometimes appear called a Document Window because they often contain pre-written documents or data files that have been saved.

In the "**Program Manager**" as shown in Figure(1) they contain groups in the "**File Manager**" they contain directories, and of course you can open several of these at the same time for a comparison. Please See Figure(2).

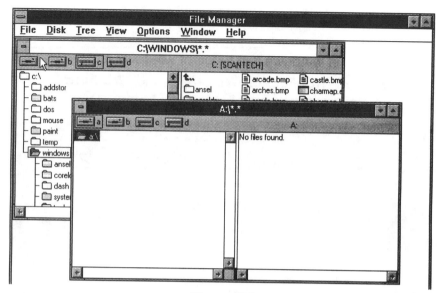

Figure (2)

Please see Figures (3,4 and 5) showing you a selection of the windows that you will come face to face with on a daily basis

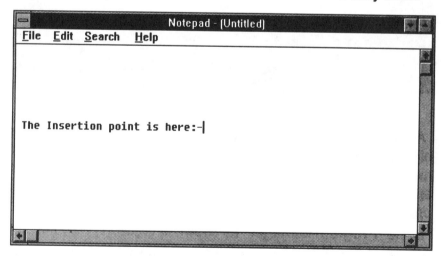

Standard Application Window

Figure (3)

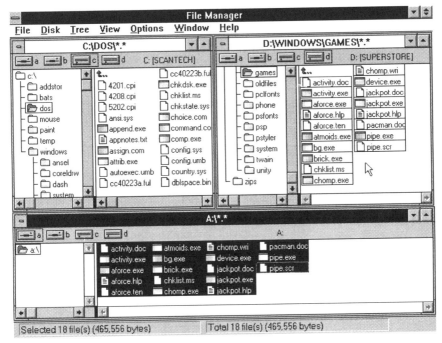

Figure (4)

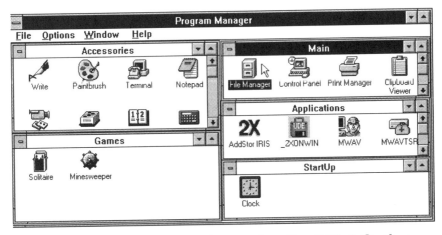

Prgoram Manager Window using the "Tile" Option

Figure (5)

BASIC MOUSE AND KEYBOARD TERMINOLOGY

From time to time in every manual about Windows that you can buy, you will be confronted with funny, strange and seemingly unreal words. With this in mind we have attempted to explain what these words mean.

If you are told to "**Click**", this means to press and release the mouse button once.

If you are told to "**Double Click**", this means press and release your mouse button twice in quick succession. We have seen people spend hours attempting to double click on an icon, through not clicking quick enough onto the icon.

If you are asked to "**Drag**" you will simply hold down the mouse button whilst you are moving an object with the mouse.

Finally if you are told to "**Point**", this means that you move your mouse arrow to a pre-selected place.

Obviously there are other terms that are commonly used but as we have already gone over them thoroughly, we feel that to go over all of them again would probably prove very confusing.

UNDERSTANDING WINDOWS APPLICATIONS
(Working with different Applications)

A major advantage of Microsoft Windows is that it is able to run two or more programs/applications at the same time i.e.

It is possible to run a spread sheet that will work out complex formulas while you are using a word processing package at the same time. This means that your computer through Windows can work out mathematical problems and type an explanation of what you are doing at the same time.

When using Windows there are four major benefits that will all immediately become evident

1.) You can quickly start your Applications and always know precisely where to find them.

2.) You can organise your applications into groups that make absolute sense to you.

3.) You can run one or more application at a time and easily switch between them.

4.) You can cut and paste information between windows applications by using a clipboard, that is to say move parts of what you have done to somewhere else.

TYPES OF APPLICATIONS

There are various types of applications that will run within the Windows operating system. Some are especially designed for Windows and others for MS-DOS.

It is important to understand the differences between them and also to remember that if you wish to load older programs created for older versions of Windows there could be problems.

The following types of applications suitable to run in Windows are;-

1.) Windows applications designed for Window 3.0+above.

**2.) Older Windows applications designed for versions   .
der than 3.0, BUT BE CAREFUL!**

**3.) Non-windows applications designed for MS-DOS,   .
' nost of them will run with Windows).**

4.) Memory resident Programs.

Windows Applications require Windows version 3.0 or later in order to run properly because they are designed to take advantage of all the windows features.

Windows automatically divides memory cooperatively between the programs that you are running in it; Which means that the Windows environment memory manager distributes your computers memory to each program as efficiently as possible.

Windows applications are generally highly graphical and their menus, commands and dialogue boxes are visually the same throughout Windows.

You will find that when you load Windows for the first time that several programs are included with it, these programs all take full advantage of the Windows environment.

OLDER WINDOWS APPLICATIONS

If you are running a program or intend to run a program designed for a version of Windows earlier than version 3.0, it is always better to obtain an update because the older programs were not designed to run correctly or to their optimum potential in the latest Windows 3.1 environment.

If you try to load a very old program it is almost certain that the following message will appear.

Application Compatibility Warning.

The Application you are about to run, PAINT-V1.EXE, was designed for a previous version of Windows.

Obtain an updated version of the application that is compatible with Windows version 3.0 and later.

If you choose the OK button and start the application, compatibility problems could cause the application or Windows to quit unexpectedly.

If it does and you still wish to carry on click **"OK"**, but remember that the program or application may not perform reliably!

NON WINDOWS APPLICATIONS

This means that the program is not designed to run in Windows, and in-fact will only run properly in our view in MS-DOS, being the system it was originally designed for.

An MS-DOS program will not take advantage of the Windows graphical interface and may not have menus or dialogue boxes or even make use of a mouse.

In our experience if you load an MS-DOS program and run it through Windows, the program tends to run slower than it would in MS-DOS, and so as a general rule we advise you not to use or run MS-DOS programs in the Windows environment, after all it is not really a problem to come out of Windows and use the equivalent start prompts through MS-DOS.

MEMORY RESIDENT PROGRAMS

A Memory resident program is a Non-Windows application and it runs differently than most other programs, when you start MS-DOS it immediately loads itself into your computer's memory and is therefore available at any time even when you are running another application, this is a form of memory resident program.

A common type of memory resident program is a **"Pop-Up"** program which when loaded into your computer memory is not visible until you tell your computer to run it, when you do it will then run in conjunction with the application you are currently using.

Memory Resident programs are sometimes referred to as terminate and stay resident programs or **"T.S.R's"**, so if you see the letters **"T.S.R."** you immediately know it refers to a memory resident program.

RUNNING TWO OR MORE APPLICATIONS

As we have already stated, it is possible to run two or more applications through the Windows environment, in effect you can start an application and keep it running whilst you start another and keep that running, and so on. When the applications run at the same time each will share your computer's resources (thinking time), the way they share these resources depends on the type of computer you have i.e. The processor chip that you posses (286, 386, 486 or P5) and the amount of memory that is available.

Please note:- if you run Windows in **"386 Enhanced Mode"** (386 and above chips only) rather than **"Standard Mode"** (286 chips and above), more applications can be run at the same time, please refer to **"Windows 386 Enhanced Mode"** later in this book.

SWITCHING BETWEEN APPLICATIONS

As we have stated, you can switch between as many applications as you like at the same time, up to the limititations of your computer's memory capabilities. Windows automatically displays the application that you are currently working on in the foreground (on top of all the other windows), this is called an "**Active Window**", the Active Window will always appear in the foreground and so it could well overlap or completely obscure the other window/s you are running.

To work on another "**Application Window**" you must select the required "**Application**" and make it active, remember the "**Active Window**" always has a coloured title bar, a "**Non-Active Windows**" does not, provided you haven't changed the colours. To switch to another application you should do the following.

1.) If you can see the application simply click on it.

2.) To return to the application you last used or in-fact switch to any open application, you can press and hold the "**ALT**" key and then keep tapping the "**TAB**" key until the required program is displayed in the window which appears. Please See Figure(2).

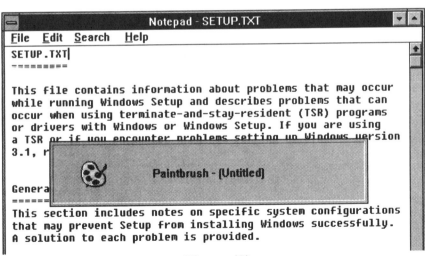

Figure (2)

MICROSOFT WINDOWS WRITE

Microsoft Windows Write ✐ is a program that is automatically loaded when you load Windows for the first time. "**Write**" is a word processing program that you can use to create letters for day to day business or personal documents. To work with "**Write**" you will need to know how to use a keyboard (type, edit), but most importantly know how to use "**Format text**" and "**Save text**" to a file, after which you will then be able to print your documents onto a printer or keep them safe for later use.

This section easily explains each task that you will have to perform as using "**Write**" will essentially help you to understand Windows more fully as you will be using all the elements of typical menus and drop down dialogue boxes. To start "**Write**" you must first of all go to your minimised program group called "**Accessories**" in your "**Program Manager**". Please see Figure(1).

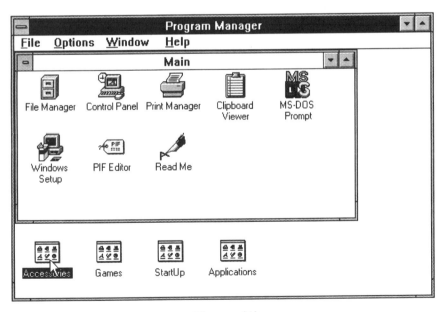

Figure (1)

Double click to view the program group. Please see Figure(2).

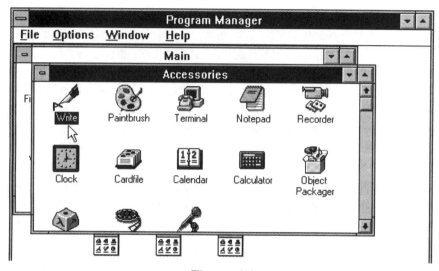

Figure (2)

Go to the "**Write**" icon and double click, you will then be into "**Microsoft Write**". Please see Figure(3).

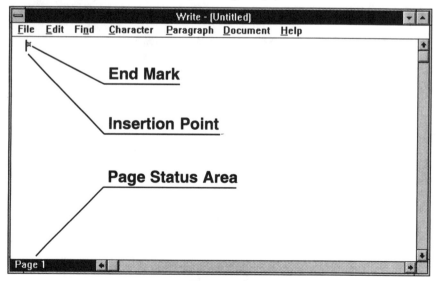

Figure (3)

Now you are ready to type. In the **"Write"** Window you will see the following items.

1.) A flashing line - called the **"Insertion point"**, that will tell you where text will appear when you start typing.

Whenever you open a **"Write"** document an insertion point will appear in the upper left hand corner of the window.

2.) The **"End Mark"** Ⴃ as shown in Figure(3), indicates the end of a document or when there is no text in a **"Write"** window. The end mark is always to the right of the Insertion point.

3.) **"Page Status Area"** Page 1 please see Figure (3). This is a black bar indicating the number of the page that you are currently working with. Please note that until you break a document up into pages you will only ever view page one.

You can use your mouse in the standard way when performing a Windows Write task. If you are ready to type your letter or document simply start typing, the words that you type will start to fill the window at the insertion point. When you reach the end of a line Write will automatically take you to the beginning of the next line; so in-fact you can just continue to type.

To start a new paragraph you must always press **"Enter/Return"** key. If you want a blank line between paragraphs you must press the **"Enter/Return"** key twice.

If you make a mistake whilst typing you should press the **"Backspace"** ← key, which will undo your mistake. Before you start to use **"Write"** it is a good idea to refer to the initial **KEYBOARD** section near the start of **"THE BOOK"** to familiarise yourself with the keyboard functions, that is, if you have not already done so. You will also need to know how to edit your document. The following section explains some of the techniques. **"Write"** includes a number of special keys and key combinations for moving around the document. These are in addition to the normal key movements such as the **"Space bar"** and **"Return"** etc.. We have compiled a table to assist your ease of use .

PRESSING	MOVES THE INSERTION POINT TO
`Ctrl` + `→`	THE NEXT WORD
`Ctrl` + `←`	THE PREVIOUS WORD
`5` + `→`	THE NEXT SENTENCE
`5` + `←`	THE PREVIOUS SENTENCE
`Home`	THE BEGINNING OF A LINE
`End`	THE END OF A LINE
`5` + `↓`	THE NEXT PARAGRAPH
`5` + `↑`	THE PREVIOUS PARAGRAPH
`Page Down`	THE NEXT SCREEN DOWN
`Page Up`	THE NEXT SCREEN UP
`Ctrl` + `Page Down`	THE BOTTOM OF THE WINDOW
`Ctrl` + `Page Up`	THE TOP OF THE WINDOW
`5` + `Page Down`	THE NEXT PAGE
`5` + `Page Up`	THE PREVIOUS PAGE
`Ctrl` + `Home`	THE BEGINNING OF A DOCUMENT
`Ctrl` + `End`	THE END OF A DOCUMENT

Please Note:- The "5" Key referred to is the 5 key on the numeric key pad, also always make sure that the "Num Lock" switch is off on your keyboard.

You will find the above commands useful even if you are using a mouse as you can sometimes perform a function quicker by using both the mouse and the keys consecutively.

If your document has several pages in it, you can quickly go to a page of your choice by pressing the "**F4**" key, or you can use your mouse by first clicking onto the "**Find**" option and then selecting the "**Go to Page**" option, a dialogue box will then appear. Please see Figure(4).

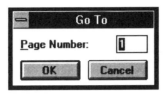

Figure (4)

Simply change the number to the page number of your choice.

You will find that the Options in "Write" are particularly easy to use and they are definitely self-explanatory, so unlike other manuals we do not intend to fill you full of useless information that you will invariably not be able to understand, these are the simple workable facts.

There is a "**File**" option, if you click once you will see Figure(5).

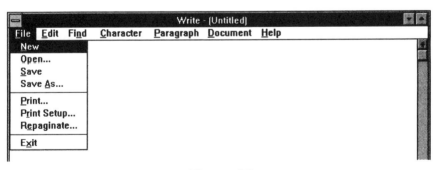

Figure (5)

There is an "**Edit**" option, if you click on it Figure(6) will appear, you will note that some of the headings in the drop down menu are a different colour (Greyed Out), this is because they will not become active until there is a document or picture that can be edited or in some cases pasted from the clipboard.

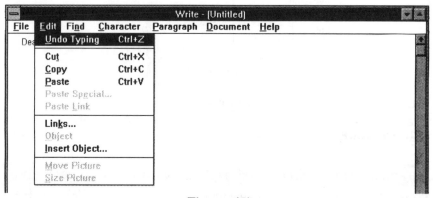

Figure (6)

If you click on the "**Find**" option, Figure(7) will appear, the contents of which are self-explanatory, however until you have text in the windows, these functions will not become active.

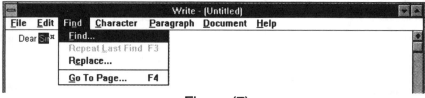

Figure (7)

If you click on the "**Character**" option Figure(8) shown overleaf will appear, the contents of which concerns itself only with "**Type size**", "**Type Styles**" and the "**Short cut keys**" to change them.

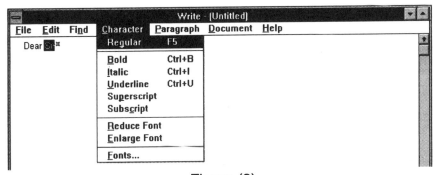

Figure (8)

Just in case you are not fully aware of the word **"Font"**, a **"Font"** is a letter or **"Type Style"**, if you click on the **"Fonts..."** option then Figure(9) will appear.

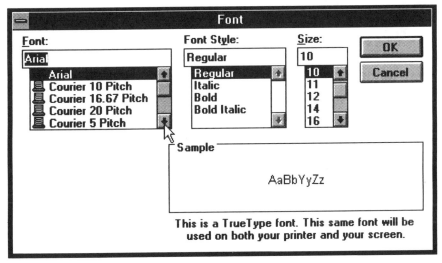

Figure (9)

You can scroll through the Fonts on the left using the up and down arrows, to choose the required **"Font"**, **"Font Style"** and **"Size"** simply highlight them, the Sample box will change accordingly allowing you to see the selected option. Once you have selected the type size and Style you require simply click on **"OK"**.

If you click on the **"Paragraph"** option, Figure(10) will appear.

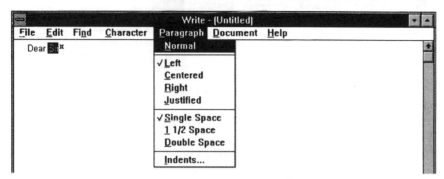

Figure (10)

You will note the contents are to do with type alignment i.e **"Left"**, **"Centred"**, **"Right"** or **"Jusified"**. There are also options to change the **"Line Spacing"** and the **"Indents"**, these are exactly the same functions you would expect to find on any conventional typewriter, only unlike a Typewriter the computer is able to change the complete format of your documents for you.

If you click on the **"Document"** option, Figure(11) will appear the contents of which are self explanatory.

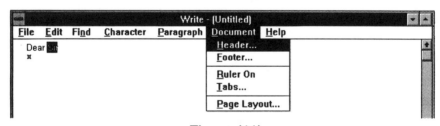

Figure (11)

Finally the **"Help"** option is as you would expect it to be in any Windows application. Please see Figure(12) overleaf.

If you have any problems please telephone (0860) 325144

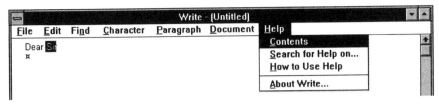

Figure (11)

We hope that this section has given you an insight as to how Windows Write works, but whilst this program is suitable for it's designed intention, there are many other word processing packages that will allow you to be more professional for example:- **"Word Perfect for Windows"**, **"Microsoft Word for Windows"**, **"Ami-Pro"**and **"Word-Star for Windows"**, will surprise you in their versatility and might I add being the proud possessor of this book, you will receive an in-depth study on how to use them in a language that you can understand, Good Luck with Write.

Paintbrush 🎨 is perhaps the easiest graphics application that has ever been produced, or at least it's very easy. As we explained earlier to start Paintbrush you need to find the Paintbrush Icon 🎨 found in the "**Accessories**" program group in the main "**Program Manager**". Please see Figure(1)

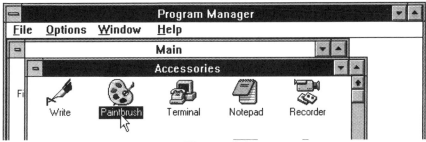

Figure (1)

Simply double click on it and Paintbrush will start, see Figure(2)

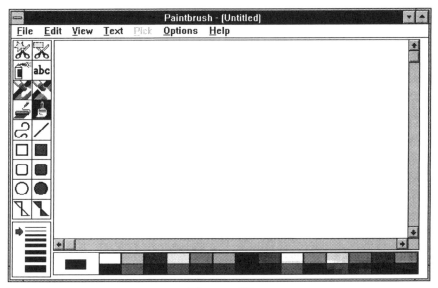

Figure (2)

As you can see you have a range of tools on the left hand side of the Paintbrush window consisting of nineteen tools, starting from the bottom working up they are as follows.

The "**Line selector**" at the bottom left See Figure(3) below simply allows you to select the thickness of line you want to work/draw with, if you take your mouse into the line selection box the arrow will change and whichever line you select will be confirmed by the green arrow opposite marking your selection.

Figure (3)

To use any of the following tools you just have to simply click onto the appropriate tool, move over onto the main screen/canvas then click and hold the mouse button down whilst moving the mouse.

The Polygon tools ![polygon tools icon], allow you to produce mathematical shapes automatically, please see Figure(4), showing examples of both filled and outline polygons. Try creating a few shapes of your own for a few minutes, remember that you can select any of the colours shown at the bottom of the screen simply by clicking onto them, use the left mouse button to select and fill objects and the right button to select the outline colour.

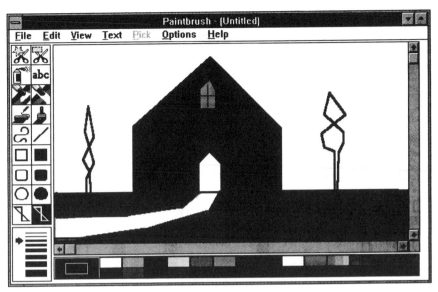

Figure (4)

These  tools are **"Circle/Ellipse"** tools which allow you to produce filled or hollow ellipses, Please see Figure(5) below.

Figure (5)

These 🔲🔳 tools are **"Rounded Box"** tools, which can be used either empty or filled. Please see Figure(6)

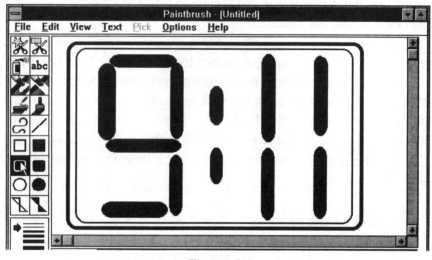

Figure (6)

These 🔲🔳 tools are the **"Box Tools"**, again you can select to have them filled or empty. Please see Figure(7) below

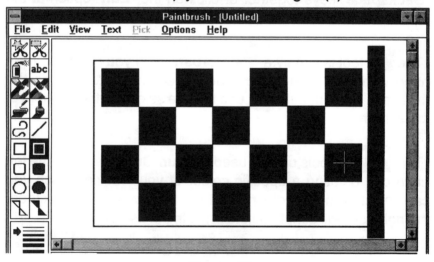

Figure (7)

These ⌐▭/ tools are the "**Curve**" and "**Straight line**" tools, both of which are slightly different from the rest of your tool box items, as in the curve has the facility to bend at straight line twice before it is set, for instance:-

If you produce a straight line by dragging your mouse across the page and take the cross cursor to the middle of the line then hold your mouse button down whilst moving the mouse it will start to bend, now let go of the mouse button in the desired position and move the cursor to another point on the line and repeat the procedure, and there you have a curve.

To use the Straight line tool simply click then move the mouse and click again.

The ▭ tool will "**Fill**" in a completely enclosed area in any colour you choose from the bottom colour palette, but be careful, if the enclosed area you wish to fill is not completely sealed, the paint will run out and may completely fill the screen.

To correct a mistake at any time simply press the "**Alt**" and "**Backspace**" keys together or click on the "**Edit**" option at the top of the screen with the mouse and select "**Undo**".

The ▭ tool is simply a "**Paintbrush**", and you can draw free-hand with it by using your mouse, remember to change the thickness of the paintbrush, use the line selector at the bottom of the screen.

The ▓▓ tools can be used to "**Rub Out**" mistakes, the left hand one deleting a specific colour of your choice, which you can select from the colour palette at the bottom of the screen, the right tool will simply delete anything in its path.

The [tool icon] tool acts just like a **"Spray Can"**, remember you can adjust the size of the Spray Can by using the line selector at the bottom of the screen.

The **abc** tool allows you to place **"Text"** anywhere on the canvas, to change the Font, click on the **"Text"** option and change the styles in the normal way.

The [tool icons] tools give you the ability to **"Cut and Paste"** any shape you wish in and around the picture, play with them to see what happens.

The Menu Options at the top of the screen are virtually the same as any Window except for the **"View"**, **"Pick"** and **"Options"** menus. Please see Figure(8) below to view their options.

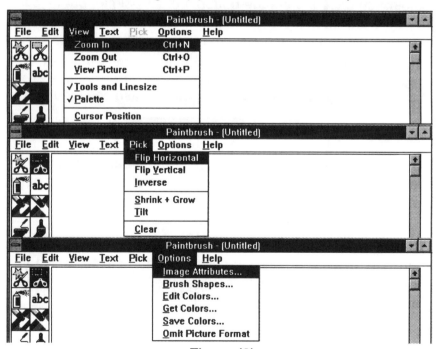

Figure (8)

As you can see you can **"Zoom in"**, **"Zoom out"**, **"View** an entire **Picture"** and even measure your **"Cursor Position"** if you wish to try precision drawing, but we would recommend using another program if you are serious about the idea.

Finally as you can see, in the **"Options"** menu, you are given several useful facilities, you change the **"Image attributes"**, as shown in see Figure(9) below.

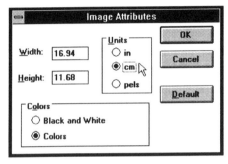

Figure (9)

You can change your **"Brush Shapes"**, please see Figure(10).

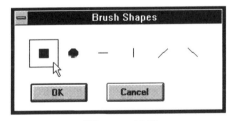

Figure (10)

You can create new colours and save or retrieve them at a later date by using the **"Edit Colours"**, **"Get Colours"** and **"Save Colours"** options please see Figure(11) overleaf showing the **"Edit Colours"** option.

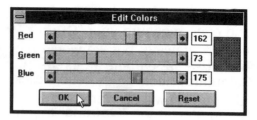

Figure (11)

As we have mentioned, there is a Colour Palette at the bottom of the screen, you can use this with most of the tools that we have just described by clicking on a selected colour, please note to select a fill colour use the left hand mouse button and to select an outline colour use the right hand mouse button, that is unless you have switched the mouse button around in the Control Panel.

Finally the best way to get used to the Paintbrush program is to use it, like most things in life, the more you practice, the better you will become.

If you have any problems please telephone (0860) 325144

In your "**Accessories**" group of the "**Program Manager**", you will find the "**Calculator**" icon 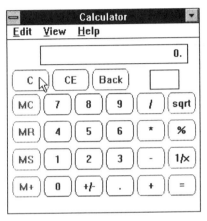, double click on it to run the Calculator, and Figure(1) will appear.

Figure (1)

You have two main viewing options on the calculator, click on "**View**" option and they will appear, namely "**Scientific**" and "**Standard**", if you click on "**Scientific**", the scientific calculator layout will appear please see Figure(2) overleaf.

To revert back to the "**Standard**" calculator simply click on the "**View**" option and then select standard, the calculator will now revert back to its standard mode as shown in Figure(1)

You can use your calculator either manually using the keyboard's numeric keypad or the numbers along the top of it or you can simply use the mouse to click on the numbers displayed, rather like you would with a normal calculator.

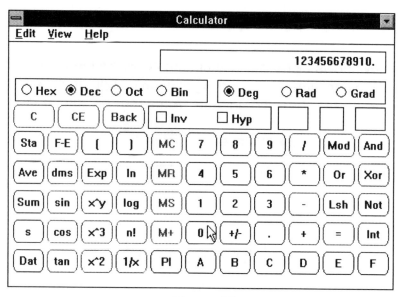

Figure (2)

Don't forget you can copy any figure which is displayed on the calculators read-out window to the clipboard, to do this simply click onto the "**Edit**" and select "**Copy**".

That's really all there is to it, however don't forget you can use your calculator at any time even if you are using another application, for instance if you were using a word processor and you wanted to calculate a quick "**V.A.T.**" return you could use the "**Alt**"+"**TAB**" commands to quickly switch between the calculator and the word processor, you could even copy the figures straight into your word processor's document if you wanted.

The Windows clock is a useful item as you have at your disposal the right time when working on your computer (provided of course it's set correctly), in your "**Accessories**" group in Program Manager you will see a "**Clock**" icon ▦ double click on it and the clock will run. Please see Figure (1).

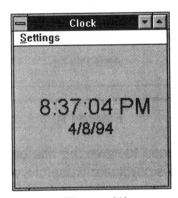

Figure (1)

You have the option of either an "**Analogue**" or "**Digital**" readout, you can select these by choosing from the "**Settings**" option on the menu bar. Please see Figure(2).

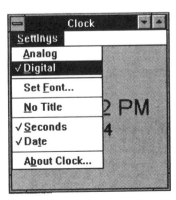

Figure (2)

You can also select the **"Font"** on the digital clock by choosing the **"Set Font"** option in the same **"Settings"** menu. Please see Figure(3).

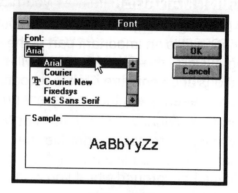

Figure (1)

Finally you can choose to have the title bar removed from the clock altogether, this is particularly useful if you want to leave the clock in, for instance the top right hand corner while you work on another program, remembering that as with any window you can stretch and reshape the clock to virtually any size.

If you constantly use the clock on a daily basis it might be a good idea to move the clock icon to the start up program group where it will automatically be activated every time Windows is started, this saves you having to click on it each time.

If you have any problems please telephone (0860) 325144

WHAT IS A PRINT MANAGER

Well the **"Print Manager"** in windows is a system that takes charge of all printing, it is an important part of the Microsoft Windows operating system, the Print Manager will take care of all printing applications and configure itself to recognise any printer, provided that it has been given the necessary printer driver.

When you print from Windows with your Print Manager turned on, the Print Manager creates a print file that effectively tells your printer what to do, if you like a Print Manager is a shadow that is always in the background whilst you work, taking notes of anything you need to do with your printer. Normally the Print Manager automatically turns on when you print from a Windows application.

Please See Figure(1) showing a simple file being proceesed from **"Notepad"** by the **"Print Manager"**.

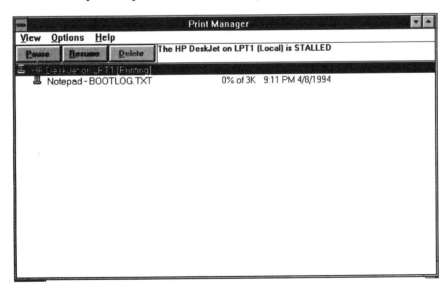

Figure (1)

Before you can print in Windows you first of all have to connect your printer to your computer, for reference you can see STEPS (14,15 and 16) in the section marked "**SETTING UP MICROSOFT WINDOWS 3.1**" as shown earlier in the book, if you did not install a printer when you first setup Windows you will need to go through some of the initial procedures again.

To do this click onto the "**Control Panel**" icon which is located in the "**Main**" group of your Program Manager and follow these steps.

STEP(1)

Select and double click on the printer icon and the following screen will appear. Please see Figure(1).

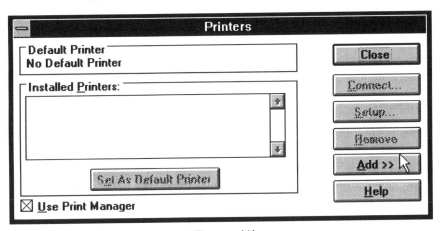

Figure (1)

STEP(2)

Click on the "**Install**" or "**Add**" option in the dialogue box and the screen will extend as shown in Figure(2) opposite.

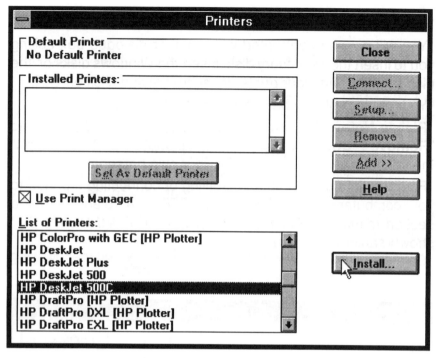

Figure (2)

STEP(3)

Use your mouse to scroll up and down the list of printers until you find your own, now click onto it with you mouse and then click onto the "Install" button.

Please note:- When selecting a printer the printer that is currently selected will be highlighted in blue, it is important to remember that there will be occasions when your printer does not appear in the list of available printers, don't panic as there are several ways to overcome this problem. For instance if you have a "**Bubblejet printer**" that does not appear on the list you can select "**HP Deskjet**" and it will almost certainly work, also if you have an unlisted "**Laser printer**" the same will apply by selecting "**HP Laserjet**" or "**HP Laserjet Plus**".

STEP(4)

You will now be confronted with another dialogue box asking you to insert the neccesary disk, insert the Windows disks or the disk supplied with your printer if neccesary and click on O.K.

Your printer will now be automatically installed.

Please Note:- You can also use the printer's dialogue box to "**Remove**", "**Connect...**" your printer to another port or "**Setup..**" the various setting applicable for your own personal printer.

For more information about installing or connecting a printer to your computer please refer back to STEPS (14,15 and 16) in the section marked "**SETTING UP MICROSOFT WINDOWS 3.1**" shown earlier in the book

If you have any problems please telephone (0860) 325144

USING CARD FILE

In the "**Accessories**" program group there is an icon representing a "**Card File**" index 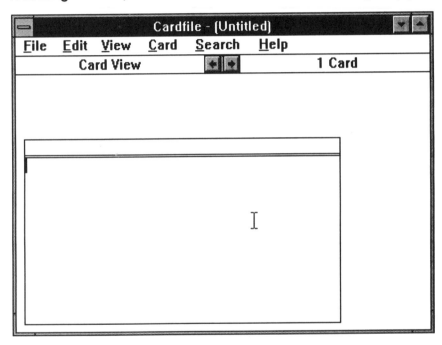. If you take your mouse pointer to the icon and double click you will then be presented with the following window, headed "**Card File**". Please see Figure(1).

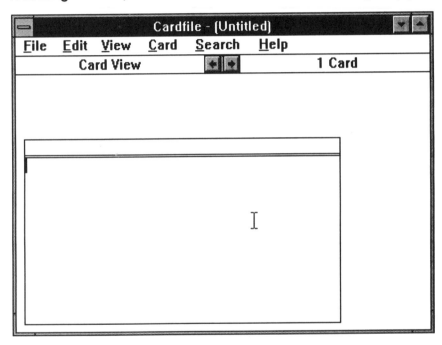

Figure (1)

It is simplicity itself and really needs no explanation. We have explored the contents of several tutors for card indexing, all of which seem to have made the whole procedure extremely complicated and when questioned, most people would have preferred a simple explanation which outlined the basics.

Microsoft Cardfile is nothing more than a simple database. You have as many cards as you wish in a box and each time you wish to enter a series of facts you simply pull out a card write on it, then give it some kind of identification and put it back in the box, it will then always be there for your personal reference. These tasks are performed by Microsoft Cardfile at lightning speeds.

Let's study the program's main window, yet again you will see the standard **"Title Bar"**, **"Minimise"** and **"Maximise"** buttons, a **"Menu Bar"** plus all the usual features of a normal window.

The words **"File"**, **"Edit"**, **"View"**, **"Card"**, **"Search"** and **"Help"** are the listed main options. When you click on any of them a drop down menu will appear. Please See Figure(2) opposite showing all of the drop down menus and their relative options.

WORKING WITH CARDFILE

Suppose that you have the need to keep a file of basic information on your clients with special notes applicable to each of them. First of all you would need a simple way of identifying each of them quickly, perhaps in alphabetical order or numerically. Secondly you would need an easily recognisable title on each of the cards and thirdly you would need an area to write the information on.

You may need to standardise the cards to make it easier to enter the information on. You can enter any information you wish e.g.. **"Names"** ,**"Addresses"**, **"Directions"** etc. You can change the size of your Cardfile window by using the minimise and maximise buttons but you cannot change the actual card size itself.

To create a Cardfile you should fill in as many blank cards as you need. Once the cards are filled out you can save them in a file, naming the file according to the type of information you wish to store. There is virtually no limit to the amount of files that you can store; however if you literally have hundred's of "Card Files" then you will notice a drop in the program's performance.

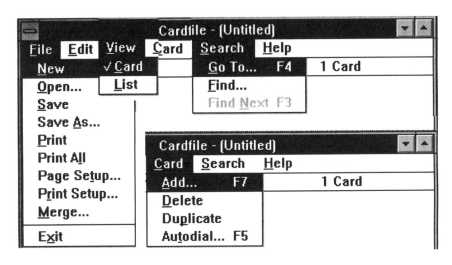

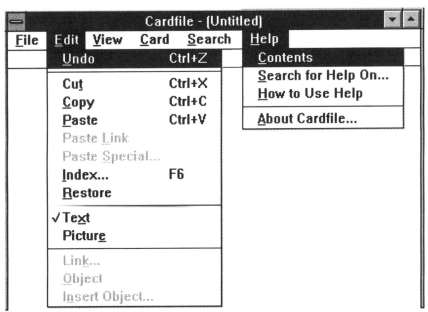

Please Note:- Some of the options shown above are not available unless you have more than one program running in Windows

Figure (1)

FILING AND ADDING CARDS

Each card's **"Index line"** is situated at the top of each card. Please see Figure(3).

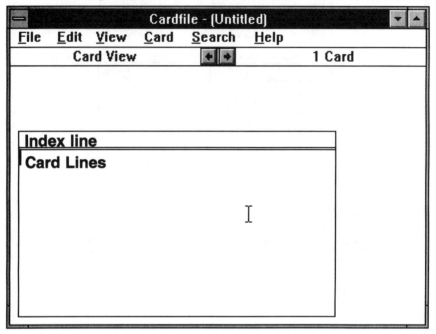

Figure (3)

Cardfile uses the text that you put in the **"Index line"** to identify each card. You could also type a name or brief description on each line to identify the card yourself. To fill in a blank card follow these steps.

STEP(1)

From the **"Edit"** Menu line click onto the **"Index"** option or double click onto the **"Index line"** itself. Please see Figure(2).

STEP(2)

Type in the Cards Name and click on **"OK"** and your card will be automatically labelled. Please see Figure(4).

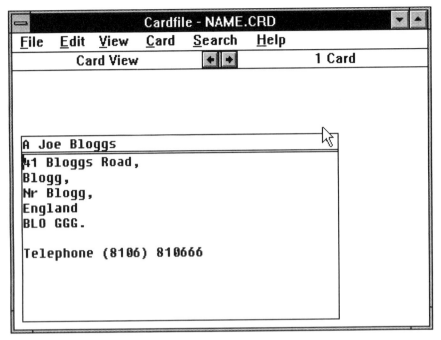

Figure (4)

STEP(3)

Type in text for each card line, you have up to fourty characters in each line.

STEP(4)

To Add another "**Card File**" click onto the "**Card**" option on the top menu and another drop down menu will appear. Please See Figure(2). Choose Add. Please see Figure(5). A quicker way of adding a card at any time is to simply press the "**F7**" key.

Figure (5)

Step(5)

Simply type the name for your next **"Index line"** in the dialogue box and click **"OK"**, and you will have added your card to the file.

VIEWING CARDS AS A LIST

From the "**View**" option select "**List**", and a tick will appear confirming your choice. You can either select the cards individually by clicking onto them or scroll through them by clicking the left and right arrows in the centre of the window. See Figure(6)

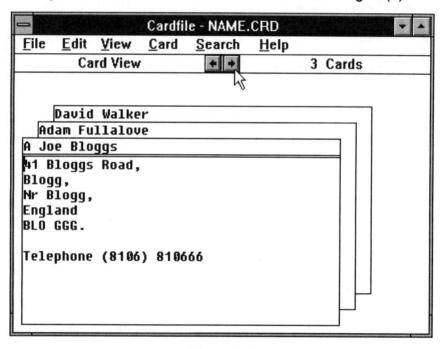

Figure (6)

If you wish to go to a specific file then simply press "**F4**" or Click onto the "**Search**" option and select "**Go To..**", Please refer to Figure(7) on the next page.

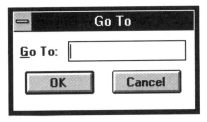

Figure (7)

Type the Index line refering to the card that you wish to view and click on "**OK**".

You can change your index lines at any time by repeating the procedure that you followed when you first created the card i.e double clicking on it, pressing "**F6**" or by clicking onto "**Edit**" then "**index**" option.

MOVING AND COPYING INFORMATION

If you want to "**Move**" or "Copy" text from one card to another you should perform the following steps.

STEP(1)

Use your mouse to Select the text that you want to copy.

STEP(2)

Select the "**Edit**" option and choose either "**Copy**" or "**Cut**" depending on what you wish to do, you can use the keyboard commands to do the same, i.e. "**Shlft**"+"**Delete**" = "Cut" and "**CTRL**"+"**Insert**" = "Copy".

STEP(3)

Select the card in which you wish to insert the text and move the "**Insertion Point**" to where you wish the text to appear

STEP(4)

From the "**Edit**" option choose "**Paste**" and the text will appear in its new location, the keyboard shortcut is to press the "**Shift**" +"**Insert**" keys together.

You can "**Delete**", "**Duplicate**", "**Restore**" or add "**Pictures**" to a card, in fact one of the most useful features of "**Cardfile**" is its ability to transfer artwork from a paint or graphics application into a card in Cardfile.

For example you could create a drawing in "**Paintbrush**", perhaps a map and then copy into a card containing information on that drawing, but please remember that each card can only contain one picture.

There are three methods of copying graphics into Cardfile

1.) "**Copy**"

2.) "**Embed**"

3.) "**Link**"

This is how you should embed or link a drawing into a card.

First Copy the drawing onto the Windows "**Clipboard**" by using the "**Edit**" and "**Copy**" option in the graphics or paint program's window, the drawing must be saved in a file if you are going to create a link to another application. Switch to the Cardfile program and then select the card in which you want to insert the drawing. Then follow these procedures.

STEP(1)

From the "**Edit**" option choose "**Picture**", click onto the "Edit" option again and you will note that a mark has appeared next to the "Picture" option.

STEP(2)

Choose "**Paste**" from the "**Edit**" menu or to link a drawing choose "**Paste Link**". The image will now appear in the card.

STEP(3)

If text appears on the card the drawing may cover it. Hold the mouse button and drag the drawing to an available space. Please See Figure(8).

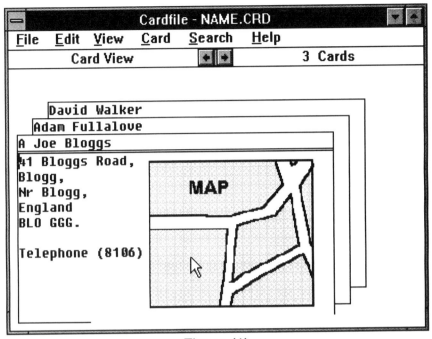

Figure (1)

There are many other functions in Cardfile that you will find useful, for instance if you posses a modem in your machine Cardfile will automatically dial the telephone numbers for you..

However, we do not propose to become involved in these techniques as comparitively very few people have a modem.

If you do require assistance with this subject **please call (0860) 325144** as we have an in-depth section on the subject.

USING CALENDAR

As we have mentioned the "**Accessories**" program group contains resident programs that will have automatically been loaded when Windows was installed for the first time. These programs are written specifically for the Windows environment and, therefore, will not corrupt your software configuration.

The "**Calendar**" ⊞⊟ program displays the time, date and a status line when you first click on its ⊞⊟ icon. See Figure(1)

```
┌─────────────────────────────────────────────────────┐
│  ─           Calendar - [Untitled]            ▼ ▲    │
│ File  Edit  View   Show  Alarm    Options  Help      │
│ ┌─────────────────────────────────────────────────┐ │
│ │  5:54 PM       ◀ ▶   Saturday, April 09, 1994   │ │
│ │    7:00 AM   |                                ▲  │ │
│ │    8:00                                          │ │
│ │    9:00                                          │ │
│ │   10:00                                          │ │
│ │   11:00                                          │ │
│ │   12:00 PM                                       │ │
│ │    1:00                                          │ │
│ │    2:00                                          │ │
│ │    3:00                                          │ │
│ │    4:00                                       ▓  │ │
│ │    5:00                                          │ │
│ │    6:00                                          │ │
│ │    7:00                                          │ │
│ │    8:00                                       ▼  │ │
│ ├─────────────────────────────────────────────────┤ │
│ │                                                 │ │
│ └─────────────────────────────────────────────────┘ │
└─────────────────────────────────────────────────────┘
```

Figure (1)

If the Time or Date is wrong or you need to change the format you can reset it by using the Windows "**Control Panel**" 🖥 . Please refer to the earlier section labelled "**USING WINDOWS CONTROL PANEL**" for more information.

The "**Calendar**" gives you the option of two views when you initially start to run it. By using the "**View**" option you can see either a full "**Day**" at a time as shown in Figure(1), or you can view a complete "**Month**" at a time as shown in Figure (2) below.

Calendar - [Untitled]						▾ ▴
File Edit View Show Alarm Options Help						
6:16 PM ◀ ▶ Saturday, April 09, 1994						
April 1994						
S	M	T	W	T	F	S
					1	2
3	4	5	6	7	8	9
10	11	12	13	14	15	16
17	18	19	20	21	22	23
24	25	26	27	28	29	30

Figure (2)

In order to use the Calendar program effectively it is a good idea to work out the amount of information you wish to record each day. For instance, if your day holds several appointments you might need more time intervals to remind you of them and likewise if you simply only have one or two long appointments each day you won't need as many time intervals, the adjustments are controlled by the "**Day Settings**" option in the "**Options**" sub-menu.

Right then let's get on. Please see Figure(3) showing all of the options available in "**Calendar**".

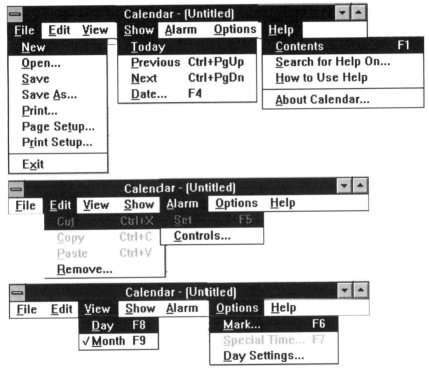

Figure (3)

The contents of the "**File**" menu are again very similar to any windows application in that you can create a "**New**" Calendar, "**Open**" an existing Calendar, "**Save**" or "**Save As...**" and "**Print**" your Calendar, you can also use "**Exit**" to exit the program.

The "**Remove**" option in the "**Edit**" sub menu enables you to remove appointments, for instance if you have a cancellation. Click onto it and Figure(4) will appear.

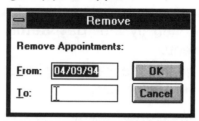

Figure (4)

You will note there are two boxes labelled "**From:**" and "**To:**" simply type in the start date you wish to remove from and then type in the date you wish to remove to. Once you are satisfied the entries are correct, click on the "**OK**" and the computer will log in your changes. Simple isn't it.

If you want to see what you are doing today, you can use the "**Today**" option in the "**Show**" sub menu. If you want to see what you did or tomorrow, you can simply click onto the "**Previous**" and "**Next**" options. Finally if you want to know what you are doing or want to enter some information on any date in the future or past, (between the years 1980 to 2099) you can click onto the "**Date**" option, and simply type in the date you require, again click onto "**OK**" to accept. Please see Figure (5)

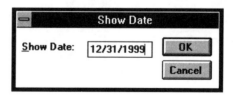

Figure (5)

Scrolling through your menu bar still further you will note the "**Alarm**" option. If you click it, yet another drop down menu will appear. If you have entered an appointment in your Calendar then the "**Set**" option will be available, this means that you can configure your computer to prompt you with your computer's built-in speaker at a specific desired time.

The next menu along is the "**Options**" sub menu which has three options in it "**Mark**", "**Special Time...**" and "**Day Settings...**".

If you click onto "**Mark**" the following Window will appear, headed "**Day Markings**". Please see Figure (6).

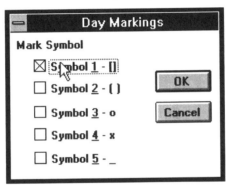

Figure (6)

This option simply allows you to mark a specific day with a symbol that you can quickly recognise when viewing in the "**Month**" option. Please See Figure(7) showing some of the days in a monthly calendar being marked by the various symbols.

The "**Day Settings**" option is particularly useful as you can adjust the intervals between your daily appointments with the options of **15**, **30** and **60** minute intervals, you can also change the "**Hour Format**" and the "**Starting Time**" that each daily appointment sheet will begin from.

You can add a special time to your daily calendar by selecting the "**Special Time**" option.

| _ | Calendar - (Untitled) | ▼ | ▲ |

File   Edit   View   Show   Alarm   Options   Help

| 7:59 PM | ◄ ► | Saturday, April 30, 1994 |

April 1994

S	M	T	W	T	F	S
					× 1	2
3	4	5	6	7	8	> 9 <
10	11	12	13	14	15	16
17	[18]	19	20	• 21	22	23
24	25	26	27	28	29	[30]

Figure (7)

Always remember there is a "**Help**" system in every Window's application. If you click on "**Help**" in the menu bar a drop down menu will always appear which is self explanatory.

This concludes your basic knowledge of the "**Calendar**" program. Always remember the best way to become an expert on any of these programs is to use them. Good Luck.

If you have any problems please telephone (0860) 325144

WHAT IS OPTIMIZING?

Optimizing is customizing your system so that is uses it's built-in resources more efficiently for the tasks you wish to perform. For instance, each program you run in the Windows environment requires a specific amount of memory. The Windows environment knows how much memory is present within your system, it also recognizes the amount of memory each of your programmes require to run at their optimum effect.

Typically optimizing involves improving one or more aspects of your system's performance, but beware you sometimes sacrifice something else by doing it. For example, you might be able to run more applications at faster speeds, but in doing so you would end up with less hard disk space available as a result of your actions. If you optimize your system for Microsoft Windows, it literally means working with the following system resources:-

RESOURCE   WHY IT IS IMPORTANT

Speed	Your system's speed affects the time it takes for Windows/Application to start up, re-display a Window, switch between applications or carry out any other task required.
Memory	The amount of memory your system has determines how many applications you can run at the same time and also how much information they can store in the memory at any given time. It can also affect Window's performance.
	(Please note Windows runs more slowly when there is little or no memory available). We strongly recommend having a minimum of 4Mb of Ram fitted in order to run Windows effectively.

Available Disk Space The amount of available hard disk space can affect your system's speed and efficiency, this is specifically because Windows needs to have somewhere to save information whilst you are running it. Some applications use disk space to store temporary files while they run. Windows can also configure some of your available disk space as virtual memory which effectively provides Windows with more memory than the computer actually has.

WHAT IS VIRTUAL MEMORY?

Just in case you don't understand what **"Virtual Memory"** is, we thought it useful to explain it more fully as optimizing your system requires your full understanding of it. Let's take a typical program, perhaps **"Paintbrush"**.

Paintbrush requires a large amount of memory in order to work, primarily because it is a highly graphical program. If your computer requires more memory for Paintbrush than is currently installed, it will automatically try to work even though it's memory is inadequate and it will effectively end up with a headache due to it becoming frustrated at not being able to run the program to its optimum efficiency, and your computer will slow down.

Therefore, your computer will look for other areas to release memory in order for it to think more clearly. Rather like people take an Aspirin for a headache, the computer's Aspirin is it's **"Virtual Memory"** which takes away the pain by using some of your hard disk space to store information when there is no more room in your computer's **"Ram"**.

The most important thing you can do to improve Windows performance is to configure your system's memory properly. This will also allow the programs installed to work faster and more effectively with one another.

After you configure your system's memory for optimum efficiency, you can use other procedures to improve its performance still further. For more information on using **"Virtual Memory"** please see the **"VIRTUAL MEMORY"** and **"386 ENHANCED MODE"** sections further on in this chapter.

The next section will help you understand your computer's memory, please also see **"MEMORY"** at the start of the book for a more basic explanation.

UNDERSTANDING MEMORY

Memory is usually added to your computer's motherboard by plugging in small boards called **"SIMMS"**, these boards usually have several chips on them capable of storing various amounts of information.

Before information can be processed by the computer or displayed on the screen it needs to be placed in memory. If you like memory is the computer's way of grabbing information, analysing it and placing it into the correct areas. When you run an **"Application / Program"** its files are loaded into memory so that they can be processed. Memory also provides temporary storage for your application's data.

It is a general rule that the more memory you have, the more applications you can run in the Windows environment. It is possible to increase the memory on your motherboard by fitting more of the small boards namely **"SIMMS"**. These boards plug into an available memory slot called a **"BUS"** and increase the system's memory capability. For example, you might add two **"1Mb"** SIMMS to your system to increase it from having **"2Mb"** of Ram to **"4Mb"** of Ram, (the minimum recommended requirement for Windows).

Your computer has the option of using four kinds of memory.

1.) Conventional Memory

2.) Extended Memory

3.) Expanded Memory

4.) Virtual Memory

We will attempt to explain what each of these memory types actually do in your computer/system.

IDENTIFYING YOUR MEMORY CONFIGURATION

The memory configuration of your system significantly affects your computer's performance. It is important to know how much and what type of memory your system has.

On most computers whenever you turn on the power you can watch the screen count how much memory your system has. You will recall that when your machine starts to boot up a clicking sound is heard and some numbers begin to count quickly, when the clicking stops a final set of figures is displayed on the screen, this represents the memory you have installed into your system i.e., **"008000 KB OK"** is **"8Mb"**of RAM.

However, this does not show you the type of memory you have, therefore, it is important to find this out. If you are using MS-DOS version 4 or later there is a built in facility that will display the amount of memory you have and what type of memory it is, you can use this facility by typing **"MEM"** return at the **"C:\ Prompt"**.

To find out your system's memory configuration you should perform the following Steps:-

STEP(1)

If Windows is running, exit from the program in the normal way. That is by choosing the **"File"** menu program and selecting **"Exit"** in the sub menu, or by pressing **"ALT"** + **"F4"**

STEP(2)

At the MS DOS prompt type "**Mem**" and then press return. MS DOS will now display all the information you require about the type of memory your computer has in it. Please see Figure(1).

```
Microsoft(R) MS-DOS(R) Version 6.20
            (C)Copyright Microsoft Corp 1981-1993.

C:\>mem

Memory Type          Total    =  Used   +  Free
----------------     -----       ----      ----
Conventional          640K        79K      561K
Upper                 147K       147K        0K
Reserved              128K       128K        0K
Extended (XMS)      7,277K     6,253K    1,024K
----------------     -----       ----      ----
Total memory        8,192K     6,607K    1,585K

Total under 1 MB      787K       226K      561K

Largest executable program size       561K (574,064 bytes)
Largest free upper memory block          0K      (0 bytes)
MS-DOS is resident in the high memory area.

C:\>
```

Figure (1)

You will note MS DOS has listed your memory into four separate categories and tells you specifically how much of each your computer is currently using.

STEP(3)

To restart Windows type "**WIN**" and then press return.

There are several other diagnostics tools which are specifically designed to display memory information, most computers and memory boards come with these tools and they are all capable of indicating exactly what type of memory your computer has and how much of each type it has. However, we strongly recommend that you utilize the "**Mem**" command in DOS as it has proven to be both simple and reliable. For more information about alternative diagnostic programs please **phone (0860) 325144.**

CONVENTIONAL MEMORY

Conventional memory exists on all computers and most computers have at least "**256K**" of "**Conventional Memory**" but are capable of accommodating up to "**640K**". You will have noticed when your computer boots up a figure will appear telling you how much conventional or "**Base Memory**" your computer has.

When you start your computer MS DOS uses some of the computer's Conventional Memory to actually perform at all. MS DOS then runs through the commands in your "**Config.sys**" and "**Autoexec.bat**" files. Running these commands also uses up Conventional Memory. Windows will then use the remaining memory (when started) to manage your system and run your programs or applications.

To summarize; Conventional Memory, is really the standard memory you use for simple tasks rather like the speech we use in every day life. You use it so much that the development of specific memory allows you to talk without really thinking about the formation of the words.

EXTENDED MEMORY

Extended memory is a general purpose memory that functions beyond "**1Mb**" on "**286**", "**386**" and "**486**" computers.

The Window's environment requires "**Extended Memory**" in order to run, however your system requires an "**Extended Memory Manager**" in order to use it. The Extended Memory Manager coordinates the use of your system's Extended Memory and actually divides the memory available in your machine for use with applications you are using or intend to use either in DOS or Windows. It also prevents an application from stealing another application's memory, which would of course cause your computer to crash.

All Windows programs use the Extended Memory Manager namely "**HIMEM.SYS**". For more information about using "**HIMEM**" please refer to the MS DOS sections at the beginning of this book.

Please note many "**286**", "**386**" and "**486**" computers come with "**640K**" of Conventional Memory and an additional "**384K**" of upper memory, for a total of "**1Mb**" of conventional memory i.e., "**640 + 384 = 1,024K**". The additional "**384K**" is not accessible by all applications and is usually used by device drivers so be careful when attempting to use it.

EXPANDED MEMORY

If installed, "**Expanded Memory**" exists separately from your systems Conventional and Extended Memory. Most, if not all computers, can accommodate or configure your system's memory as "**Expanded Memory**". If your computer does not then our advice is to update your computer, as it will not be capable of running all of the programs available on your computer i.e. "**Games**" etc.

Expanded memory is located on an Expanded Memory Board and comes with yet another memory manager called "**EMM386.EXE**". Applications must request access to this type of memory through the "**Expanded Memory Manager**", most programs are unable to use Expanded Memory because they were not designed to interact with it, as the Manager gives applications access to only a limited amount of memory at any given time, using Expanded Memory is slower than using Extended Memory, and for this reason it is always important to select the minimum amount of Expanded Memory you will require.

Windows and Windows applications do not use expanded memory, however, if you have a "**Non-Windows**" application that requires expanded memory you should still be able to run it within Windows by changing its "**PIF**" file to use expanded memory.

For more information on "**PIF's**" (Program Information Files") please **phone (0860) 325144.**

When running Windows on a 286 computer most applications that require expanded memory will only be able to access if it physically exists on the computer, i.e. in the form of an expanded memory card; However if you are running Windows on a 386, 486 or above computer you can configure some of your computer's Extended Memory as Expanded Memory by changing the "**EMM386.EXE**" command line in your "**Config.sys**" file, please see the "**TWEAKS**" section, later in the book.

Some expanded memory boards such as "**AST RAMpage!**", "**AT**" or the "**Intel Above board**" can be set up with Extended Memory, Expanded Memory or with both. Windows runs best if you configure your Expanded Memory board as Extended Memory.

VIRTUAL MEMORY

Virtual memory is a space on your hard disk that Windows uses as if it were actual memory built into your computer. Windows does this through the use of a file called a "**Swap File**". It is important that you understand what a "**Swap File**" is and how it works, as it will give you insight in defining or recognizing any problems that may occur though its use in Windows.

If you can imagine you are in a classroom studying an extremely difficult course of teaching, all of which is too much for you to handle at any one time in your head, it is therefore logical that you would write down some of the facts on a piece of paper so that you can refer back for future reference.

A Windows Swap File is used by the computer in exactly the same way by it having the ability to transfer any excessive amounts of information that it cannot handle in its Ram, onto the computer's hard disk whilst the lesson is still going on, to do this efficiently your computer creates a "**Swap File**" on your hard disk which it use to write it's notes on.

The benefits with Virtual Memory are that your are able to run more programs than your computer's memory is normally capable of handling.

The drawbacks are that the space on your hard disk is reduced, and a program's execution time when swapping information to a Swap File rather than memory is slowed down. In short if you use too much Virtual Memory your machine will slow down.

For more information about creating a Windows **"Swap File"**, see **"386 ENHANCED MODE"** section later in this chapter.

We have spoken in depth about the different types of memory and we are quite sure there will be some of you panicking at this volume of information. It really isn't that difficult, but the terms can be extremely puzzling and for this purpose you really only have to totally understand the following four facts:-

1.) Conventional Memory:-
Exists on all personal computers.

2.) Extended Memory:-
Is the general purpose memory beyond 1 Mb.

3.) Expanded Memory:-
Is slower than and exists separately from your system's Conventional and Extended memory.

4.) Virtual Memory:-
Is a space on your hard disk that helps your computer to think.

UNDERSTANDING DISK SPACE

We have already explained that disk space provides storage for programs, files and data used by your computer and that the information stored on disks will always remain there even if you switch off your computer. The two most common types of disks are "**Floppy Disks**" and "**Hard Disks**". Most personal computers will possess a Hard Disk on which applications and other files can be stored.

We feel that to become involved with configuring your hard disk is particularly technical and for the general purpose of this book we have chosen to omit these procedures, however, if you would like to receive a section on the configuration of your Hard Disk, please **phone (0860) 325144** and we will supply accordingly.

CHECKING YOUR SYSTEM'S DISK SPACE

It is a good idea to know how much hard disk space is available on your computer. To do this please follow these steps:-

STEP(1)

Make sure that you are in Windows.

Start "**File Manager**" 📇 from the "**Main**" Program group.

STEP(2)

View the drive you want to check by clicking onto it's respective icon i.e. 💾a , 💾b , 💾c , 💾d etc.

For example: to find out how much space is available on Drive **D:** you would click onto the 💾d icon, or if you wanted to find out how much space is on Drive **C:** you would click onto the 💾c icon.

A number in the status bar at the bottom of the File Manager window indicates how many bytes of disk space are currently available on that disk. Please see Figure(2) overleaf. It will read **C:** together with the amount of Kilobytes (KB) free together with the total disk size in Kilobytes (KB).

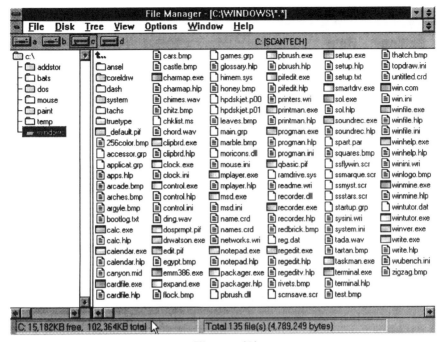

Figure (2)

It will also tell you how many files are in your current directory and their total size in KB. Often there is less free disk space when you are running Windows than when you are in DOS, this is because Windows uses some of your hard disk to store its temporary Swap Files, which obviously take up disk space.

386 ENHANCED MODE / PERMANENT SWAP FILES

If you start the **"Control Panel"** by double clicking on it from the Main program group in Program Manager, the following Window will appear. Please see Figure (3). You will note there is something resembling a scrubbing brush with the letters 386 written on it in blue with the title **"386 Enhanced"** underneath it. By the way the scrubbing brush is supposed to be a chip but we didn't think that it was very good.

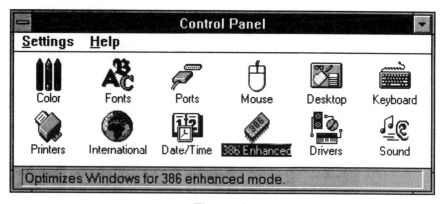

Figure (3)

Double click on the 386 Icon ![icon] and you will be presented with a 386 Enhanced Window. Please see Figure (4).

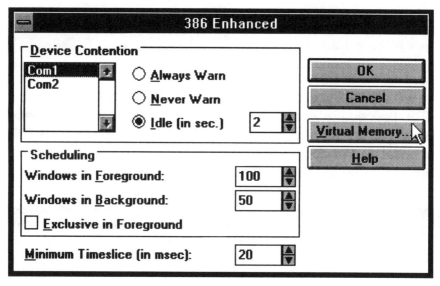

Figure (4)

The 386 Enhanced window is actually quite easy to explain but its purpose is more involved.

We will try to make this as painless and as simple as possible.

You will note that there are two main areas in this Windows "**Device Contention**" and "**Scheduling**". These do not need to be altered as the default settings for Windows are more than adequate in 99% of all cases, the same goes for the "**Minimum Time-slice (in msec):**" option.

CREATING A PERMANENT SWAP FILE.

If you click on the button marked "**Virtual Memory**" the following Window will appear. Please see Figure(5).

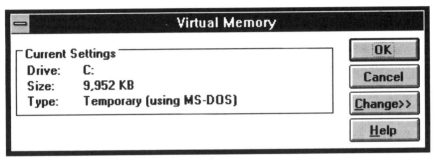

Figure (5)

The dialogue box will display the "**Temporary**" or "**Permanent Swap File**" that windows is currently using, if windows displays a temporary Swap File, then click onto the "**Change**" button to change it, the windows will now expand to accommodate your "**New Settings**". Please see Figure(6) on the next page.

You are now able to select which of your hard disks you would like your permanent Swap File to be on by using the "**Drive**" option, (that is if you have more than one hard disk). You should also note the "**Type**" option which refers to the type of Swap File you are about to create, this can also be changed from in this case "**Temporary**" to "**Permanent**", we recommend choosing a "**Permanent**" setting as this will give Windows the sole usage of the Swap Files disk space and will therefore increase the overall speed of Windows.

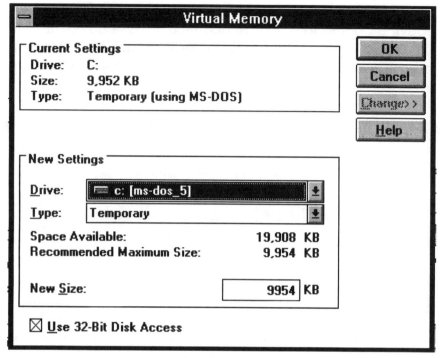

Virtual Memory

Current Settings
Drive: C:
Size: 9,952 KB
Type: Temporary (using MS-DOS)

OK
Cancel
Change>>
Help

New Settings

Drive: c: [ms-dos_5]
Type: Temporary
Space Available: 19,908 KB
Recommended Maximum Size: 9,954 KB

New Size: 9954 KB

☒ Use 32-Bit Disk Access

Figure (6)

After Windows has told you what its **"Recommended Size:"** is, ensure the **"32-Bit Disk Access"** switch is on and then confirm the new Swap File by clicking onto the **"OK"** button.

After confirming your new setting you will be asked if you are sure that you want to make your changes to the Virtual Memory settings. You should confirm by clicking onto **"YES"**.

If you have never used the 32-Bit disk Access option before then you will be prompted by another screen, warning you that some Portable Computers may not be reliable in power saving modes. If you use a laptop with these power saving features then click onto **"NO"** if not click onto **"YES"**. You will now be presented with the following screen, click onto the **"Restart Windows"** option as shown in Figure(7).

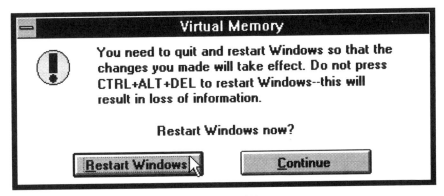

Figure (5)

Windows will now automatically reload after asking if you would like to save any changes to the various programs that are open.

The "**386 Enhanced**" icon will only appear in the Control Panel if you are running in Windows "**386 Enhanced Mode**", this can only be run on computers which are 386's or above.

To check which Windows mode your computer is running in click onto "**Help**" in the main "**Program Manager**" window and then select the "**About Program Manager**" option, Figure(9) will now appear showing you who the Windows program is licensed to and which mode it is currently running in.

If you are using a 386 or above style computer, and it is not running in "**386 Enhanced Mode**" (usually due to lack of memory) you can force load Windows into the 386 Enhanced Mode by typing the following at the Dos prompt: Type "**Win/3**" return.

As you can see the 386 Enhanced mode allows you to make your computer run more effectively in windows. It automatically sets the parameters of your system and creates better available resources to each of the applications by changing the settings for their Swap Files.

Changing the Swap File settings generally will give you better results, however, we strongly recommend that wherever possible you leave these settings at their default values. Primarily because when the Windows program was written most of the resident programs were designed to run with the installed default settings.

If you would like more information on this section then please dial **(0860) 325144)**. We have dedicated this help line for configuration and optimization, all of which is on a one to one basis.

You will note in your Windows "**Accessories**" Program Group there is an icon labelled "**Terminal**" .

This icon will activate the terminal program which primarily is involved with networks and inter-connective systems. Whilst we believe it is an important function there will be not too many people owning "**The Book**" that will be using a Modem link or a Networked system.

However, you will be delighted to know that a separate publication will be marketed in the Summer of 1995 concerning itself only with the Networking and the surrounding areas. We need to know the demand for this publication together with its updates before we can decide how comprehensive it needs to be. If you are interested in receiving such a publication, please telephone **(0860) 325144**

Please note: The new publication mentioned above is not part of the original enhanced book price and will be sold separately.

Before we start this Chapter you must understand that Microsoft Windows **"BackUp"**, **"Anti-Virus"** or **"Undelete"** will not work unless you have installed MS-DOS 6 or higher onto your P.C. this is because when you load MS-DOS 6 or above onto your computer Windows understands that it is present and creates Icons and their own program group for them to work in. The group is called **"Microsoft Tools"** and it holds the referring icons to the next three Sections of **"The Book"**.

This is the **"Microsoft Back-Up for Windows"** Icon:

This is the **"Microsoft Antivirus for Windows"** Icon:

This is the **"Microsoft Undelete for Windows"** Icon:

CONFIGURING MICROSOFT BACK-UP FOR WINDOWS

In this section we will explain how to configure Back-Up for windows so that you will be able to make reliable disk copies of your hard disk, and hopefully prevent any future loss of information.

You will find it comforting to know that if your computer does suffer from a catastrophic crash you will be able to restore any Microsoft Windows Back-up files without reloading Windows by using the MS-DOS 6 Backup/Restore program, this will save you time by not having to reinstall windows.

To configure Microsoft Back-up for Windows click on the respective "**Back-Up**" 🖳 Icon and follow these steps:

STEP(1)
If a message similar to Figure(1) appears proceed to **STEP(2)**.

```
┌─────────────────────────────────────────────────┐
│  ▬              Microsoft Backup                 │
├─────────────────────────────────────────────────┤
│                                                  │
│  Microsoft Backup is not properly installed on this   ┌─────────┐  │
│  system.                                         │  OK  ▷  │  │
│                                                  └─────────┘  │
│  Please reinstall Microsoft Backup, or make the   ┌─────────┐  │
│  following changes to your SYSTEM.INI file:      │  Help   │  │
│                                                  └─────────┘  │
│                                                  │
│     [386Enh]                                     │
│     DEVICE=[ms-dos path]VFINTD.386               │
│                                                  │
│                                                  │
│  If you change your SYSTEM.INI file you must be sure that    │
│  VFINTD.386 is in the Windows system directory.  You will    │
│  need to restart Windows for these changes to take effect.   │
└─────────────────────────────────────────────────┘
```

Figure (1)

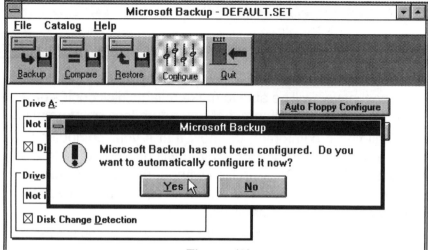

Figure (2)

If a screen similar to Figure(2) appears proceed to **STEP(10)**.

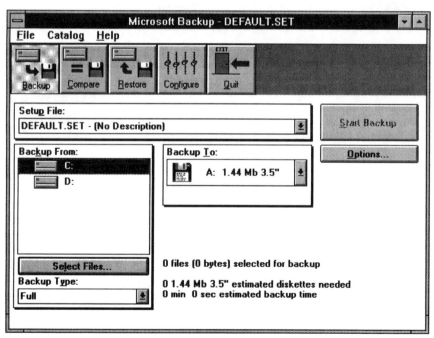

Figure (3)

If a message similar to Figure(3) appears go to the next section marked **"MICROSOFT BACK-UP FOR WINDOWS (DOS6+)"** as the Back-Up program has already been configured for you.

STEP(2)

A screen similar to Figure(4) will now appear.

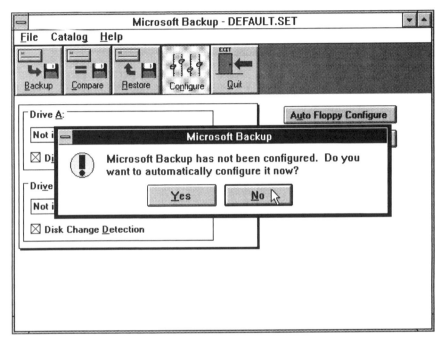

Figure (4)

Click onto the **"NO"** button as the MS-DOS 6 device line has not yet been added to your windows **"System.ini"** file.

Now exit the Back-Up program either by double clicking onto the ⊟ switch, by Clicking onto **"File"** then **"Exit"**, or by simply pressing **"ALT"** and **"F4"** together.

A message will now appear informing you that **"You are about to exit Microsoft Back-Up"**, make sure that the **"Save Settings"** box is **NOT** highlighted by clicking onto it once, then Click onto the **"OK"** button or press return to exit. Please See Figure(5)

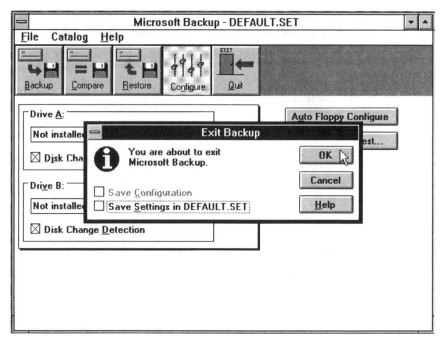

Figure (5)

STEP(3)

Now that you have come out of Back-Up you need to edit your Windows "**System.ini**" File, this file is one of the key players in the overall setup of the Windows operating system and contains vital information which is needed to load and run Windows, in other words act with extreme caution when editing this file.

The easiest way to edit your "**System.ini**" file is to use Microsoft's own "**System Editor**" called "**Sysedit**", this small program is not usually documented in Windows manuals, Why? We don't know!, but it is extremely useful for editing your major system initiation files i.e. "**System.ini**" and "**Win.ini**" for Windows, "**Config.sys**" and "**Autoexec.bat**" for DOS.

To run "**Sysedit**" click onto your "**File**" menu in "**Program Manager**" and select "**Run**", now simply type in "**Sysedit**" and press return or click on "**OK**", Windows will do the rest. See Figure(6).

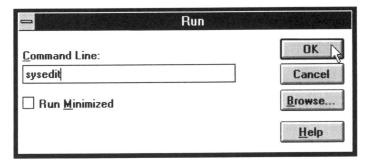

Figure (6)

STEP(4)

As you can see in Figure(7) below **"Sysedit"** really stands for **"System Configuration Editor"**, but we'll stick to **"Sysedit"** as it's much easier to remember; Anyway as we have just explained **"Sysedit"** loads up the four main configuration files which are generally associated with your computer, for now we are not interested in any of them except for the **"System.ini"** file which is hidden behind the other windows at the top of the screen.

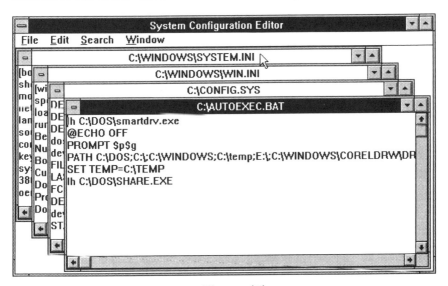

Figure (7)

Click onto the "**System.ini**" window and Figure(8) will appear.

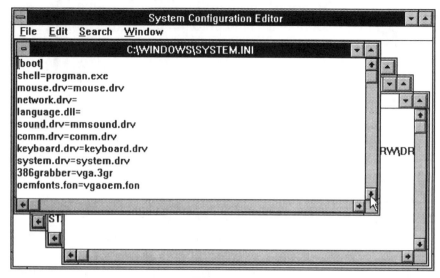

Figure (8)

STEP(5)

As you can see in Figure(8) the mouse pointer arrow has been placed over the scroll down arrow ⬇, do the same and click on the arrow to scroll down through the "**System.ini**" file.

When you get to the "**[386Enh]**" section insert an extra line anywhere underneath and type the following:

"**Device=C:\windows\system\vfintd.386**". See Figure(9)

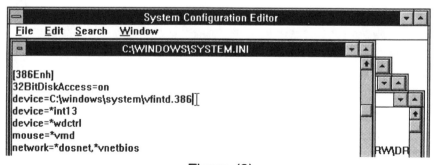

Figure (9)

STEP(6)

Now exit the "**Sysedit**" program by either pressing "**Alt**" and "**F4**" together or double clicking onto the program's switch ▱, or by clicking onto "**File**" and the selecting "**Exit**"; when asked if you want to "**Save current changes?**" click onto the "**Yes**" button and the "**System.ini**" file will be updated.

By changing the "**System.ini**" file you have told Windows to look for and use the "**Vfintd.386**" file whenever it starts. Which leaves you with one problem, where is the "**Vfintd.386**" file, well it's in your DOS-6 directory which should usually be named as "**C:\DOS**", and you need to make a copy and put it in the "**C:\Windows\System**" directory.

STEP(7)

Exit out of Windows by either pressing "**Alt**" and "**F4**" together or by double clicking on the Program Manager's switch ▱ ,or by clicking onto "**File**" and then selecting "**Exit**".

STEP(8)

At the DOS prompt type:

"**Copy C:\dos\vfintd.386 C:\windows\system**" return

This will copy the necessary "**vfintd.386**" which Windows needs to find in its system directory when it loads.

STEP(9)

Restart Windows by typing "**Win**" return

Now start the Windows "**Back-Up**" program again by clicking onto its 🗄 Icon. A window will appear telling you that:

"**Microsoft Backup has not been configured. Do you want to automatically configure it now?**"

STEP(10)

Click onto the "**Yes**" button and a window will appear asking you to "**Remove all diskettes from your drives to perform the disk change test**". Do so and Click onto the "**OK**" button.

A further window will appear. Please see Figure (10).

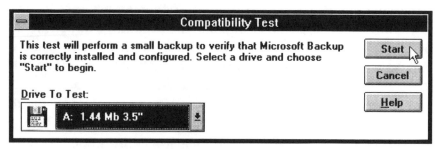

Figure (10)

Back-Up will now ask you which drive you wish to perform the test on. "**Drive A:**" is in nearly all cases the correct drive, but you can choose any other floppy drives that are available by clicking onto the down button ⬆.

STEP(11)

When you have selected the floppy drive click onto the "**Start**" button. The following window will appear. Please see Figure(11).

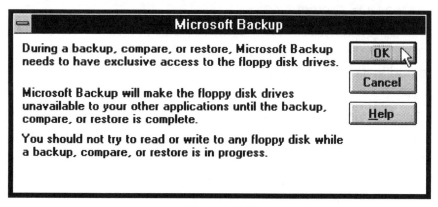

Figure (11)

Click onto the "**OK**" button and the compatibility test will run. You will now as prompted on the screen need to insert a blank or unwanted floppy disk into the correct drive which in this case is "**Drive A:**". Please see Figure(12) overleaf.

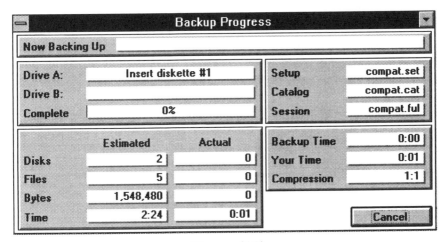

Figure (12)

If you insert a disk with information still on it Microsoft Back-Up will tell you that you have done so by presenting you with a message similar to the following. Please see Figure (13).

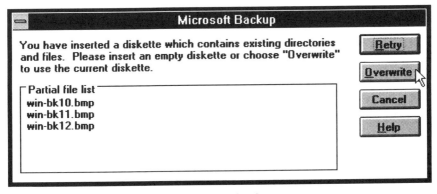

Figure (13)

If you do not want to keep the information on the disk you can choose the **"Overwrite"** option, if you are at all unsure you can put another floppy disk into the drive and select the **"Retry"** option.

STEP(12)

When you have either chosen to "**Overwrite**" or "**Retry**" with a blank disk another screen will appear as Back-Up starts to perform a test back-up on your floppy disk. Please see Figure (14).

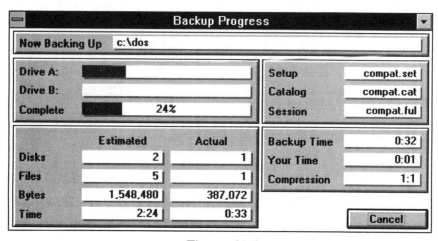

Figure (14)

Two red bands will now start to appear, the top one showing how much the disk in Drive A: has been filled, the bottom one showing the amount of the test back-up completed so far.

When the disk in Drive A: is full, you will be asked to insert a second clean or unwanted disk. You can do the same as shown earlier if you want to "**Overwrite**" or "**Retry**" with another disk.

Insert the second disk and after a few seconds the test back-up will have been completed.

STEP(13)

A further message will now appear first telling you that the back-up has been completed, then asking you to insert the first floppy diskette back into Drive A:.

Do so and then click onto the "**OK**" button or press return, MS Back-Up will now start to check that the files held on the test back-up match those held on the hard disk. See Figure (15).

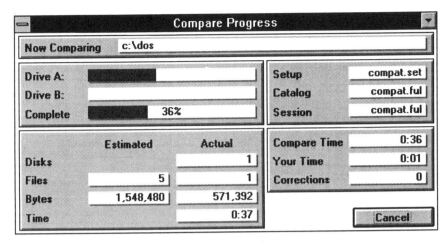

Figure (15)

When the first disk is finished MS Back-Up will ask you to put in the second disk, again do so and click on **"OK"**, after a few seconds more a message will appear informing you that the **"Compare phase of the compatibility test is complete"**.

Click on **"OK"** and a further message will appear telling you that **"The compatibility test completed successfully. You can now make reliable disk backups"**. Click on **"OK"**.

MS Back-Up will now be configured correctly and you will be able to make safe back-up's.

Click onto the **"Backup"** button situated near the top left of the Back-Up windows and proceed to **STEP(1)** in the next section for instructions on using **"MS Back-Up"**.

If you have any problems please telephone (0860) 325144

If you are starting MS-Back-Up for the first time and it has not been configured, you should refer to the previous section namely **"MICROSOFT BACK-UP FOR WINDOWS FIRST TIME USERS"** before continuing. To start the **"MS Back-Up"** program double click on the **"Back-Up"** Icon found in the **"Applications"** program group, inside the **"Program Manager"**.

USING WINDOWS TO BACK UP YOUR HARD DISK

If you don't understand backing up you hard disk please refer back to the MS DOS section of this book labelled **"BACKING UP YOUR HARD DISK"**. When you start **"Back-Up"** the Backup option will already be highlighted for you. Please see Figure(1).

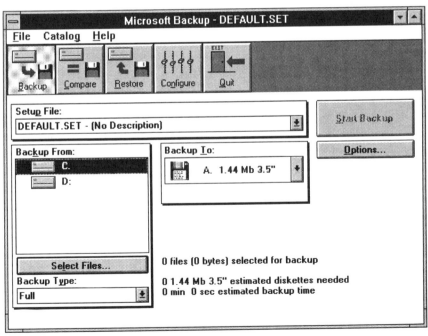

Figure (1)

STEP(1)

First of all you need to make sure that the "**Backup To:**" option box has the correct floppy drive selected, this is usually drive **A: 1.44 Mb 3.5"**. You can change the drive by first clicking onto the down arrow ⬇ button, and then clicking onto the available floppy drive/s options shown.

STEP(2)

Now click onto the "**Select Files**" button near the bottom left of the window and a screen similar to Figure(2) will appear.

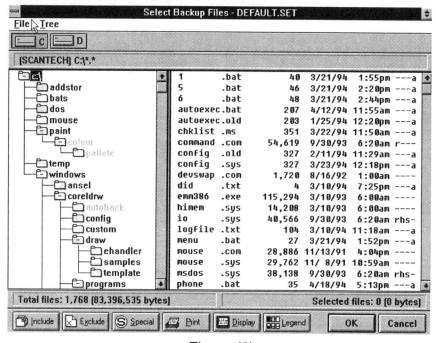

Figure (2)

If you want to Backup the whole of your hard disk go to **STEP(3)**.

If you only want to backup part of your hard disk, by choosing which directories or files to backup go to **STEP(4)**.

STEP(3)

To backup the entire contents of your hard disk, simply click onto the **"File"** option near the top left of your screen and then click on **"Select All"**. Please See Figure(3).

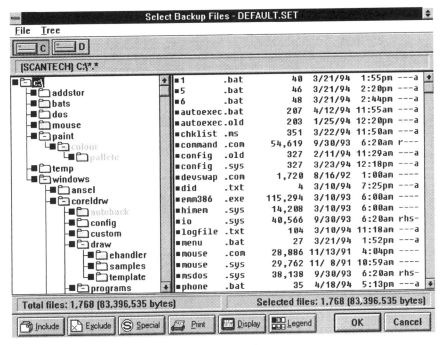

Figure (2)

All of the files and directories on your hard disk will now be tagged shown by black squares to the left of them and the amount of files selected and their overall size will be shown near the bottom of the screen. Click on the **"OK"** button and go to **STEP(5)**.

STEP(4)

To backup only part of you hard drive all you need to do is first use your mouse to click onto the directory you want to backup, and then double click to select the entire contents of the directory or double click on each of your selected files in the directory windows on the right hand side of the screen. See Figures(4&5)

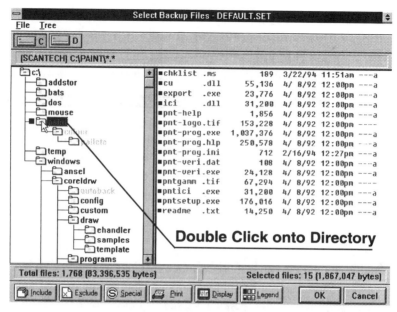

Figure (4)

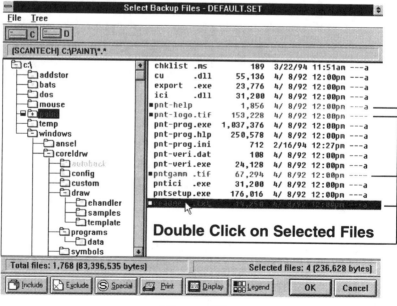

Figure (5)

A good thing to know is that whilst you are selecting your files or directories, the amount of files and their overall size is shown at the bottom left of your screen.

When you have finished selecting your files/directories click onto the "**OK**" button and proceed to **STEP(5)**.

STEP(5)

You can now start your backup, again the amount of files selected for backup are shown at the bottom of the screen together with their overall size, however the approximate amount of floppy disks required to perform the backup is now also shown together with the approximate time it will take to perform the backup. Please see Figure(6).

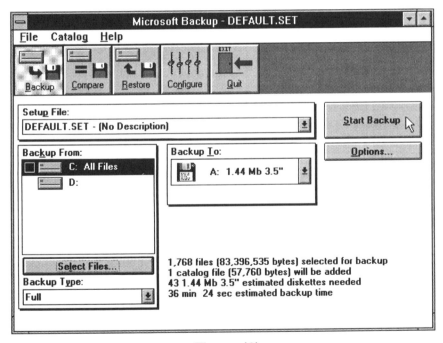

Figure (6)

Start your backup by clicking onto the "**Start Backup**" button which will now be properly highlighted. Please see Figure(7)

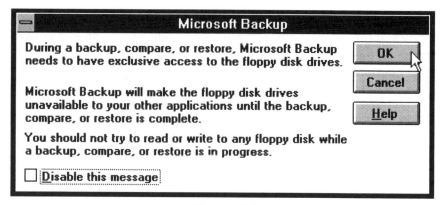

Microsoft Backup

During a backup, compare, or restore, Microsoft Backup needs to have exclusive access to the floppy disk drives.

Microsoft Backup will make the floppy disk drives unavailable to your other applications until the backup, compare, or restore is complete.

You should not try to read or write to any floppy disk while a backup, compare, or restore is in progress.

☐ Disable this message

OK | Cancel | Help

Figure (7)

STEP(6)

Before we go any further, now would be a good idea to start labelling all of your disks in numerical order, as you will need to know the correct disk order when you come to restore your files at a later date.

Click onto "**OK**" and the backup will begin. You will now as prompted on the screen need to insert a blank or unwanted floppy disk labelled "**Disk1**" into the correct drive which in this case is "**Drive A:**". Please see Figure(8).

Backup Progress

Now Backing Up

Drive A:	Insert diskette #1		Setup	default.set
Drive B:			Catalog	default.cat
Complete	0%		Session	cc40504b.ful

	Estimated	Actual		
Disks	2	0	Backup Time	0:10
Files	37	0	Your Time	0:00
Bytes	2,811,414	0	Compression	1:1
Time	1:07	0:10		Cancel

Figure (8)

If you insert a disk with information still on it Microsoft Back-Up will tell you that you have done so by presenting you with a message similar to the following. Please see Figure (9).

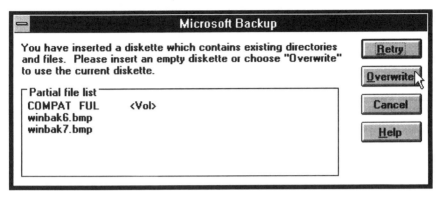

Figure (9)

If you do not want to keep the information on the disk you can choose the **"Overwrite"** option, if you are at all unsure you can put another floppy disk into the drive and select the **"Retry"** option. When you have chosen to **"Overwrite"** or **"Retry"** with a blank disk another screen will appear as Back-Up starts to backup your hard disk onto your floppy disk. See Figure (10).

Backup Progress		
Now Backing Up	c:\addstor	

Drive A:			Setup	default.set
Drive B:			Catalog	default.cat
Complete	30%		Session	cc40504c.ful

	Estimated	Actual		
Disks	2	1	Backup Time	0:22
Files	37	19	Your Time	0:04
Bytes	2,811,414	860,826	Compression	1.8:1
Time	1:07	0:26	Cancel	

Figure (10)

STEP(7)

Two red bands will now start to appear, the top one showing how much the disk in Drive A: has been filled, the bottom one showing the amount of backup completed so far.

When the disk in Drive A: is full, you will be asked to insert a second clean or unwanted disk. You can do the same as shown earlier if you want to "**Overwrite**" or "**Retry**" with another disk.

Insert the second disk labelled "**Disk2**", keep on putting in the relative disks and when the bottom red bar is at 100% a message similar to the following will appear. Please see Figure(11)

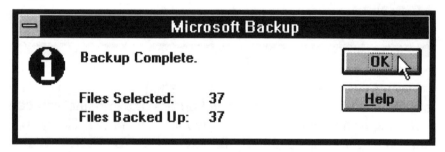

Figure (11)

Click onto "OK" and you will be left back at the main Microsoft Back-Up screen.

Now would be a good idea to store your backup disks in a safe and separate place away from your computer, preferably in another room or even another building, just remember where you put them just in case you need them at a later date.

If you have any problems please telephone (0860) 325144

Restoring files using "**Back-Up**" is relatively simple, provided the Back-Up program has been configured correctly, if it has not been configured you will need to configure it before your files can be retrieved safely. See previous section labelled "**MS BACK-UP FOR WINDOWS - FIRST TIME USERS**"

Start the "**Back-Up**" program by double clicking on the 🖴 icon usually found in the "**Applications**" program group inside the "**Program Manager**". Now follow these steps.

STEP(1)

When the initial "**Microsoft Back-Up**" screen appears, the "**Backup**" option is automatically highlighted. Use your mouse to click onto the "**Restore**" option. Please see Figure(1)

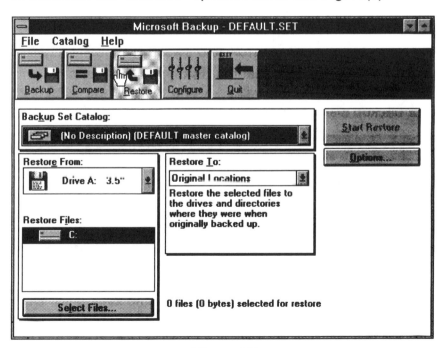

Figure (1)

STEP(2)

Please note the three options at the top of the screen. Click onto the "**Catalog**" option and select "**Retrieve**". You will now be presented will a message similar to Figure(2).

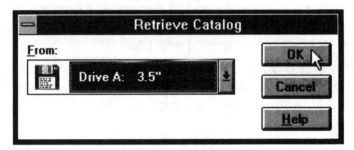

Figure (2)

STEP(3)

Make sure that the "**From**" option shows the correct type of floppy disk that you want to restore from, you can change it by clicking onto the down ⬍ arrow and selecting the correct type.

When you are satisfied that the disk type is correct click onto the "**OK**" button, and you will be asked to insert the "**LAST**" of your backup disks. Please See Figure(3)

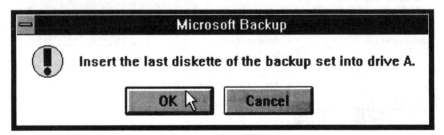

Figure (3)

Insert the "**LAST**" of your backup disks and click onto "**OK**". Back-Up will now retrieve all the information about the backup from the last disk and will display a message telling you that the "**Retrieve is complete**". Click onto the "**OK**" button.

STEP(4)

You will now revert back to the main Back-Up screen, as shown earlier in Figure(1). Take the last disk out of the floppy drive.

Click onto the **"Select Files"** button near the bottom left of the windows and a screen similar to Figure(4) will appear.

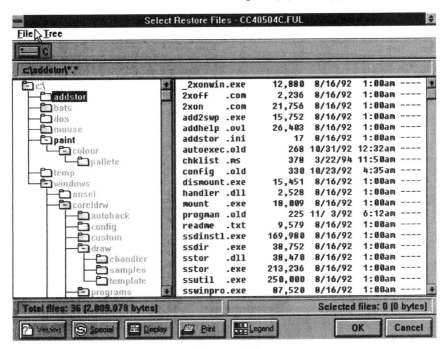

Figure (4)

As you can see in Figure(4) only two directories are highlighted in black, this is because only two directories were selected for backup in this demonstration.

You can select all the files available on your disks by clicking onto the **"File"** option at the top of the screen and then selecting the **"Select All"** option, however if you want to restore some not all of you files/directories you can double click onto them as seen earlier in STEP(4) of the previous section labelled "**MICROSOFT BACK-UP FOR WINDOWS (DOS6+)**".

STEP(5)

When you are satisfied that you have selected all the files you want, see Figure(5) and have checked that you have enough room on your hard disk by noting the size of the files selected shown at the bottom right hand corner of the screen, and click onto the "**OK**" button.

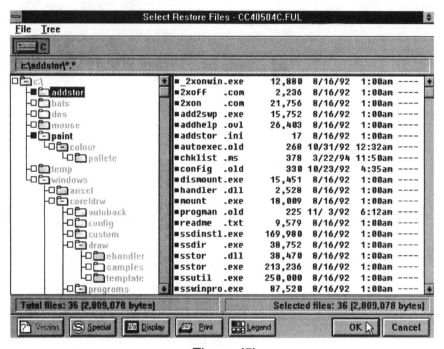

Figure (5)

Now click onto the "**Start Restore**" button and a further screen will appear, click onto the "**OK**" button and you will be asked to insert the first of your backup disks labelled "**Disk1**" do so and windows will start to restore your files.

When asked, remove "**Disk1**" and insert "**Disk2**" and so on, until a message appears saying "**Restore Complete**". Click onto the "**OK**" button and exit "Back-Up" in the normal way.

If you have any problems please telephone (0860) 325144

You will have no doubt noticed in Microsoft Windows that there is an icon labelled "**ANTIVIRUS**" or "**MWAV**".

If you double click on the icon the following window will appear. Please see Figure(1).

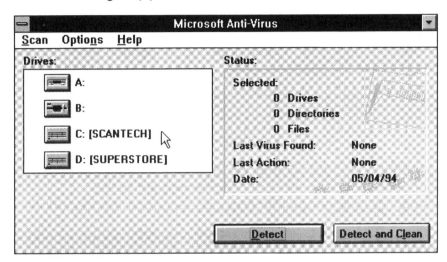

Figure (1)

If you then click onto the button referring to your drive i.e. in this case either "**A:, B:, C:** or **D:**" your computer will automatically conduct a status check on your selected disc and display the information about it on this right hand side of the window.

In order for Microsoft Anti Virus to find any viruses present on your computer or an inserted floppy disk it needs run a detect process. Try it now with "**Drive C:**" selected by clicking onto the "**Detect**" button. The following window will appear, as Anti Virus checks your computer's memory for known viruses.

Please See Figure(2) overleaf.

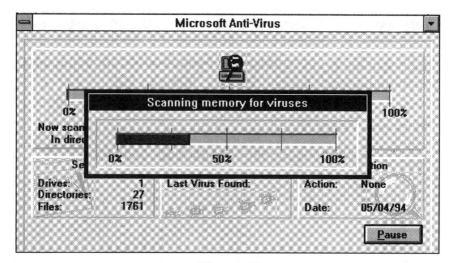

Figure (2)

A green line in the window will gradually fill the bar from left to right until it reaches the one hundred percent mark.

Upon completion another window will appear. See Figure(3).

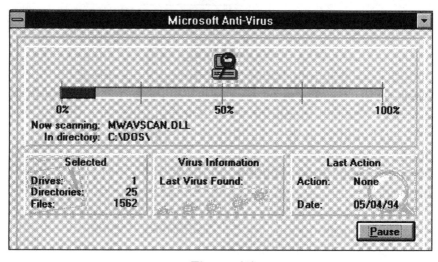

Figure (3)

Anti Virus will display another bar as it starts to scan through the selected drive for viruses, it will prompt you if any important configuration files have changed along the way. When the bar has reached the one hundred percent mark yet another window will appear. Please see Figure(4).

	Scanned	Infected	Cleaned	
Statistics				OK
Hard Disks	1	0	0	
Floppy Disks	0	0	0	
Total Disks	1	0	0	
COM Files	35	0	0	
EXE Files	143	0	0	
Other Files	1595	0	0	
Total Files	1773	0	0	
Scan Time	00:02:43			

Figure (4)

This window labelled statistics simply records what your computer has found and what it has done about any problems found. Click on the "**OK**" button and you will return to the original Microsoft Antl Virus window.

If you do detect a virus you can use the "**Detect and clean**" option which performs in exactly the same way except that if it finds a virus it will eradicate it.

Finally you will note that near the top of the initial screen there is an "**Option**" function, Click on it and select "**Set Options**".

Please see Figure(5) overleaf.

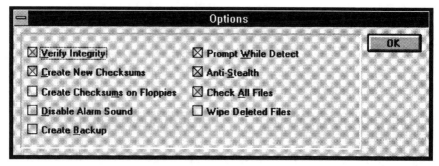

Figure (5)

As you can see there are nine separate options displayed. Next to each title is a box. You can activate or deactivate each of the options by simply clicking onto the box next to them, options are activated when its corresponding box has a cross in it.

The default option should be left as shown in Figure(5) above but sometimes you might find it useful to use the **"Wipe Deleted Files"** option for added system integrity, but always remember to turn it off after you have scanned the disk. Click on **"OK"**.

You will note also that there is a **"Scan"** option in the menu bar, the contents of which are self explanatory, except for the **"Delete CHKLIST Files"**, which will delete all of **Anti Virus's** notes about the files and directories held on your hard or floppy disk the last time it was scanned.

The **"Help"** option is as usual self explanatory and that is really all that there is to Microsoft's Anti Virus.

However it is possible to load up Anti Virus's TSR program whenever you switch your computer on, this in our view is a questionable facility, and we do not recommend it.

For more information about virus's phone (0860) 325144

MICROSOFT UNDELETE FOR WINDOWS
(MS-DOS 6+)

Microsoft's "**Undelete**" for windows can be a particularly useful tool, not only can you recover mistakenly deleted files without exiting the windows environment, but the whole process is user friendly and very simple. All you have to do is open "**Undelete**", choose the directory which held the deleted file, select the file, click on the Undelete button, and finally type in the first character of the filename. Simple isn't it. Well just to make sure that you can't go wrong with the basic functions of "**Undelete**" we have prepared some simple STEPS which should help you understand.

STEP(1)

Double click onto the "**Undelete**" or "**MWundel**" icon.
Normally found in the Program Manager's Applications window.
Microsoft "**Undelete**" will now start. Please see Figure(1).

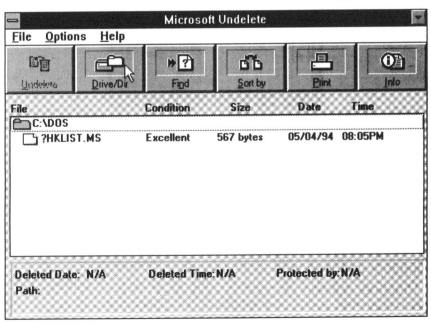

Figure (1)

STEP(2)

By default **"Undelete"** usually displays the **"C:\DOS"** directory, so unless you have deleted a file from **"C:\DOS"** (Strongly NOT recommended) you will need to change the directory shown.

For our example we have deleted some files in the **"C:\PAINT"** directory of our computer's hard disk.

Change to the directory where your file was last stored before it was deleted. You do this by clicking onto the **"Drive/Dir"** button which is displayed along the top bar.

A window similar to Figure(2) shown below will appear.

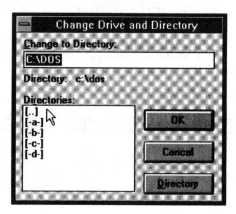

Figure (2)

STEP(3)

All you have to do now is type in the correct directory pathname where your file was last held (in our case "C:\Paint") then press return or click onto the **"OK"** button. Alternatively you can use your mouse to double click on any of the drives shown, using it to change directories by double clicking on the **[..]** symbol or a directory that is shown, when you are satisfied click on **"OK"**.

Undelete will now go back to it's original window and display a list of files that can be undeleted, together with their ratings against the success of their undeletion.

Click onto the file that you want to undelete and **"Undelete"** will display the information about its possible undeletion at the bottom of the window. Please see Figure(3) below.

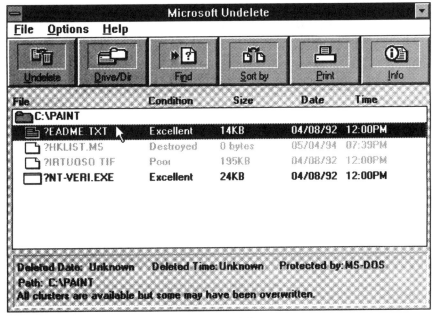

Figure (3)

STEP(4)

Now click onto the bright red **"Undelete"** button which is displayed along the top bar.

You will now be presented with another window asking you to type in the first letter of the file that was destroyed, in this case typing **"R"** for **"?EADME.TXT"** will recover the file **"README.TXT"**

Please see Figure(4) overleaf.

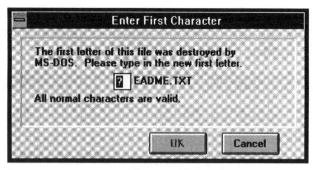

Figure (4)

When you have typed in the correct character click onto "**OK**" or press return.

Your file will have now been undeleted, you can check to see if it has been recovered correctly by looking at the "**Condition**" column next to it. Please See Figure(5) showing "**README.TXT**" having been successfully undeleted.

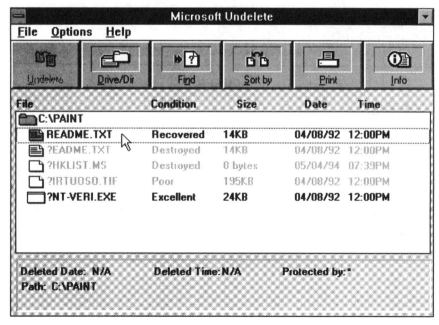

Figure (5)

Well that's just about all you need to know about "**Undelete**", there are several options which you can explore all of which are self explanatory and of course user friendly.

If you have any problems please telephone (0860) 325144

This section is designed to list all the keyboard functions which are available in Windows allowing you to run at optimum speed.

The following list shows key combinations you can use in the Microsoft Windows Operating System.

Many of these commands can be seen on the menus giving you instant visual access to their functions.

It is important to remember that using these key short-cuts whilst using your mouse will free up your mouse enabling you to run operations whilst executing other commands, this will thereby increase your overall computer working speed. Take time to learn as many as basic functions as possible and watch your performance increase.

The key functions shown on the next page can be used whether you are working in a Window or a Full Screen and will work in any application run under Windows:-

PRESSING	DOES THIS:
F1	Starts help provided the application has help
Ctrl + Escape	Switches to a task list
Alt + Escape	Switches to the next application
Alt + Tab	Switches to the last application used
Shift + Alt + Tab	Switches to previous application by pressing and holding down "**Alt**" and "**Shift**" keys you can repeat the process by using "**Tab**" key.
Print Screen	Copies an image of the screen onto a clipboard.
Alt + Print Screen	Copies an active windows image.
Alt, Spacebar	Opens the Control Menu.
Alt, Hyphen	Opens the Control Menu for the document window.
Alt + Spacebar	Opens the Control Menu for a non-Windows application.
Alt F4	Quits an application or closes the current Window.
Ctrl F4	Closes an active group, or document window.

PRESSING	DOES THIS:
Alt + Enter	Switches a Non-windows application between running in a window and running in a full screen.
Arrow key	Moves a window after you choose "**Move**" from the Control menu.

MENU KEYS	PRESSING THEM DOES THIS:
Alt + F10	Selects or cancels selection.
A character key	Selects the menu for command.
Left Arrow or Right Arrow	Moves between menus.
Up Arrow or Down Arrow	Moves between commands.
Enter	Selects a Menu name or command.
Escape	Cancels the selected Menu name or closes the open menu.

DIALOGUE BOX KEYS	PRESSING THEM DOES THIS:
Tab	Moves from option to option
Shift + Tab	Moves between options in reverse order
Alt + any character	Moves to the option or group whose letters or numbers match the ones you type.

DIALOGUE BOX KEYS	PRESSING THEM DOES THIS:
An arrow key	Moves the selected cursor through the options.
Home	Moves to the first item or character in a list or text box.
End	Moves to the last item or character in a list or text box.
Page up or Page down	Scrolls Up or Down one page at a time, when viewing a list.
Alt + Down Arrow	Opens a List
Spacebar	Selects an item or cancels an item in a list
Ctrl + /	Selects all items in a list
Ctrl + \	Cancels all selections except for the current one
Shift + an arrow key	Extends or cancels the selection in a text box or character one at a time
Shift + Home	Extends or cancels the selection to the first character in a text box.
Shift + End	Extends or cancels the selection to the last character in a text box.
Enter	Carries out a command.

DIALOGUE BOX KEYS	PRESSING THEM DOES THIS:
Alt + F4	Closes a dialogue box without completing a command, and will also if pressed again close the program.

CURSOR MOVEMENT KEYS

By using the following keys you can move the cursor or insertion point in text boxes or other places to enable you to insert text into different programs.

PRESSING	MOVES THE INSERTION POINT
Up Arrow	Up one line
Down Arrow	Down one line
Right Arrow	Right one character
Left Arrow	Left one character
Ctrl + Right Arrow	Right one word
Ctrl + Left Arrow	Left one word
Home	To the beginning of the line
End	To the end of the line
Page Up	Up one screen
Page Down	Down one screen

PRESSING	MOVES THE INSERTION POINT
Ctrl + Home	To the beginning of the document
Ctrl + End	To the end of one document

EDITING KEYS

You can use these keys to edit text in a dialogue box or window.

PRESS	TO
Backspace	Delete the character to the left of the insertion point.
Delete	Delete the character to the right of the insertion point
Ctrl + Ins or Ctrl + C	Copy the selected text and place it onto a clipboard
Shift + Delete or Ctrl + X	Delete the selected text and place it onto a clipboard
Shift + Ins or Ctrl + V	Paste text from a clipboard into an active window
Ctrl + Z or Alt + Backspace	Undo the last editing action

If you have any problems please telephone (0860) 325144

PROGRAM MANAGER KEYS

PRESS	TO
An Arrow key	Move between items within a group window
Ctrl + F6 or Ctrl + Tab	Move between group windows and icons
Enter	Start the selected application
Shift + F4	Arrange the group windows side by side
Shift + F5	Arrange the open group windows
Ctrl + F4	Close the active group windows
Alt + F4	Quit Microsoft Windows

There are many other function keys that can be used, however, we have thoroughly tested them and in general have the same functions are the ones already listed.

A couple of extra commands that usually work when you are using an application are "**Ctrl + S**" to save your document, "**Ctrl + P**" to print your document or file, and finally a quick way to exit out of any program is to press "**Alt + F4**".

Remember that when you are using a program, if available the short-cut keys are always shown in the option menus next to the command itself. I.e. In the "**File**" menu the "**Save**" option will usually have a "**^S**" next to it, the little arrow means that you can use the "**Ctrl**" key with the letter shown in this case "**Ctrl + S**".

Well you are now at the end of the Windows puzzle and we hope very much that you have learned more than you would have done from a conventional manual. It has been our intention to use words throughout the book that are understandable to everyone that has the desire to run a computer. Some of these words and phrases are completely basic and are not intended for technical specification.

Unfortunately whilst you will be able to use your computer in a manner pleasing to you, you still need to understand some of the difficult terms, especially for when you are talking to so called experts. Terms such as **"MS-DOS"** **"Config.sys"**, **"Autoexec.bat"**, **"Win.ini"**, **"Smart Drive"** and so many more are used by the boffins to puzzle and confuse the would-be user.

However, you can look forward to receiving your regular updates of workable program information written in a language you can understand provided you have purchased a copy of the advanced book (ring binder version). You can purchase the updates if you have chosen to initially use the paperback version of the book. We strongly recommend that you do so as by now the facts will have become clearly evident in that the puzzle was indeed made easy by using this unique teaching program.

When we conceived the book it was always our intention to allow the user to understand **"DOS"** and **"Windows"** before anything else; Primarily because nothing else will work unless you understand these two major working environments. Having taught many people how to use computers, we have found that almost every one tends to skip from manual to manual rather than specializing in the DOS and Windows environments, to the end that each manual having been written in a more different and complicated language than the last confuses people more and more, the end result being mass confusion and nothing learned at all.

The book clearly realises that to become proficient with other programs which work within "**DOS**" or "**Windows**" you must first know how to use the initial system as every other program relies upon it. This is why we are despatching, one by one, over eighteen months, each of our selected program training courses, enabling the user to become familiar with them one by one in an order that they can understand. In this way it is hoped that you will be able to concentrate and learn each application as there will be nothing else to distract you.

We have always felt that the future depends upon people understanding and working more fully with computers, as this is indeed the future. Society will always need to save time as the pressures of business become more harassing. i.e. by "**Access to Information**", "**Graphics**", "**Faster Production**", "**Quicker Publications and Newspapers**", "**Improved Services**", in fact the list is endless and we will all eventually rely on computers. As a direct result of this we are sure that in the future there will be few jobs available that do not rely upon a reasonable computing knowledge. To this end we wish you every success in the future and look forward to dispatching our next updates.

Finally, as part of the service we have consulted and carefully checked both the value and quality of many suppliers of different products and services who have agreed to offer their expertise to the users of the book. Special offers and opportunities will be forwarded to you free of charge. Each offer will come in the form of a page that will neatly fit into your binder for quick reference.

For instance we have made contact with a stationery supplier that will provide suitable discounts purely by being the owner of the book.

Again we hope you have enjoyed the book, don't forget to use our **"on-line help service"** if any problems occur. You have no doubt realised the value of such a publication and with this in mind we have incorporated in the rear of the book an introductory slip that you can give to a friend. If they forward that to us we will return either a registered ring binder copy or a paperback version depending upon their requirements.

THANK YOU FOR PURCHASING THE BOOK

INDEX

INDEX

INDEX

Registration Form

Please Register me as a "SIMPLY THE BOOK" owner. I would be interested in being sent details of any special offers that might become available.

My special interests are...

Name..

Address..

....

Phone No:...

Please return to:- **John Daw, Walden Premier Ltd C/O Kuma Books Ltd, 12 Horseshoe Park, Pangbourne, Berks RG8 7JW**